Advance Praise for *The Campaign Within*

"Neil Giuliano is an American gay rights hero. His personal story, beautifully told in his memoir, is an often dramatic tale about the darkness and fear of the closet and the light and freedom of coming out—to family, friends, voters and most of all to yourself. It is a story about politics, media, gay rights, and most of all, about integrity. *The Campaign Within* is a landslide winner."

—Richard Socarides, former Special Assistant to the President and Senior Advisor, The White House, Administration of President Bill Clinton.

"A shockingly honest memoir; I was riveted by Neil's transformation from secretive politician to proud advocate."

—Marc Cherry, Creator and Executive Producer, *Desperate Housewives*

"It's a challenge and blessing to be a pioneer, and Neil plumbs aspects of this unenviable role in his engaging and highly readable memoir. I've known Neil as a colleague, but knew few details of his full story. *The Campaign Within* is enthralling and left me grateful to know him as a friend and fellow activist."

—Kate Kendell, Executive Director, National Center for Lesbian Rights

"Neil Giuliano has crafted a story about conscience, integrity, and the importance of living one's truth. His journey has taken him to the heights of political power and through the minefields of the entertainment industry. With unsparing honesty and unexpected humor, he lays down a blueprint for living life in the public eye without sacrificing self-respect or authenticity."

—William Mann, best selling author of *Kate: The Woman Who Was Hepburn*

"*The Campaign Within* is a searing story of coming of age and coming out, but—even more than that—it is an inspirational testament to the power of service to causes greater than oneself. It is a memoir that will not simply let you see the world through someone else's eyes, but change the way in which you look at it yourself."

   —Andrei Cherny, author *The Candy Bombers* and president of *Democracy* journal

"Neil's peak behind the curtain of public service is as open and honest as his life. Sharing his historical journey with us is a gift, one that should be required reading—if such still exists—for all civics and LGBT studies courses."

   —Chuck Wolfe, President/CEO, Gay & Lesbian Victory Fund and Institute

"*The Campaign Within* is a fascinating inside look at one man's personal journey as a leader. Going behind the scenes of the Mayor's office and his personal life, Giuliano takes us along as he steps forward to reconcile the two. We see the negative side of politics and the bigotry that still exists, but ultimately we are left with a high appreciation for his demonstrated courage and strength of character."

   —Grant Woods, Arizona Attorney General, 1991-1999

"Neil Giuliano's remarkable ability to be both personally confident and dispassionate in describing his journey, and becoming a highly successful and respected mayor along the way, speaks to the uncertainties and possibilities of all of us. *The Campaign Within* reflects a profound level of self-awareness which makes it an especially relevant story for anyone serving in or preparing to run for public office."

   —Don Borut, Executive Director, National League of Cities

The
Campaign
Within

The Campaign Within

A Mayor's Private Journey to Public Leadership

Nancy —
thanks for all
your support!,
Neil Giuliano

Neil Giuliano

MAGNUS
BOOKS

This book is dedicated to the memory of my parents, Neil and Jackie Giuliano, to my sister Kim and brothers Greg and John. To David Mixner and other activists whose hard work enabled my success. And to the people of Tempe, Arizona, who trusted me to serve them as I journeyed along my campaign within.

"Ah, but a man's reach must exceed his grasp,
or what's a heaven for?"
—*Andrea del Sarto*

Table of Contents

PROLOGUE

On Saturdays when I was a boy, my father would take me with him to his office, the Jersey Loan Company in Bloomfield, New Jersey. I would explore and twirl on the desk chairs in the empty office while he worked. My tendency then, as now, was to find the largest desk: the one made of wood in a room full of steel-grey metal desks. My father said it was the boss's desk, but I could sit there on Saturdays. I was happy to oblige.

After one such Saturday of "working," we were walking together downtown. As we passed the Royal Movie Theater on Bloomfield Avenue, my father met an acquaintance, an older man who wore a long, black suit coat, buttoned all the way up. They shook hands and stopped to chat. The sun was bright but the air was crisp enough that I had on my favorite blue windbreaker, zipped to the top. I looked up at the man in between watching the cars go by. His mop of thick gray hair blew in the wind.

Noticing me, the man smiled. His hand came to rest on my

head for a second, giving me the "pat the child on the head" routine that all children hate and I have refused to administer ever since. "This young boy," the old man told my father, "he's a smart and special boy. He is going to do good things someday."

As we separated and continued our walk, my father told me the man was an elder rabbi, adding, "He is a very wise and spiritual man. He knows there is something special about you."

Something special, which to me meant something different.

There *was* something special, and definitely different, about me, and I would spend many years trying to shed, understand, and ultimately accept and embrace that truth.

CHAPTER ONE

July 1996

"A person on the city council specifically told me about the sexual preference of one of the members on this council. And they are quite different from mine, and they are quite different from the person who gave me this information."

The speaker at the lectern just twenty-five feet away paused, staring at me, waiting for my reaction. There was none. Years of practice—four on the city council and two more as mayor of Tempe, Arizona—had helped to perfect my "poker face" at public meetings. But while I knew my face betrayed nothing, my insides were in turmoil.

Deep down, I knew some aspect of this set of circumstances had been inevitable and now it was happening; for the first time, in a public setting, someone was intimating that I was gay.

There had been nothing unusual about this day, and I had had no reason to suspect that tonight's council meeting would be any different from the hundreds of others I had sat through during my public service and political life. Scattered groups of people, mostly city staff, dotted the chambers that night. As we did each week, the other six members of Tempe's city council and I sat facing the audience. As mayor, I sat in the center on a high-back, mauve-colored leather chair with three members of the council on either side of me, my attention focused on the man at the lectern in front of me, as it was for all who came forward during "Unscheduled Public Appearances" at the close of the meeting each week to share their thoughts on one topic or another.

His name was Fritz Tuffli and until that moment, I had regarded him as little more than a nuisance. He was a long-time political gadfly, sometimes candidate for city council, and far-right fanatic. He was also a former city police officer. He'd held that post for a short tenure but, nonetheless, we taught him how to use a gun, among other things. Years later, after my tenure as mayor, he truly went postal and walked into a local hospital firing a weapon. He was sent to jail for that and has since passed on, but before that crazy turn, he usually came to the council meetings to use the three minutes allotted to each citizen to drone on about whatever bee was circling his bonnet that week.

Every community has a Fritz or two or three. They make it their life's calling to follow the minutiae of city government. They come to city council meetings to share what they know (or what they think they know) and more than anything else to let their elected officials know they are paying attention. Fritz's commentary meandered around the various issues of the day and on this particular summer night he'd started out as usual, using his three minutes of time to rage about one issue and then comment on others. As he began, I arranged my face like I was listening, but my mind was sailing on to other things. I thought about the red-eye flight I was about to catch to the 1996 Olympics in Atlanta. I thought about the friends I would see and the good times we would have together. I caught bits and pieces of what Fritz was saying, but for the most part, his words swirled around me almost unheard.

"…the sexual preference of one of the members on this council. And they are quite different from mine and they are quite different from the person who gave me this information."

My thoughts snapped back to the present. I wanted to look around, I wanted to assess the reaction of the room to this man's allegations, but I knew that breaking eye contact with Fritz would look weak and be noticed. I fought down the impulse and stared him in the eye. I said nothing and did nothing, which by law was what I was required to do. After a moment, Fritz concluded while I struggled to suppress my rising sense of panic.

I knew he was talking about me, and apparently the source of his information was one of the people beside me, a council member. I couldn't fully turn to look at my colleagues, left and right, but I wondered which one of the six people flanking me was his source. I glanced to my left as I shifted my weight in my chair. Councilwoman Carol Smith glared at me with tight lips, her trademark tightly-wound white hair framing the irritation etched into her face. I couldn't determine if her anger was meant for Fritz or me. Since she had supported my opponent, Don Cassano, in the 1994 mayoral election, I guessed at least some of her reaction was meant for me; we weren't yet the allies we would become in later years of serving together. Councilwoman Linda Spears, on the other hand, was a good friend and fellow Kiwanis Club of Tempe member. It was only her second year on the council, and it was clear that the focus of the fury on her face was directed only at Fritz. I read her expression as clearly as if someone had dropped a sign around her neck: she was struggling between challenging his bigotry and ignoring his stupidity. If she could have spoken to me, I'm pretty sure she would have said, "What an idiot."

I could imagine what the other council members—Ben Arredondo, Joe Spracale, Joseph Lewis, and Dennis Cahilll—were thinking, too: emotions ranging from annoyed to downright pissed off. I knew them well enough to understand their thoughts. It wasn't so much that Fritz was accusing me of being a gay man—I suspected that each of them, with varying degrees of clarity, already assumed that I was. That I might be gay wasn't the issue for my colleagues. The issue for the council members was more political. Fritz's rambling innuendo would put them on the hot seat, too, and their own views about sexuality and gay public policy issues would be sought, topics few elected officials in 1996 were comfortable addressing. Up until that moment, my fellow city council members and I had enjoyed an unspoken "Don't Ask, Don't Tell" arrangement, but with only a quick glance across the panel, I could read in each of their faces that now there was no way that deal would endure.

And now, too, thanks to Fritz's comments, there would be political hell to pay.

I had known for a long time I would one day have to face the music for having spent my career—my whole life—dividing my world into neat boxes. In one box, I was a dedicated public servant who seemed to have no personal life and who lived the life of a solitary bachelor. In the other world, I indeed was a gay man.

Initially, I kept those worlds separated by thousands of miles. The journey of them uniting at last was long and arduous, for reasons you'll come to know. It was an internal campaign; longer and tougher than any I had ever had for public office.

Just four months earlier, in March 1996, I had been re-elected mayor of Tempe without opposition. No one else had even considered running. After my first campaign for mayor in 1994, a very competitive election that I won with 53% of the vote, breezing to victory for my second term as the only name on the ballot was a politician's dream. Serving as mayor of Tempe, a dynamic and attractive city of about 175,000 people, bordering Arizona's capitol city of Phoenix, suited me. My life was solid: I was young, not yet forty years old, had a successful professional career (then as Director of Federal Government Relations at Arizona State University, my alma mater) and had been re-elected mayor with no opposition. Professionally and politically, things were pretty darn good.

Although I was still in the closet, I was starting to feel more comfortable and much less concerned about managing my sexuality as a part of my public political image. I was finally feeling secure enough to lower my political guard. I assumed more and more people in Tempe had quietly "figured out" that I was gay: I was in my late thirties, was not married, and routinely showed up at events without a female trophy date. It seemed pretty obvious to me.

Since serving as mayor was technically not full-time, my Director of Federal Relations position at ASU frequently took me to Washington, D.C., where I was anything but in the closet. In fact, my friends had nicknamed me the "Mayor of 17th Street," referring to the area widely known as home for the gay community in that city. In the mid-1990s I was in D.C. as often as a couple times a month for a few days at a time, working on Capitol Hill on behalf of ASU and enjoying a real social life with a cadre of gay friends. My personal life there was everything it couldn't be at home in Tempe.

I was strangely comfortable with this arrangement. I was rather openly gay and social in the city where I often worked, closeted and socially isolated in the one where I served as mayor.

But there were signs that trouble was on the horizon and looking back, I know I should have foreseen that my dual life wouldn't last as long as I thought it might.

Earlier in the year, in the spring of 1996, Arizona Central Pride (ACP), a gay community group based in Phoenix, applied for a partial fee waiver for the annual Gay Pride festival it had been holding for many years at Tempe Diablo Stadium's soccer complex. Because the soccer complex is city property, the issue of determining if a fee waiver was appropriate came before Tempe's Sponsorship Review Committee. The committee granted a partial waiver, knocking $1,500 off the $8,100 fee, as it frequently had done for non-profit groups holding events in Tempe. ACP received the same kind of waiver given to the Miss

Tempe Pageant and more than fifty other events each year.

After approving the fee waiver, the Sponsorship Review Committee forwarded its recommendation to the city council for routine approval. As long as the group requesting the waiver had a good track record for respecting city property and paying its obligations to us, the council rubber-stamped the committee's recommendations without comment. We knew that by the time the matter reached the full council, the citizens of the sponsorship review committee had already discussed the matter thoroughly and made a fair determination.

That should have been the end of it, but it wasn't.

A week or so later, a brief newspaper article detailing recent city council action included a listing of groups that received fee waivers, including Arizona Central Pride. The article was routine in every possible way. But that tiny announcement was enough to set off a firestorm of controversy.

Conservative religious zealots seized on the issue. The $1,500 grant was twisted into yet another nefarious plot to pervert the population and poison the common decency of the community. By granting the waiver, the city council of Tempe had begun its descent into becoming a modern day cesspool of sin. Everywhere in local politics, sexual orientation was a topic of discussion. The city council couldn't avoid the fallout of what had been seen at the time as merely a routine approval, conducted according to our usual policies and procedures. Sexual orientation and gay politics had become an issue for the city council, and for me, the still-closeted mayor.

The issue rallied citizens with strong religious views about gay people and gay rights. It offered them an issue they could now exploit: a connection between city business and what they long suspected was my hidden sexual orientation. As far back as my first mayoral campaign, some religious community members had threatened to share their belief that I was gay and had attempted to make their beliefs about my sexual orientation an issue. But they had stopped short of publicly outing me. Was that about to change?

With the Arizona Central Pride fee waiver non-issue, I started to receive angry voicemail and email messages, including one from a Baptist minister who wrote that we had hastened the day when signs would read, "Welcome to Sodom and Gomorrah and Tempe."

Before the issue had even reached the city council for routine approval, some fundamentalists were flocking to council meetings to condemn the fee waiver. At the first city council meeting after the article ran, they challenged us about waiving the fee with more fiery speeches. They returned the next week and the next. For four or five consecutive meetings, religious conservatives used their three minutes to make their disapproval known. People of the anti-gay establishment trudged into the city council chambers on those hot summer Thursday nights, signed in under "public appearances" and then, when their turns came, unleashed tirades about battles and holy wars and fighting the evil they believed was around every turn. I assumed they had set their home VCRs to the cable access channel, recording their part in the great noble fight against "the gays," who in their minds were overtaking the city at that very moment.

The issue got my attention, of course, but I didn't believe their anger—however righteous—was sustainable. As mayor, I had to sit, feign interest, and listen to whatever they unleashed. I was always polite, sometimes entertained, but mostly I just let them exercise their right to speak, avoiding any kind of wider discussion about the issues with them. Beyond the minor irritation of having to listen to them rant a few minutes, their concerns were moot. The decision had been made. Procedurally, all they could do was complain.

My matter-of-fact handling of their concerns infuriated them further. Their faces grew red with rage as they preached sermons to the council and decried our blasphemous ways of ruining the city, endangering children, and leading our town straight down the road to hell, pun intended. They really knew how to work themselves up. As they exercised their First Amendment rights, we looked on, fascinated that human beings could muster such vitriol and hate. A quote I remembered from my own religious upbringing popped into my head: "Forgive them, for they know not what they do."

What I underestimated, however, was their fervor and resolve. Even more than that, I didn't fully connect the impact their ranting would have on my personal situation. I was fairly comfortable in the closet and did not think they would ever make their issues directly personal. I didn't think they would make it about me. I was wrong.

For all of my carefulness, for all of my compartmentalizing, the rumors and whispers were growing louder and could not be ignored for much longer. While I had known for years that this moment would one day arrive, nothing in that knowledge had truly prepared me for the profound shock and terror that welled up inside me on July 18, 1996, when Fritz Tuffli stood up and directed his innuendoes at me, in-person and broadcast live on our Tempe 11 TV channel.

I tore my eyes away from Fritz and casually looked out into the audience. Three familiar faces: Tempe's city manager, the city's director of communications, and my own chief of staff- stared up at me with stunned expressions. A few other people from the community were seated throughout the room, but what their reaction was, I couldn't tell. I focused on the man at the microphone again, while struggling to appear nonchalant. I leaned forward on my elbows, shifting my weight to better conceal and settle my nervousness and shaking legs. Outwardly, my gaze implied that I was paying rapt attention, but I was barely hearing the sound of Fritz's words.

He stopped at last, his time finished.

"Thank you," I heard myself say as I had a thousand times before, even in this moment of complete shock and fear, sounding calm and professional. When a speaker finished, I always thanked them and called for the next person. It was a perfunctory process, yet an important one for public discourse. Everyone received the same level of polite attention.

Another person rose to speak. I don't remember who it was or what he said. When that person was done, I knew I couldn't sit in that room another minute. I seized the moment and quickly stated, "Seeing no other members of the community wishing to address the council the meeting is adjourned, thank you," without taking a breath or inserting proper grammatical pause, and provided a harder than usual rap of the gavel. I sat frozen in self-conscious fear, nearly immobilized by the conflicting emotions spinning inside me. I wanted to look at my colleagues, but I didn't want to see the angst and frustration in their faces. I wanted to run out of the room, like a frightened child, but I knew that was the last thing I could afford to do, or would do. In fact, I had to do just the opposite. I had to move slowly and deliberately and behave calmly and professionally. Somehow, I had to find it in me to even smile a bit. I knew everyone was watching me. I was the mayor.

Instead, I tunneled my vision to the small red "microphone off" button I had tapped moments ago. I concentrated on that little piece of the world as I slowly gathered my papers and packed up. My head was pounding, and the urge to bolt from the chambers was overwhelming. I resisted it. I had to appear in control, unaffected. Later I would learn that Councilman Dennis Cahill jumped from his seat, chased Fritz into the outside courtyard, and threatened to deck him, but the others silently shuffled their papers into order, just like me.

Finally, Councilwoman Spears said to no one in particular, "This is just ridiculous."

Carol Smith added an irritated "Yeah" with a huff and shot a disgusted look my way. Any second, I feared, Carol would vent her feelings about the entire situation. She was never shy about sharing her opinions. Whether supportive or accusatory, I knew I could not handle hearing them at that moment. My composure, held together by habit and necessity, had frayed down to its final seconds. I was struggling just to breathe without having to take deep breaths.

Joe Spracale, a fatherly man in his seventies, put a caring hand on my shoulder and looked right at me. "These people are crazy, Boss." Joe often called me "Boss" and his use of the term at that moment indicated to me that our relationship was unchanged.

I just nodded. His face told me that he knew the score. I darted a quick glance at the others and saw the same knowledge in every face. They all knew. Everyone knew. I felt exposed, like I had somehow let them down, although the only thing that had changed was a public implication of what I assumed had long been a private understanding. Their faces mirrored my own uncertainty and frustration. Sexual orientation was once again going to be a political issue in Tempe, only this time it was going to be one particular person's sexual orientation.

Mine.

I couldn't say anything. My throat was tight and my stomach ached. I managed a weak smile, grabbed my papers, and pulled open the exit door behind us. Normally, I took the elevator up the four floors to my office, but on this night building renovations had closed us out of our usual spaces. Instead, we were housed in temporary offices on the third floor of a commercial office building next door to City Hall.

I left the chamber and exited the building, walking quickly across the parking lot toward the outdoor stairwell, where I took three steps at a time to distance myself that much more from my colleagues and anyone else who might try to ask me any questions. Anxiety twisted my insides and heightened my senses. I noticed that the stairs had not been cleaned to the corners, and made a mental note to speak to the city manager about the cleaning service. The stale air smelled of fresh paint. Fluorescent lights buzzed above me, beaming down with an absurd yellow intensity. My world was crumbling around me, but my usual attention to detail had not been shaken. If I had been able to, I might have laughed at myself. I'd just been publicly outed, for all practical purposes, confronted in front of my colleagues and on live TV, my political future compromised and headed into realms unknown, but by tomorrow evening, these stairs would be clean.

I arrived at my temporary office on the third floor, certain of one thing: I had to get as far away from the mayor's office, from Tempe, and from all the uncertainties surrounding me as quickly as possible. A moment of comfort flashed through me when I remembered my red-eye flight to Atlanta was only a few hours away. In the private hell of the last thirty minutes, I'd forgotten that I was going to visit friends and attend the 1996 Summer Olympics. I had spent $625 for a ticket to witness the opening ceremonies and had a $270 ticket for the men's gymnastics finals. I was not going to miss those. I know; the opening performance and men's gymnastics. Of course I'm gay. First, though, I had to get out of the office without being confronted by Fritz and his friends, or anyone else for that matter, and especially without meeting any members of the council.

I knew I didn't have anything to say yet. I knew I needed to think.

Usually after council meetings, I would touch base with my staff to discuss any issues raised in the meeting. I might even make a few phone calls if the hour wasn't too late for business. This night was different. I saw and talked to no one, and no one talked to me. I tidied my desk in a lonely, heavy silence. I hadn't wanted company, true, but the completeness of my solitude made it clear: I was being avoided. I was being left to rearrange the deck chairs on my own sinking ship; no one else was about to get on board.

I waited, sitting numb and quiet in my office, watching the clock over the door tick down the minutes. When I was sure that everyone had gone, I took the elevator to the first floor and left the building.

The sultry night air assaulted me with its heat and weight.

My car was the lone vehicle in the desolate parking lot. *Thank you*, I thought, gratefully, shedding my jacket and tie, as the remains of the summer day's triple-digit heat swelled up off the asphalt, engulfing me.

Once I was secure in the safety of my car, the vague, queasy knot in my stomach turned into a sharp, focused pain. As I started the engine, cranked the air conditioning, and rolled out of the lot and into the night, I told myself to breathe. I focused on pulling air in and out of my lungs with deep breaths. I knew that if I didn't keep my attention on breathing, I'd lose control of myself and surrender to an anxiety attack so debilitating I'd never make it home.

I drove, automatically heading east on Fifth Street and then south on College Avenue. I sat waiting for the light to change at College and University Drive. Directly in front of me, across University, was the campus of Arizona State University. To my left were some dorms. On my right, I stared at the historic brick of the All Saints Newman Center, the Catholic Church where I had been a member since 1975. It was the first time in a long time that I had even noticed the church on my daily drive home. I turned left, headed east on University Drive and passed under the pedestrian bridge marked with "Arizona State University" in letters that span the six-lane street.

"This is my life," I said out loud, almost as a prayer, an appeal. "But where is it heading?" My entire adult life revolved around first studying and then working at Arizona State University, around the same Catholic Church and Tempe politics. I had walked over and driven under that bridge thousands of times. The university had always given me a sense of place, of connection, of home. The church and my Christian beliefs had been the very foundation for me wanting to serve others and make a difference in their lives. As crazy as it might sound, I had long thought and felt that serving others was what I was supposed to do with my life.

Yet, tonight, passing the places I found most comforting

did little to quell the anxiety growing inside me. Stomach acid bubbled and burned in my throat. My confusion and anger morphed into emotional free fall.

"You're different."

The voice came from deep within. It wasn't a stranger: I'd known, lived with, and sometimes feared that voice my whole life. At times I'd tried to push it down; I'd tried to ignore it. I'd tried to bury it in a mountain of responsibilities and obligations. And yes, sometimes it was my only friend, too. Other times, I'd even convinced myself that it was gone forever.

It wasn't. That voice was back and stronger than ever. And worse, it was no longer one voice: it sounded like the voice of an entire community: *We know about you. We know who you* really *are.*

My stomach lurched and I knew I wasn't going to make it home. I had controlled myself for the others, but the effort had weakened me. I was about to puke. Head spinning, stomach throbbing, I caught a green light at Rural and University and wheeled into a gas station on the corner, hurrying inside, to interrupt the customer already at the register and get the attention of the cashier.

"Key to the men's room?"

That was rude, but the rising liquids and lumps in my esophagus were moving upwards, still burning and still bubbling, held back only by the sheer determination that the mayor of this city would not redecorate that candy rack or counter with vomit.

Inside the restroom, I pushed open the stall door and reached for porcelain all in one frantic motion. The vomit came in a few waves of gut-wrenching spasms. Spitting acid saliva and smelling the stench from the bowl, I found myself thinking of my tie, safely tossed with my jacket in the backseat of my car. The craziness of the thought brought a giddy smile. My tie? My career was probably over, and I was thinking about my tie? I gulped for air, filling my nostrils with the stale smell of old urine and disinfectant. The rank smells sobered me. *I've got to get out of here.*

Breathing through my mouth and trying to steady myself, I realized I was still clutching the restroom key: a bit of brass chained to a foot-long wooden dowel that had been wrapped with black electrical tape. I just stared intently at the key, as though it might offer some advice or counsel. Finally, I stood and washed my hands at the sink and wiped my mouth with a wet right hand. I looked into the stainless steel mirror that was so badly scratched I could only make out a blurred image of myself, like I might see in a trick mirror in a carnival.

We quickly learn in politics that we cannot help but think of our lives, both private and public, in terms of how events will play in the press. "Mayor wins re-election," a headline might read. "Tempe gives mayor nod." Only now, the headline I imagined read, "Messed-up, stressed-out, closeted fag mayor pukes in gas station." How attractive.

Minutes later, I made it home and sank into the comfort of my couch. What would happen next? How was I going to handle all this? And then reality really sank in: this was just the beginning.

Ready or not, the day was imminent when what I had long hidden would be made public. *What should I do? What could I do? What did I want to do?* As inevitable as it was, I should have thought of a plan for coming out of the closet as a gay man. I hadn't. This was 1996; there weren't a lot of openly gay elected officials yet, and no mayors outside of gay enclaves such as West Hollywood or Wilton Manors, Florida, that I knew of anyway. Tempe was about to become the largest city in the United States with an openly gay mayor and remain so for nearly six years. I might have been even more fearful had I known that fact, as I sat there, contemplating my future and feeling the isolation of my circumstances.

As the mayor, an elected official and public person, proclaiming my gay identity openly was walking into the void of the political unknown. As a young, moderate Republican in Arizona (becoming a Democrat would take place later) and elected to a non-partisan local office, I would be like a piece of raw meat lowered into a shark tank. Sure, my friend Jim Kolbe, a congressman from southern Arizona, had been outed a couple months previously. But he had decades of political service and relationships to fend off any challenges. My adversaries would surely swoop in, cut me up, and render me unworthy by the next election. In local politics, any type of glaring vulnerability is exploited and exaggerated by one's adversaries. That was despair speaking, and those thoughts did not persevere. Frustration would pass fast, and rage would swiftly transform into determination.

I would come up with a response, a plan. Somehow, I would figure out how to survive this. But at that moment, all I could think about was getting out of town. I showered, quickly packed a single carry-on bag, and headed to the airport, hours early. I sat in the boarding area alone with my arms folded across my chest and a baseball cap pulled low over my eyes, lost in my thoughts.

Thirty years peeled away as I waited for my flight in Sky Harbor airport, slumped anonymously in a black plastic chair. My mind slipped back to my earliest memories of the journey I had traveled, the one I was still on, to the beginnings of my beginnings and the first moments that I knew I was indeed "different."

CHAPTER TWO

Beginnings

He was riding a lime green Sting-Ray bicycle with a white banana seat and chopper handlebars.

I knew who he was and had seen him around the neighborhood plenty of times, but my memory locks on that moment, on that image of him: sitting on the bike, confident, laughing. I knew something different was going on inside me. I didn't understand it. The feeling wasn't sexual. It was more like a stirring deep inside me, an attraction and awareness, an interest I had not felt before.

It was late afternoon on a sunny and crisp fall day. School was done for the day, and my friends and I were hanging out in my backyard. Just beyond our property line was a vacant lot where neighborhood kids would gather, and I could see a bunch of boys on bikes gathered there. The sun was throwing long shadows on the piles of changing leaves as the boy glided his bike into the lot and stopped by his friends.

He had whitish-blonde, shoulder-length hair and wore a

white tank top. At thirteen or fourteen, he was a few years older than me, and I remember being fascinated by his shoulders and arms and the sloping curves of his biceps and triceps. It wasn't that I wanted to have sex with him—I didn't have any inkling about sexuality or sex at all—but I was enthralled by his physique and presence. There was something about him that drew me in. I stared, wanting to be closer to him.

That was the first time I remember being attracted to guys.

That's when I began noticing their faces, smiles, chests, and shoulders more than in passing. That's when I started to notice little things that a particular boy did or wore that made me take a second look at him. As I grew older, when I noticed something about another boy that attracted me—whether it was his body or his mannerisms or his clothes or whatever—I'd check myself to see if what was going on inside me was the same feeling as I had about the boy on the green Sting-Ray. And more often than not, it *was* the same feeling. But as I grew older, I was taught from all directions that boys who looked at or thought about other boys were not okay. In fact, they were very bad, sick people.

* * *

Much as I would like to tell you that I had a boring, normal childhood—and as much as I would like to believe that myself—it's not entirely true.

Most of my childhood was simple, wonderful, and uncomplicated: a nice suburban, middle-class Italian American family life filled with love. But a series of events and influences drove me to a perplexing and dark place for a period of time, and I realize now that those experiences shaped me considerably over the years, in ways that have left indelible marks on who I am and how I see the world. Fortunately, I came out the other side and found a good, satisfying, and successful place in the world.

I was around ten the first time it happened; it was an

experience that changed me forever.

A couple of kids from a few streets up the hill, just over the border of Bloomfield, New Jersey, started hanging around down in my neighborhood. They seemed really cool. They seemed my age, too, but when they invited me to their "show" and started to take off their clothes, it was obvious they were older. They had a lot of hair in places I didn't yet. I watched what they did, both fascinated and shocked, as they put on their show for me. They said what they did was something all guys did with each other. They said I was lucky they chose me. It was all very casual at first.

That's how it started. I'd go up the hill, into the other neighborhood, and watch the show, always feeling a little scared, but also strangely curious and happy to be included.

One day they made me a part of the show. They did things to me—and made me do things—that felt wrong when forced, and hurt, especially at my young age.

After that experience, I ran home, shaking, my little tan shorts now soiled in the front and back. My former Marine father was standing near the doorway when I burst into the house, sobbing. I couldn't avoid him.

"What happened? What did you do?" he cried when he saw me, scooping me into his arms. "What happened?"

I couldn't answer.

He carried me quickly upstairs, into the bathroom, stood me in the tub and helped me take off my ruined clothes. He ran a bath and washed me.

"What happened, Neil? What happened?" he asked over and over again.

I never told him. All I could do was cry and mumble "I don't know," over and over again too, between sobs.

He stayed with me until my bath was over, and then let me go to my room alone.

We never spoke of it again. Ever. He never mentioned it or asked me anything about it the next day. I was afraid he would ask again, and I wasn't sure what I would say, but I knew I didn't want him to know the truth. I never had any indication that he told my mother, either. I still don't know whether they ever discussed it. I doubt it.

I also don't know exactly why, but when the kids came down the hill another day looking for me, I went with them. I went back a few times, with three or four others too.

One Saturday morning those older kids brought a new kid. I got to stand with them and watch the new kid become the recipient of "the show."

It was years before I understood that I had been abused—and that I'd been a direct, though ignorant, participant in the abuse of others. It was quite a while before I understood this wasn't something that "all guys did" as kids. For a very long time, even after it stopped, I tried to chalk it up as little more than an exaggerated version of the age old children's game of "I'll show you mine, you show me yours"—after all the oldest boy in the group wasn't more than twelve or thirteen. But in my heart, I always knew it was beyond that. If it had truly been innocent play, why did it stay with me so? If it were truly innocent, why had I always thought less of myself for being involved in the first place? Even worse, I hated myself for doing to others what had been done to me. Did they run home in tears, too? Why had the experience left me shaking and sobbing, too filled with self-loathing to talk to my father as he implored me to tell him what had happened over and over again?

Those experiences left me a cipher when it came to any intimate personal relationships for many, many years. Family life went on as usual around me, but I spent a good part of my later childhood somewhat withdrawn, alone in my room reading or listening to music. And it wasn't until much later, in my thirties and with the help of a professional, that I came to understand how those experiences, now over forty-five years ago, thwarted my emotional and interpersonal development in such significant ways.

"You've internalized all of this in ways that really shaped you and had a significant impact, so it is good you are facing it now," she said. "And you've done better than many men who were victims of sexual abuse." She went on to say that I was fortunate to break away, that I might easily have continued the activities, then turning my shame and anger against others in much more harmful ways, becoming unlikeable and cruel, even violent into adolescence and beyond.

The statistics, I've learned in the period since, are truly startling. Men who were victimized in the way that I was as child often end up in prison, as drug addicts, or as long-term abusers themselves.

Instead, I was able to break away, though not before hurting others, for which I am profoundly sorry. It took me many years to forgive myself for those experiences. Yes, I've become successful. At the same time, however, most of my life from the moment of that abuse onwards has been about hiding my shame and trying to convince others—and myself—that I'm not bad or unworthy. So much of my life has been about trying to reconcile that ugly memory with the rest of my childhood, which was otherwise steeped in pride in its Italian-American, deeply Catholic tradition.

* * *

Since I was very small, I've heard the story of how my paternal grandmother crossed the Atlantic as an infant. Maria Pagano, my father's mother, was born in 1903 and remembered nothing about her voyage to America: nothing of the euphoria of sailing or of watching the ship carve a path through Mediterranean waters or even of the stagnant smells and seasick nights of fifteen days on the Atlantic. Grandma Giuliano, the name I would know her by many years later, would not remember being dropped into the ocean and, miraculously, being plucked from the salt water and pulled to safety, even though she often told the story decades after her tiny body was baptized by those cold waves.

She didn't remember the journey, but she understood later in life what it must have meant to her parents for the ship to pull into New York Harbor: opportunity. Sleepless with anticipation, the steerage mob would have been crowded on deck since before dawn, clutching bundles, babies, and wicker baskets, waiting. I try to imagine what it must have been like for passengers to catch that first glimpse of the Statue of Liberty, who was then a newcomer herself to the harbor, having only been erected seventeen years before. In my mind's eye, the crowded deck falls silent as the Statue of Liberty comes into view, as each of the new immigrants imagined the new future they hoped the green lady would have the power to grant.

* * *

Though I can visualize my Grandma Giuliano's passage vividly, my memories of my own childhood are much less clear. I don't remember much about growing up, largely because it seems unremarkable in many ways. Other than what I previously shared, I had a normal, basic, middle-class upbringing in a New Jersey suburb, with two parents, three siblings and relative safety and comfort. By comparison, my parents and grandparents' lives seemed to have had much more drama and intrigue.

Both of my parents lost their fathers at a young age.

My father's father, Roberto Giuliano, immigrated to the United States in 1911. He was sixteen years old when put on the boat with his two younger brothers by their parents: Carmonella Gabaciona Giuliano and Angelo Giuliano. They did not send their daughter Francesca Giuliano over to the new world. Eventually, Roberto married Maria Pagano and they settled in Bloomfield, New Jersey, where he worked as a street sweeper. Then, when my dad was ten years old, Roberto Giuliano had a heart attack while driving the street sweeper.

He died instantly at the age of forty-one. He had fathered nine children in his seventeen-year marriage, my father being the fourth. There were five other pregnancies that did not survive. He kept my Grandmother pregnant fourteen of their seventeen years together.

In a way, it turned out to be a family curse—not the pregnancies, but death while working for the city. Roberto's son, Charlie, one of my dad's brothers, became a street sweeper and suffered the same fate. He died of a heart attack driving the street sweeper when he was forty-four. As devastating as both these losses were, the joke in our family became, "Don't get a job with the city. It'll kill you."

Many years later, I ended up working for a different city in a different state in a different capacity—and suffering a few tragedies of my own as a result, none fatal of course. Maybe I should have heeded that advice.

My mother, on the other hand, lost her father in a completely different way. Her father, August Enright, deserted his wife, Anna Sinsel, and my mom and her older brother when they were young kids. After being abandoned by her husband, my maternal grandmother sent her daughter and son to an orphanage, something my mother resented for the rest of my grandmother's life. Mom felt her mother should have tried to take care of them; being given over to the orphanage felt like a double abandonment. But without her husband, Grandma Enright really had no way to care for her two offspring. She had little education and no skills. When she worked at all, she took in laundry or helped with chores at the rectory where the priests lived. She barely made enough to feed and shelter herself, let alone two growing children.

I can only imagine what my mother's life was like in the orphanage. She was around twelve when she was sent there and though she lived there for over a year, she never spoke of it. I can only suppose that the memories were complicated and painful, and like most mothers, she saw no reason to burden her children with them. I do know that it was difficult for her to resolve her feelings about her own mother, my Grandma Enright. About her father, her feelings were very clear: she had nothing to do with him for the rest of her life, even though she knew where he lived in New England and could have mended fences with him in the years before he died. We heard through distant relatives that he remarried in 1952, and then died when he fell and hit his head, while drunk, in 1971. He had never reached out and my mother's anger and resentment over his abandonment was very strong. She did try, however, to forgive her mother, though that certainly wasn't always easy for her.

Years later, after my mother was married and had her own family, Grandma Enright would come to live with us from time to time. The tension between them was palpable, spilling over into little family dramas that were never, ever completely resolved. After my parents left New Jersey for Arizona in 1973, Grandma moved to Arizona, too. She lived in her own apartment in a senior complex until she died in 1993. For many years, I went to see her at least once a month and to me, at least, she showed none of the behaviors that made my mother's blood boil. All I ever saw was a gentle calm that was nice to be around. For Christmas every year, even after I had my master's degree and was on the city council, she gave me a card with $20 inside as if I was still a boy.

One year, I gave her a red picnic basket filled with her favorite soup mixes, the hard candies she liked, and other little treats that I knew would brighten her days. It became a tradition: each Christmas for the next fifteen years, I re-filled the basket and gave it to her, freshly re-loaded with soup, candy, and any new favorite items she had become fond of. I still have the basket, and I put it under my Christmas tree each year in her memory.

* * *

My mother had been studying to become a pediatric nurse

when she met my dad, likely a result of having cared for the younger kids in the orphanage. But after they were married, she became a stay-at-home mom, who, other than a part-time job at the grade school, didn't work outside the home. She took care of the house and us kids and eventually grew into the role of political wife to my father when he began his career in public service. She didn't necessarily love that role, but she accepted it and was good at it.

While she was not an overly emotional or affectionate mother, she let me know I was loved by taking good care of her children. She was a den mother for my Cub Scouts pack, volunteered for school field trips, and did most of the things that many stay-at-home Mom's did in those days.

She also knew about me.

Truth leaves mothers clues, and my mom knew my truth long before I was ready to accept that she knew it. Growing up, we never discussed personal things. I probably would never have brought it up, even as an adult. That depth of conversation and sharing was not ever a part of our relationship. But in the early 1990s, at my brother Greg's commencement from his doctorate program she asked me point-blank: "Are you gay?"

By then I was in my mid-thirties. My father had been dead for fifteen years, and since his death I had grown increasingly distant from my family as I grew sure about who I really was. And there was my mom, trying valiantly to bridge the wide divide.

Without making eye contact with her, I said nonchalantly, "Yeah, why?"

"No one knows you, Neil, you're a stranger," she said. "And no one cares if you are gay."

She spoke warmly and I knew she meant to be reassuring, but her words made me uncomfortable anyway. *We spend decades avoiding any kind of deep personal connections or conversations and she wants to jump to this one about me?* She was telling me point blank that no one in my family cared that I was gay; she was telling me that it changed nothing in her love for me, even if that is not how she verbalized it. But it didn't matter that she had accepted me for who I was: I still couldn't fully accept myself, and I certainly didn't want to discuss it with my mother. It was complicated beyond her knowledge, going back to those "shows" and my role in them. It was complicated by my own confusion, by my own shame. It was complicated by decades of feeling that being gay was a cause for shame.

It was easier for my mother to be relaxed and open about my sexual orientation than it was for me. For years she felt my distance, and thought it was just that I didn't want to come out to her. My issues were deeper and I was working on them, but she wanted me to know it was okay, so she just laughed and said, "I don't know how I got two!"

She was referring to my younger brother, John, and me. I don't know that John had come out to her, either, but, as I've said, mothers always know.

Later in life, when I was an elected official and out of the closet, Mom became one of my biggest fans and public defenders. I accept now that neither of us was perfect as son or mother, but mother and son we were. There was always love.

But I've gotten ahead of myself. When I say that my parents' families had all the drama, I mean it. There's more.

Grandma Enright had a sister, my mom's Aunt Jean. Aunt Jean was single, but she and her "best friend" traveled together and acted in every way like an old married couple—which was fine, except that her "best friend" was the local Catholic Monsignor. As a child, I never put it together, but now, looking back, I realize they were probably having an affair. In fact, my siblings and I now have a theory that Aunt Jean was actually our mother's mother, our Grandmother!

Our theory goes like this:

Aunt Jean, who was my Godmother, got pregnant by her friend the priest and had the child, my mom. That could have been the truth of the orphanage right there. If that were true it would explain the strained relationship my mother and "Grandma Enright" had all those years: their entire history was based on a lie.

Of course, all of this is pure conjecture on our part, and now all of the parties involved are long dead. But I can tell you this much: Aunt Jean often acted more like the grandmother than Grandma Enright. My mom looked like her much more than Grandma Enright. And shame makes people do and say strange things, I know that from my own experiences.

I loved being with Aunt Jean. She chain-smoked and covered the heavy odor of smoke with a distinct perfume that permeated her body and her apartment. The scent was neither particularly pleasing nor offensive. Rather, it was something strong and unique. I never asked her what the perfume was; instead I accepted it as Aunt Jean's signature scent.

She would take me out to lunch and inquire about my life: my school, my friends, and activities in a way that always made me feel special. She wasn't exactly glamorous, but she was fashionable and up-to-date and had a presence and style about her that made her different from most of the other women I knew. She was unique largely because she never married, and her being different resonated with me. She lived by herself in our town's only modern, high-rise apartment building, which, compared to our suburban neighborhood of single-family homes, seemed cool.

When I was in junior high school, she got sick with lung cancer. My mother moved her into my bedroom so she could be better cared for. A few months later, while Dad and us kids were vacationing on Pelican Island at the Jersey Shore, my dad got a call that she had died. We hurried home, cutting the vacation short. There was a funeral, but the kids were not included at all. I never learned why but it seemed almost like her family wanted to bury her quickly and move on. I never had a final good-bye with Aunt Jean—and whatever her secrets were, they died with her.

* * *

Where as my mother's family was fairly small, my father's side was the opposite. Aunts or uncles, there were a lot of them. As I've said, Grandma Giuliano had had an astounding fourteen pregnancies in her life, resulting in nine living children: five boys and four girls, one of whom was my father, Neil Anthony.

I don't remember hearing my father talk much about his upbringing, but my brother, Greg, remembers the stories told of physical abuse. Grandpa Giuliano's idea of discipline, in his short time as a parent, was to beat the hell out of his children. My father was a survivor of that abuse in many ways. As Greg put it, we are a family of survivors: my mother of the abandonment of her childhood, my father of the abuse of his, and me of the experiences I had with the kids up the hill. In spite of those deficits, they made the best life they could for us; and I've made the best life I could for myself.

My father's impact on my life was deeply important in many ways, although we were as different as father and son could be.

He was a full-blooded Italian football player who played under the legendary coach Amos Alonzo Stagg at Susquehanna University. At five feet, eight inches, he had a stocky build and seemed always to play the part of the likeable, gregarious jock that everyone admired. Dad went to college for two years, but never graduated. He enlisted in the Marines and served a couple of years before returning to Bloomfield. He was strong, outgoing, and social—the kind of person who really cared about people. Everyone knew my father and almost everyone liked him.

He worked all the time. Bloomfield was his hometown— he had been born and raised in the community—and in many ways he became the "local boy who makes good." He ran for city council against an incumbent and won. He even ran for mayor in a Republican primary, against the political machine in

town, and almost won. He would have loved my political life—
or most of it. His involvement in the community clearly set the
example for my own.

It would have been interesting to know him as an adult and
share some of my experiences in the world of politics, but it
wasn't to be. My only campaign for office while he was still
alive was for International President of Circle K International,
a collegiate service and leadership club sponsored by Kiwanis
International, while I was a junior at ASU. By then, I had been
living on my own since I was sixteen. The distance had grown
between us since that awful day when he scooped me into the
bathtub. I didn't share much about that campaign in August
1977 with him until after I won, and then only after my mom
took me aside during a weekend visit.

"Why don't you tell your father about your campaign and
how you won? He'd love to know more."

He had never asked much about my college experience, and
never about the leadership posts I held in Circle K, but I did
share with him about the campaign and how I won and I could
tell he was very proud of me. Did he know the real truth from
the very beginning about me? Was that why he didn't want to
get closer to me and engage with me? I honestly don't know,
and now it does not matter.

At home, he was an authority figure and definitely the "head
of the household." He was the old-school model of the strong
father figure whom no one questioned. Although he wasn't tall,
his thick, muscular build made him physically imposing. I don't
remember now if that contributed to the emotional distance
between us, but truthfully, I never longed for a deeper emotional
connection to him; I never felt like there was anything missing.
I understand now there probably was something missing, but at
the time I figured that was how it was supposed to be between
fathers and sons. I thought ours was exactly what the father/son
relationship was supposed to be: a very formal one.

As far as the issues of sex and sexuality, nothing was ever

spoken about it, one way or the other. My father never sat me down for the birds-and-bees talk about what went on between men and women. For a 1960s-era Catholic, sexual development, identity, and experimentation were things that happened through osmosis and accident.

Dad laid down the rules by which we lived but Mom was the day-to-day disciplinarian. She was the one who might deliver the backhanded slap for some misbehavior or the other, who might have ground a bit of soap into our back teeth when we swore. I can remember only one time when my father hit me: when I was in seventh grade, pretty old for such discipline. I had yelled at Grandma Enright, who was living with us in our house on Benson Street. Mom and Dad weren't home, but I was yelling and screaming at her about something while she stood at the stove. She did not respond: she just took my disrespectful outburst in stoic silence. But later, Grandma told Mom who told Dad who took me down to the basement.

His fury was evident. "Don't you ever yell at your grandmother like that again!" he yelled, hitting me exactly twice on the bottom with his belt. "Now, get out of here." As I ran to the steps to do exactly as he commanded, he punched his fist through the wall, leaving a gaping hole in the drywall. That hole stayed there for a long time, serving as a clear reminder to me to respect my elders. I never yelled at my grandmother ever again, but I yelled at my siblings plenty, I am sorry to say. I'll admit it: I did my share of teasing and fighting with them. I wasn't always the "loveable big brother." There were times when I terrorized my siblings, for no real reason other than control. That youthful drama is all so much easier to understand now, watching from up on the balcony of time lapsed and through the distance of years.

I have three siblings, I am the second oldest, and though we share a family of origin, we would each grow up to see the world differently as evidenced by our Presidential choices of 1992. Yes, it was a long time ago, but I chose that year because

of the unique choices that were available to voters that year—
and that haven't been as available to us since then. More on the
political landscape later, but in the 1992 Presidential elections,
my siblings and I voted as follows:

- John, my youngest brother who is also gay and who
  now lives in Key West, FL, voted for Bill Clinton.
- Gregory, my other younger brother who is married
  with two kids and lives in Rancho Santa Margarita,
  California, voted for the National Green Party candidate.
- My older sister Kim is a single mother. She adopted a
  baby girl from China, Jia, who is now sixteen and has
  been a part of our family since she was three. They live
  in San Ramon, California and in 1992 her vote went to
  Ross Perot.
- I voted for George H. W. Bush. He seemed smart,
  diplomatic and a no-nonsense guy, and I thought he
  deserved another term. He would be the only Bush and
  last Republican I would vote for as President, other
  than in the 2000 primary when I voted for John Mc-
  Cain; in the general I voted for Al Gore.

My interest in politics began with my father and grew from
there. By June 1968, I was fascinated by anything political. From
the solitude of my room, I wrote to campaign offices asking
for buttons and stickers for my collection. I clearly remember
being eleven years old and watching Robert Kennedy deliver
his victory speech in California. I was alone, it was very late
and everyone else was in bed, in our wood-paneled family room
built as an addition onto the house. I sat cross-legged on the red
shag carpet, watching the TV intently, fascinated by Kennedy's
ability to speak to people, to move their emotions with only his
words, to call them action. That was the only room in the house
with an air conditioner, so on hot summer nights the family

would migrate down from upstairs and sleep there. That night, however, was not so hot and I was by myself. After the speech, RFK was shot as he left the Ambassador Hotel. I stayed up all night watching the TV news coverage of his assassination. I remember crying, even being a bit afraid. I remember thinking of his young children I had seen on TV, wondering what would happen to them. I remember worrying: *What would this mean?* Even as a kid, I could see things were a mess. Martin Luther King, Jr., had been shot earlier that year, and now another Kennedy had been shot. The next morning my father would say that events that were happening all over the world were making people do crazy things here. He was thinking of Vietnam. He was a former Marine, but he was not a war hawk.

My political interests were definitely stronger than those of my siblings, but all of us were impacted by my father's political career. My own interest led me to join in walking the neighborhoods of Bloomfield as my dad campaigned for his seat on the city council in the fall of 1969. I was now thirteen.

Dad knew everyone. Everyone. Watching him shake hands, asking questions and making it a point to remember the details about everyone he met taught me about public service. My father wasn't a hard-core, win-at-all-costs, take-others-down politician—and I hope I never have been and won't ever become one, either. My dad was a public servant, and he took his responsibilities to his community very seriously. He was the perfect role model in that sense, a servant-leader long before the term was popularized.

I walked with him again in his Republican primary mayoral bid in 1971: he lost in a very close race against the establishment candidate, John Kinder, and I remember feeling bad for him as people expressed their sadness at what was suppose to be a victory party. He just shrugged off the loss. And I walked with him when he ran for re-election to city council in 1972. I loved being included for those few hours on Saturdays. It was during those times when I felt we were closest, and they too shaped me. I was proud of my dad: he was someone important to the community. He was someone who was trying to help people, and people responded to him, worked hard for him, and supported him in very positive ways.

My father's district was Ward One and as we walked the neighborhoods together, I got an up-close-and-personal education about Bloomfield and its residents. "Walk with Me" was his slogan for his campaigns, and people did. Politically moderate and mostly middle-class, Bloomfield was an ethnic community with one main drag, Broad Street, running from north to south through the length of town. Most residents in the city were either Italian or Polish, and so, too, was my father's ward. Although he was Italian, Dad enjoyed solid support from both groups. In his first election, he unseated a twenty-six year incumbent riding a wave of ethnic support that he worked diligently to maintain.

My father was a very moderate Republican. He was a good Catholic and he raised his family in the church—but he wasn't a right wing, "live the way I do" Republican. Today, he would have to be in order to carry the party banner, especially in the West and the South, where "Republican" and "religious conservative" have practically become synonyms. But that just was not him.

Dad never wore a suit. He knew he didn't need one to serve his community, and he knew without having to be told by a focus group or a media advisor that his constituents would trust him more if he stayed true to himself. He was a casual guy, usually wearing khakis and a blue, short-sleeved buttoned shirt. "Dressed up" for him meant he added a blue blazer. Nothing flashy. When he and I walked the neighborhoods of Ward One, he had on his khakis and his blue shirt: familiar, comfortable, and easy. On these outings, his political style was old school: the outgoing, backslapping, approachable, relationship-building campaigning that suited the era, before technology and media became the tools to sway voters that they are today. I believe we need more of that style of campaigning today. Dad wanted people to feel like they knew him. He wanted to know them. Dad believed that the relationship was as important as the issues he would be elected to address, that trust was more important than the issues. And in those Saturday afternoon talks with our neighbors, it was rare that issues were ever discussed. Instead, he asked about people's families and jobs. He talked about marriages and christenings and graduations and that day's slate of college football games He listened to what was going on in the lives of the people in his district.

While policy is important, it turned out that Dad's approach is as important now as it was then. My own life of public service has taught me that it's all about building and maintaining relationships and helping people. If you want to be a successful politician, you really *do* have to be a public servant. To serve, you have to be available to the people. You have to listen to them. You have to be just as concerned with what's going on in their lives—with their children, their families, their workplaces, and their neighborhood—as you are about getting their vote.

When the game becomes solely about vote-getting, you're a politician and not a public servant. People aren't stupid: they know the difference. They know who has taken the time to really build a relationship with them and who hasn't. That sort of relationship building may seem too old-fashioned for a digital age—and perhaps some aspects of it belong to a bygone era when schedules were simple and people interacted more easily. But other parts of it will always be relevant. Today's public servants may build relationships via Twitter or on Facebook, but however it's done, the need for personal connection remains the same. That's one of the most important lessons my father taught me as we traversed up the stairs to wide wrap-around porches and across the green lawns of Bloomfield on crisp Saturdays in the fall.

One of my most vivid memories of my dad's tenure on the city council came one summer night in the early seventies when riots erupted in Newark, which is on the southern border of

Bloomfield. I'll never forget piling in the police car with Dad as we raced to the edge of town. He took me along on these excursions because he knew I had an interest in politics—he saw me collecting the bumper stickers and posters from national political campaigns—so he exposed me to as much as he could of his city councilman experience. And I ate it all up. The Bloomfield police had formed a blockade of patrol cars and barricades separating the town from the Newark city limits in an effort to keep the violence from spilling over into our community. From the back seat of the squad car, I watched a tank roll down the street on the Newark side of the barricade. I could see people running as smoke curled up into the sky from the riot fires.

It was terrifying and fascinating at the same time. It was another thing I loved about being with my dad: his position gave me a window on a world much bigger than my own. Being his son broadened my self-esteem in ways I needed. In the annual community parades on Memorial Day or the Fourth of July, I would walk next to him as everyone waved. My community knew me as the councilman's gangly and quiet son and when I was with Dad, I was a part of something important. He was always doing things for people and often said that the job of a councilman was to help people. He was right.

He believed in what he was doing, and he was good at it, but that didn't mean he was without his own oddities. As an Italian Catholic family, we counted Christmas as the focal point of the year. We always had a wooden nativity set complete with a porcelain Baby Jesus who never appeared until Christmas morning. We also had a tradition of waiting until Christmas Eve to get our Christmas tree. On that night, we'd decorate the tree together and Mom always made sloppy joe sandwiches. Always. That was our special family tradition every year.

Years later, in 1975, I figured out the truth about the Christmas tree tradition.

By then, the family had moved to Arizona, and that

Christmas, I volunteered to work at a tree lot as a fundraiser for the Kiwanis Club of Tempe, which sponsored my Circle K Club on the ASU campus. People bought trees as early as the day after Thanksgiving and throughout the month of December, but when the clock wound down to the last few days before Christmas, we began giving Christmas trees away. By Christmas Eve, we were just happy to be rid of them.

A light bulb went on in my brain when I realized my dad had waited until Christmas Eve all those years not because of some family tradition—but so we could get a free tree! Until then, it had never really occurred to me that we could have had a tree three or four weeks *before* Christmas. We certainly weren't rich, but I'm pretty sure we could have afforded a Christmas tree. My dad wasn't the kind of man who believed in wasting money, but he certainly wasn't miserly either. It was just odd that he waited to get a free tree.

What was my dad thinking? I don't know. It certainly wasn't a big deal, but it's one of those little things that now I look back on wonder about.

Free tree or not, whenever my father's family gathered, you could bet on a loud, stereotypical, Italian event. Since my father was one of nine children and most of them had kids of their own, Giuliano Christmases meant kids everywhere. They also meant *food*. If you picture a scene out of *Good Fellas* with constant activity and people coming and going continually, you've got a Giuliano family gathering.

On Sundays, Grandma Giuliano was always in the kitchen. She lived in the same house from the time I was born until she died, at age ninety-four, in 1996. The house was tiny, with a comforting smell of marinara sauce and fried meatballs that lingered in my young mind no matter what she was actually cooking. On the way to her house, we would stop at Brookdale Bakery where the warm air and aroma from the bread ovens would swirl around us as soon as Dad pulled open the door. We bought fresh crumb buns and several loaves of bread to go with whatever delicious thing Grandma was cooking. But as wonderful as the bread smelled, the real anticipation began when we arrived at her house and saw the ravioli board on the table.

"The board's out!" my siblings and I would yell in our excitement. "Grandma's making ravies!"

It was no less exciting the five hundredth time than the first. For home-made ravioli, there were two official posts for young hands: (1) cutting the ravioli from the dough Grandma rolled out on the board; or (2) at the other end of the operation, putting the fork marks on the dough to seal the edges shut. Grandma always did the middle step—wrapping the cheese inside the dough—herself. I loved making ravies, but I never ate them: I didn't like ricotta cheese. Still, my mouth waters when I recall those Sundays at Grandma Giuliano's house. There was always salad, fresh Italian ham, two or three jugs of wine, and some kind of homemade pasta that melted, like butter, in our mouths. Then, for the main course, there were pan-fried pork chops or fried chicken breasts or meatballs or pounded veal, each perfectly breaded and fried until it was crispy and flaky on the outside and moist and tender inside. I can still smell her marinara sauce laced over homemade pasta. Her huge dining table comfortably sat fifteen people, and all day long family and neighbors came and went, sitting down to eat in shifts.

My siblings have all of Grandma Giuliano's recipes and as adults have actually learned to cook. Unfortunately, I never paid close attention to all that went on in the kitchen. To this day, I have only a limited knowledge of how to prepare good meals. I am very good at ordering them, however, and know what I like, and much of that comes from those early days at Grandma's house.

Those Sunday afternoons rank as one of my most significant childhood memories: eating all day and running around Grandma's house with all my cousins. Grandma Giuliano was very important to me and had unbelievable patience with all of us. Even with all that chaos at her house every Sunday, week after week, only once in my entire life did I ever hear her raise her voice.

In addition to my family, my two maiden aunts—Aunt Francis, "Aunt Fran" as we called her, and Aunt Julia—were fixtures at these Sunday gatherings. They shared a bedroom in that same house with Grandma for many years. Aunt Fran kept plastic on the couch and, for thirty-two years, worked with machine-like regularity at her data entry job at an insurance company. She could be extremely firm—very strict and disciplinary—a trait that didn't always endear her to us kids.

"Watch that ice cream," Aunt Fran would yell. "Don't let that fall." Or it was "Stop that running!" or "You're making too much noise."

But as stern as she was, she could also be very funny. She was also a huge Jerry Lewis fan. "I would marry Jerry Lewis," she would say. Many years later, I gave her a picture of me with Jerry Lewis on the national Muscular Dystrophy Telethon. Even later, she developed a crush on Dan Quayle. By then, I was in a position to ask his staff to send her an autographed glossy photo, which, to this day, I'm certain, hangs on a wall somewhere in her home in Franklin, New Jersey, where she still lives with Aunt Julia. They're both in their late seventies now, and despite some health challenges, still going strong.

Aunt Julia, or Aunt Gigi as we called her, had a much more laissez-faire approach with us kids. She was slighter, soft-spoken, shyer, enjoying little of life outside of her work at the Schering Drug Company, her family members, and going to church.

There was one exchange between them when I was a kid that I can't forget.

"Liberace?" Aunt Fran said. "He's a fag. Everyone knows he's a fag."

I don't remember now how that topic came up, but I remember the words very clearly, and the sound of disapproval in Aunt Fran's voice.

"That's not nice, Fran," Aunt Gigi said.

"Well, you know he is."

"It doesn't matter, that's not nice."

"Oh Julia!" Aunt Fran sounded exasperated with her sisters' gentleness. To her mind, she was simply telling the truth the way she saw it, no slur intended. Still, I logged it down deep inside along with the hundreds of other quiet digs and negative comments about homosexuals that kept my closet door tightly shut. No matter what I had experienced or what I feared deep down about myself, I would keep it all hidden.

Religion made those feelings of shame and fear stronger.

Like any good, traditional Italian family, we attended Sacred Heart Church on Sundays and sat through Masses. I tried being an altar boy a couple times, but I just thought it was weird and boring. Going to church as a kid was a chore and while I credit my church going and Sunday school catechism as a child with giving me a moral center that governs much of what I believe about right and wrong, the Catholic Mass never brought me a connection to God. That connection for me came many years later when I discovered the Catholic Newman Center on the ASU campus.

The church played its role in keeping me sealed in my personal closet, though it was far subtler than it might have been if I had belonged to a more evangelical faith. It wasn't so much that the Bible was quoted to me chapter and verse, but more that there was "a way things are supposed to be." Watching the rippling muscles of the neighborhood boys—as fascinating as that was for me—wasn't written anywhere in "the way things are supposed to be." The omission made it perfectly clear to me that those feelings and attractions weren't anything I should ever speak of out loud. Not to mention the things I had done with and to other boys.

* * *

I find it fascinating now to read my report cards from those years, and the written exchange between my teachers and my parents. My fourth grade teacher, in January of 1966, wrote: "Neil's standards have greatly faltered in these last few months. He does not take pride in the neatness and correctness of his work as he once did. Neil has lost also some of the fine spirit of 'awareness' that he once brought to classroom discussion. Can you suggest any personal reasons there may be for this situation?"

My father's note on the report card, dated February 4, 1966, is telling: "Mrs. Kuras—regarding your comment—Neil was hesitant in our father-son discussion, however, I think the problem lies at school. I believe some of his classmates are pressuring him. Mrs. G. will be glad to meet with you to discuss this further. I believe Neil is trying to do better." "Pressuring him"? "Personal reasons"? What exactly were they trying to communicate, but wouldn't say, to each other? I don't recall much about the time, and don't remember "Mrs. G." ever raising the topic with me.

A year later, my fifth grade teacher, Mrs. Jacobi gave me an "N," meaning "needs improvement," for every quarter in the category of "claims only his share of attention," along with another written appeal for a parent-teacher conference. "He needs to continue to work toward mature behavior," she wrote. Mrs. Jacobi left Bloomfield School after that year, not because of me I hope. Her attention to me made a real impact. She had me stay after school to help her with things in the classroom, and gave me special assignments that were very easy, perhaps as a way to improve my confidence and receive her approval, and therefore build trust and respect that had not been present. And I did improve and I wouldn't disappoint her now that we had a special relationship. We exchanged letters after she left

Bloomfield and was teaching in Brick Town, New Jersey. In one
of her letters to me dated October 25, 1967, she wrote:

> How happy I was to receive your letter! I really miss
> you, Neil. Do you help Mr. Linkin after school the way
> you helped me? What are you doing in school now? I
> hope no one sees the flowers on the envelope of this
> letter. They'll think you have a girlfriend! Please write
> again.
>   Love, Mrs. Jacobi

We did write further, not for long, but that extra interest she
showed in me left a mark for good, although I would continue
to get "needs improvement" on "citizenship" into junior high,
in four of my seven classes in seventh grade. Was my acting out
in class somehow related to what I had experienced with the
boys up the hill? Probably, although I chose not to delve into
that aspect when I finally faced it all as an adult.

I was starting to pay attention to what was going on in the
world. I had a pen pal, arranged though a national organization,
with an Air Force Captain serving in the Vietnam War, stationed
in Thailand. I found it very cool and exciting to be in touch with
a real soldier, although as an eleven-year-old, I didn't grasp it
very well. In a letter dated July 18, 1967, Captain D.B. Deigan
wrote the following to me:

> Sorry to take so long in answering your letter. I'm glad
> to know that you are aware that I am in Thailand. Most
> people don't realize how many men are flying into
> Vietnam from here. So far we have been lucky enough
> not to have been attacked here. We are flying planes
> that your dad might remember. We have no jets. The
> air commandos fly mostly night missions, attacking
> truck routes, which bring supplies from North to South
> Vietnam. It's hard to explain to you why I would like

to be in Vietnam. When I was your age I used to play soldier with toy guns. Several of the boys I grew up with in those days have died in Vietnam. They gave their lives fighting Communism thousands of miles from home in a hot, dirty jungle. I feel as though I owe them a debt to carry on the fight. Maybe you will never have to fight. I hope you won't. I am sure your parents hope you will never have to go to war. We all look forward to the day when it will all be over and we can go home to our families. Well, it's late and I have to be up at 5am, so I'll close. Write if you have time.

Your pen pal, Captain Deigan

I kept more and more to myself as I grew older. It was when we moved from 18 Barnett Street to our house on 36 Benson Street that I got my own room, which made my "life as a loner" even easier. If I was home, I was in my room by myself, where I would remain through my last years of elementary school, through junior high and most of the way through high school. The house was a similar to our old one only with more bedrooms. It was one of many like it in a suburb filled with spacious homes with big grass yards without fences and with basketball hoops on the garage.

I carved my name all over that house.

I carved "Neil" on the garage door and on the overhang to the basement entrance. Perhaps I was already beginning the long process of trying to carve out some type of clarity and identity for myself in a world that was beginning to make less and less sense to me. But I couldn't have explained it that way at the time. I couldn't explain why I did it, only that it was just something I liked to do.

The junior high school years added to my confusion. More and more, I felt I didn't know who I was, what I was good at, or how to be the person I wanted to be.

Toward the end of ninth grade, I helped a friend clean out

the apartment of an old relative of his who had passed away. The job consisted of carrying boxes down to the car, nothing difficult at all. One of the boxes was open and full of paperback books. I stole one. I didn't plan to, it was just right there, a yellow book with the title *Everything You Always Wanted to Know About Sex**. The asterisk was key: "**but were afraid to ask*" was added at the bottom in smaller print. I was afraid to ask anything about sex, so the book just seemed to speak to me. I grabbed it and stuck in my pants at the small of my back so my coat covered it up.

When I got home, I went straight to my room and locked the door behind me. I had a lot of questions I wanted to ask, but had never asked them. I didn't have close buddies for such conversations, and such talk would never have taken place at home. I mainly wanted to know what the book said about homosexuality, since deep down I was afraid I might be one, even though all I had ever heard was that they were sick men. I was definitely different than my friends, but was I a homosexual? I found the chapter I was looking for began on page 159.

What I read terrified me.

"What is male homosexuality?"

"Male homosexuality is a condition in which men have a driving emotional and sexual interest in other men." There was an explanation about the anatomical features involved and then: "In the process they often transform themselves into part-time women. They don women's clothes, wear makeup, adopt feminine mannerisms, and occasionally rearrange their bodies along feminine lines."

Oh shit.

"Do all homosexuals act this way?"

"Not all of them. There is a wide range of variation in homosexual behavior; however most homosexuals at one time or another in their lives act out some aspect of the female role."

Oh shit.

"Couldn't homosexuals just be born that way?"

"A lot of homosexuals would like to think so… Actually for

those who want to change there is a chance."

"How?"

"If a homosexual who wants to renounce homosexuality finds a psychiatrist who knows how to cure homosexuality, he has every chance of becoming a happy, well-adjusted heterosexual."

The questions and answers went on for another twenty-seven pages and with each page I turned, I became more and more fearful. If I was homosexual, I was more than just different. According to author Dr. David Reuben, I was really, really sick.

Today, I know that Dr. Reuben's explanations are completely false, shameful lies—even for his time. Thankfully, scientific and behavioral studies over time have proven how wrong he was, and how wrong those who still hold such views are. Unfortunately, even forty years after I read those words in *Everything You Wanted to Know About Sex**, there are still people out there who believe in Dr. Reuben's explanations—I have discovered that again and again in my career, both in politics and while serving as president of the national Gay and Lesbian Alliance Against Defamation, (GLAAD) later in life. Unbelievably, some of these anti-gay voices have even risen to the point of being considered as credible candidates for the office of President of the United States. They are careful not to use language like Dr. Reuben's in public, but I would bet that in private they do believe homosexuality is a disease. They have not evolved as our knowledge of sexual orientation has been enhanced.

In the early 1970s, however, what I read in that yellow book seemed to be the sum total of knowledge about homosexuality. It weighed on me as I tried to navigate junior high school.

I went to North Junior High School. It was a roll of the dice that I ended up at North: our family lived right on the border between North, the more well-to-do, WASP junior high, and South Junior High, which was the more ethnically diverse and rougher school. To attend North Junior High, I had to ride the bus every day, a first for me—along with the experience of being around more kids whose backgrounds were very different from my own. These were the kids from what I now realize were wealthy families, with parents who had college degrees.

To my surprise, I made the junior varsity soccer team and immediately learned the first lesson of competitive sports: being *on* the team and *playing in games* were two different things. I ran endless practice laps around a field the size of Rhode Island in relentless sun and suffocating humidity. When it was time to play, there was usually a spot for me—on the bench. We were barely two games into the season before everyone knew that Number 26 would only enter during "garbage time": when our team was either too far ahead to lose or too far behind to win. During one such time, I entered late in the game on a dreary, overcast day. The grass was wet and somehow I ended up with the ball deep in the opponents' territory, so I crossed to the middle, and kicked the ball into the net. I scored! My success didn't matter: we were already way ahead. No one seemed to notice the goal made by the skinny kid in a uniform that was so clean, it looked as if it was still warm from the dryer.

Unfortunately, the skills required in soccer—strength, agility, and coordination—just weren't in excess for me. Looking back, I had a better shot at becoming fluent in Portuguese by Thanksgiving than ever being one of the starting eleven. I wasn't the only one; there were three or four of us in that situation on the team, working to the best of our abilities and yet always frustrated by an innate lack of skill. We didn't let that dampen our spirits: our hearts and minds still brimmed with the desire to excel. My body, however, could not match my determination. At soccer camp in 1970, each of us went home with a little trophy with the inscription "World Cup Junior Soccer Champs." It was my first and last athletic trophy. You didn't have to win to receive one, you just had to be there. I still have it.

The trophy was nice and I cherish the lessons of being on the soccer team: determination, persistence, and team spirit, even if I didn't have the skills to offer much as a player. But in spite of my best efforts to be "one of the guys," I failed miserably—as

I would in most other social settings in high school and young adulthood. On the Junior Varsity soccer team, the other kids insinuated that the only reason I was there at all was because my dad was a city councilman. Looking back, they may have been right. But I knew—though I couldn't have articulated it then—there was much more than co-ordination and speed standing between my teammates and me.

My brilliant soccer career culminated after two seasons, most of which I spent huddled on the far end of the bench feeling alternately hopeful and thwarted. I wanted to be one of the cool athletes, but knew I wasn't. I watched the others play while inside, deep in my psyche, a voice told me the truth about myself. A truth I couldn't deny. I was unlike them beyond what they could ever know and it left me afraid and timid. I felt that I would have to compensate for it somehow, that I would have to make amends for what and who I was, without telling anyone. And that even doing so wouldn't change my emerging and fearful reality.

CHAPTER THREE

Slow Progress

I saw my first *Playboy* magazine in Tommy Debold's garage.

His house was on the next street over, Osborn Street, and at the back of the garage, there was a loft where we hung out. As we flipped through the magazines, looking at photographs of naked women, I was intrigued only because everyone else seemed to be. Even kissing Jamie, a cute, raven-haired girl, when we played spin the bottle at a boy-girl party in fifth grade hadn't excited me. I didn't want to play that game or have to kiss the girls; I didn't want more of any of that "fun stuff" the other guys enjoyed. Those types of games, like reading *Playboy*, were only exciting to me because we were doing something forbidden and I got to be with the guys.

At this point, however, it wasn't like I was thinking of transferring that kind of "fun stuff" interest to boys; I couldn't think in terms of *Playgirl* or of kissing a boy during a session of "Seven Minutes in Heaven." I just knew I got no thrill from the things that got the other boys my age excited—or at least no thrill beyond the novelty of it all.

Politics, however, continued to intrigue me. On my bedroom walls, which I had painted royal blue, I hung political posters of Richard Nixon and Edmund Muskie and pasted candidate bumper stickers. "Tricky Dick," as Nixon was known at the time, fascinated me far more than any girl and not because of his name. I loved politics, but I never thought of myself as a possible candidate. My father was so busy with politics; I doubted I would ever choose that work for myself. I didn't think I would be smart enough for that, but I could campaign for others and be a great helper. I had helped my father enough to know I could do more of that kind of work.

Politics consumed my father's life. After he became a city councilman, he was never home. He was always "going to a meeting." When he was at home, he was entertaining an endless parade of community leaders, political peers, and power brokers at our house while my mother served as chef and I acted the role of waiter and busboy. Dad was constantly campaigning, trading on his image as a "regular guy" in the community. Often, that meant packaging us as the "perfect little Italian family" and carting us with him from one event to the next. The dizzying number of activities and the toll it took on what was already for me, not entirely a "normal" childhood, made me swear that I'd never become a politician myself. Politics meant never having any peace. Politics meant always having to play my "role." Politics meant never being free to be myself. I felt painted into a corner by the requirements of my Dad's political career—and painted into a different corner by the changes and expectations that high school brought me.

By my sophomore year of high school, after leaving North Junior High and ninth grade, I knew I didn't have any desire to interact socially with girls, other than a few friends. What I wanted was to know the guys and to be close to them, but I hadn't connected that desire to my sexuality. I wasn't one of those "queer" kids, so being gay wasn't even a concept I considered. I declared myself a "late bloomer" and tried not to worry about it.

I had tried very hard to have an interest in girls, especially Christine Haese. We were very close, our small group, and I think she thought we were in love in high school, even though we were never "a couple." I knew I wasn't in love, but I didn't discourage her, even though I figured she had visions of a white picket fence and 2.5 little Giulianos in our future. After high school, she even transferred to ASU to be near me. I considered us to be great friends, but nothing more. While she was hopeful for a long time, in the end, she realized we would never be a couple. What's funny is that she had also had a crush on my Key Club buddy Ed Miller, who was also gay. Christine sure knew how to pick 'em.

My closest male friend during high school was Clayton Sanford, a tall, geeky, blond kid who, like me, didn't really fit into any of the social cliques. He lived next to the Debolds on Osborne Street, and his mom was a hot divorcee who oozed sexiness. My mom was just a regular mom, but Joyce Sanford was something else altogether. She was young and single and had short, blond hair. She dressed stylishly and was up on all the latest pop culture. In a word, she was hip.

Clayton didn't know where his dad was, and they lived with his mom's parents. I was over there a lot, or with him at his family's beach house at Ocean Beach, Unit Two, down at the Jersey Shore. We spent endless summer days on the boardwalk, crabbing or speeding around the bay in a motorboat. If I had to call someone my "best friend" during those years, it would be Clayton. But even with Clayton, I held back. I didn't feel I could be completely myself with anyone.

I was on the periphery of high school life at first. Though I wanted to be one of the leaders, it never happened. I tried: I ran for student government and for class offices, but I never won or got elected to anything beyond homeroom representative, which no one else really wanted. I sought positions my sophomore, junior and senior years of high school and lost each and every time.

Even though I'd walked the neighborhoods with my politician father, watching him campaign and glad hand and ask for votes, I just didn't have the confidence or interpersonal skills to connect socially with my peers. I was too guarded; I didn't fit in. I wasn't popular and, of course, being popular is how you got elected to anything in high school. I'm sure it probably still is. It wasn't that I was disliked; I just wasn't "in," and I had no idea how to change that status. If I could have, I would have transformed myself into John Stanford, the captain of the football team. Or I would have become a kid named Maurice, from the soccer team. These guys were cool in a way I never was. They were "studs" as we said back then. I watched in awe as they cruised the hallways of Bloomfield High School. My most heartfelt and intense desire was to be just like them. That was my attraction to them; sexuality had nothing to do with it.

The harsh reality for me was that at Bloomfield High in the early 1970s, I wasn't cool. Don't get me wrong, though. These days some kids are bullied mercilessly for being different, but I can honestly say that wasn't my experience. I was never hazed or teased. I was never rejected or ridiculed. I even interacted with the cool guys; I was the councilman's kid after all, and they liked me well enough to sign my yearbook with a detached, brief and vague "best wishes." They weren't cruel to me, but they weren't my friends either. I always knew that when I moved in their circles I was a visitor, not an insider.

If it hadn't been for the Key Club, I might have felt far more isolated and alone in high school than I did. Quite honestly, I view getting involved with Key Club as the single most significant turning point for my young adult development. I am not sure where or how I might have ended up as a person had I not made my way to that first meeting at Bloomfield High.

Key Club is an international high school organization that provides young people the opportunity to serve their communities, build character, and develop their leadership abilities. It is the high school equivalent of the collegiate Circle

K International, and also sponsored by Kiwanis International.

My high school Key Club was where I found my opportunity to blossom and grow. What I lacked in corner kicking skills for soccer or hitting the right octaves for chorus, I developed in organizing events and people and learning about leadership in Key Club. Where I languished on the athletic fields, I found my first sense of belonging in Key Club. My high school Key Club led to my Circle K International experience in college. That in turn led to my becoming involved with the Kiwanis Club of Tempe. Combined, those experiences prepared me to run for city council and then mayor. Key Club at Bloomfield High was the foundation for my entire political and public service future, the foundation for a life of purpose and accomplishment.

I went to the first informational meeting at the encouragement of my father. Early in my sophomore year, I brought home a packet with information on the various high school activities. As dad was walking through the kitchen, he couldn't help but notice the jumble of papers spread out on our big, wooden table.

"What's all this?" my father asked, seeing all the papers spread out on that table.

"Brochures and information about the clubs in school. I don't know what I should join," I said. "Maybe one of these sports, but which one?" No, I hadn't given up on sports. I guess I was still in denial about the body I inhabited and its absentee athleticism. I still hoped that if I could pick the right sport, I might do better. Like many high school guys, I viewed sports, any sport, as the only entry into the magical kingdom of the high school elite. I was wrong, but that's what I believed during those years.

"Well, let me see," Dad said, searching through the papers and pointing at a brochure. "What about this one?"

"Key Club?"

I was a little surprised that he hadn't selected a sport, but I knew he was right. My dad had been a collegiate football player.

He'd also been a Marine. I wanted badly to be like him, to be the stud jock that he had been, but I wasn't. Yet he never once pressured me to try out for any sport: that was all my idea. He was the one who told me it was okay to drop out of soccer in ninth grade. He saw me trying with all I could muster, and I think he understood the limits of my athletic abilities better than I did. He probably knew how desperately I wanted to be an all-American son and how deeply I believed becoming a sports hero would make him proud. By selecting Key Club for me instead of a sport, I believe my father was sending me an unspoken message of love and support in my effort to develop an identity separate from his own. Thanks to his gentle encouragement, I grudgingly loosened my grip on my sports fantasy.

Dad continued, "Yeah, it's sponsored by the Kiwanis Club, which is a men's group with some influential people that does community service in Bloomfield."

That sounded promising. "Okay," I said nodding. "I'll go to the meeting next week and check it out."

I would never be the son that I imagined he had hoped for when I was a little boy. None of his sons would be in all truth. He would never see me lead a fourth-quarter drive or hit the winning home run in the bottom of the ninth. I didn't know I could make him proud in other ways. I had no idea, sitting at the kitchen table in the early fall of my sophomore year of high school, that my political involvement and my life of community service would soon begin.

* * *

Mr. Michael Pinadella, the Key Club advisor, was a forty-something, stocky man with a shock of thick, white hair. I'm older now than he was then, but at that first organizational meeting, Mr. Pinadella seemed ancient to me. He dressed like most of the men who taught at my high school, in a beige sports coat and dark green pants.

I looked around the room and was buoyed by the unusual mixture of geeks, jocks, and some "lost" children like me: the kids who were neither cool nor un-cool. We were the faceless ones who drifted mostly anonymously through high school, but not entirely.

"Key Club is a good way to get involved," he told the small group of students who made up his audience. "Belonging to this club will develop your leadership skills through our many community service projects."

He went on to outline the kinds of community service we'd be doing: car washes, picking up garbage in the park, and things like that. Nothing earth shattering, but each important in its own way. What I remember most was the sense of camaraderie that I felt at that very first meeting. I felt welcomed and at home, and those feelings were good. *Finally*, I remember thinking. *Finally, a place where maybe I belong.*

My "new member" certificate is dated December 15, 1971. I still have it. One would think I was planning for a presidential library the way I have saved things, including journals and letters over the years that form a great deal of my ability to tell my story now.

I've saved much from my days in Key Club, because there I was no longer faceless. Key Club became my social anchor through the various events we planned. I ran for club vice-president at the beginning of my junior year and lost. I contemplated running for lieutenant governor of our division, which encompassed seven area schools including actor Tom Cruise's alma mater, Glen Ridge High School.

"You can't run for lieutenant governor, we already have people running," Lou Kallas, an older kid with a broad face and glasses, told me. He was a Key Club regular, the New Jersey District Treasurer and he understood the politics of the club better than I did. "You'll never win. There are plenty of people running more popular than you. Kids who've done more with the Club, too."

Ouch.

Lou wasn't going to win any beauty contests, but he was definitely bright and wielded a certain power in Key Club. He spoke from his seat at the long cafeteria table where several of us had gathered. Mr. Pinadella was there, too, listening to our conversations about the upcoming district convention and elections that would take place.

"Here's what you ought to do, Neil. Run for district treasurer."

I'd never thought of running for treasurer, Lou's current post. Mr. Pinadella didn't say a word, but he nodded his agreement. The club president was there, too, and he nodded as well.

"Okay," I said. "I'll do it. I'll run for district treasurer."

I had only the vaguest notion of what the district treasurer did. Something to do with money, I assumed. I didn't have a bank account of my own, and I wasn't very good at math either. In fact, I wrote numbers backwards all the time in my math classes and got my homework back with so many red circles that it looked more like art than my homework. No one had ever told me that my troubles with numbers might actually be a learning disability, though now I know that it probably is. Left to my own devices with that problem, though, I have compensated and covered for it throughout my life.

Because of my issues with numbers, I was hardly the perfect candidate, but in March 1973, I launched my first official political campaign at the New Jersey Key Club District convention held at Mount Airy Lodge in Pennsylvania's Pocono Mountains. I had learned a great deal in my speech class with Mr. Harry Berkheiser, so once I learned the right things to say in my presentations to the voting delegates—from Lou, of course—I performed well and was pretty impressive for a kid running for the first time. Somehow, even with "financial acumen" and "understands numbers" conspicuously missing from my resume, I won.

Later I realized how it had happened. The popular leaders of the district, graduating seniors on their way out of office, didn't want some of their younger peers to win, so they got behind a slate of candidates who would be considered "outsiders," and we all won the top four positions of the district.

I was ecstatic. I wanted to do a great job, and knew I had it in me to work well with the other leaders. But there soon was a glitch that put my fledgling political career in grave jeopardy.

My parents gathered us kids around that big kitchen table for a family conference.

"Kids," my father said, "we're moving to either California or Arizona."

What? What the hell is this about? I thought.

Later, I'd understand: my father had already suffered a mild heart attack, which he hadn't told us kids about. The health scare had made him re-evaluate his priorities in life. He had decided to resign from the city council and follow his dream of living out West.

For years my dad had read Zane Grey novels, and had always said he wanted to follow his own personal manifest destiny and move to San Bernadino, California, or Phoenix. I remember thinking San Bernadino and California sounded a whole lot better than Phoenix in Arizona, but no one asked me my opinion. This was not a family decision: it was a family *announcement.*

Even later, I learned from my adopted Godfather Bud, who had been my dad's campaign manager, there might have been even more to the story than the heart attack. My father, an elected official and a rising star, had refused to play ball with the powerful and corrupt leadership of northern New Jersey. Did he get crosswise with the wrong family? Did he vote against a big zoning issue that some influential people really wanted? I don't know the details. But I know it was very odd that even health issues would compel my father to resign a city council seat and move far, far away from all his family, to essentially restart his life in his mid-forties. The health issues were real, but was there more to the story of his sudden departure from the town where he had been born and raised and invested so much of his life?

I don't know for certain, but knowing what I know now about politics, and New Jersey politics in particular, I think so. I found an article in the local paper, dated May 24, 1973 but it was pretty vague:

> The councilman has accepted an offer to go with a national firm as a regional credit manager. He will move to either Arizona or Southern California. "This is a step up the ladder," said Councilman Giuliano, "Although it will mean re-shuffling my whole life."

Then the telling quote:

> "They can take Neil Giuliano out of Bloomfield, but they can't take Bloomfield out of Neil Giuliano."

My dad was not the most eloquent man, but I am guessing even he knew the saying is "You can take…" not "they can take…" His choice of pronoun is interesting to say the least. And when he got to Phoenix? He did not have a job. He eventually found a good one, as a branch manager for First National Bank of Arizona, which became First Interstate Bank and is now Wells Fargo. He bought a house on Bloomfield Road in northwest Phoenix, almost as if he were trying to stay as close to Bloomfield, New Jersey as he could.

These facts, which I learned as an adult, led me to conclude that my father didn't leave Bloomfield by choice. But at that family meeting, Dad simply announced his plans to move. He completely omitted any mention of his ailing health or any other issues. If he had told us, I might have understood. But in the absence of that detail, my reaction was pure teenaged fury.

"I'm not moving anywhere," I said. "I'm a state officer in Key Club now, and this is going to be my senior year."

Everyone got quiet and just sat in silence. Mom looked at Dad, who looked at me. I looked at everyone else around the table in disbelief.

A decision was made. But I didn't have to fight as hard as I thought I might in order to stay in Bloomfield.

That evening I dialed the Key Club district administrator, Fred Briggs. I had told him I might have to resign to move with my family, but was holding out hope that would not be the case. He had a positive influence on me and his calm but firm manner taught me a lot about working with other people and getting things accomplished. I would seriously disappoint him a year or so later with some teenaged hijinks, but that night in 1973, I had good news for him.

"Mr. Briggs, I talked with my parents, and they are going to let me stay and live with my grandmother so I can graduate from Bloomfield High. I don't have to resign as district treasurer of Key Club, sir."

"That's great, Neil," I remember Mr. Briggs saying, "I'm glad you don't have to resign. You were elected because you can learn and do a good job, and I am sure you will."

And so it went. Early that summer my family moved to Arizona. I stayed behind in Bloomfield.

I was probably the only senior at Bloomfield High who lived with three women: Grandma Giuliano, Aunt Fran, and Aunt Gigi—and yes, I was spoiled. I would stay in Uncle Al's old room, which was about the size of an area rug, literally maybe nine by twelve at most. Uncle Al had died several years earlier, we were told of a massive heart attack, at thirty-six, while still living in that house with his mom and two sisters. Hmmm. That sounded strange to me, even at that age. None of us kids went to his funeral services either. The same had happened when Aunt Jean died; it seemed the single adults who died had speedy burials that few attended. Uncle Al's old room, my new room, had two windows, a small heat radiator and nothing else.

It didn't matter to me. My father was born in that house, and my grandmother had lived there for close to seventy years. If ever there was a place that could be my second home, Grandma Giuliano's house was that place. I knew the house well: it had two stories, with three tiny bedrooms upstairs, a living room, dining room and kitchen on the main floor and a basement. The smell of years of Grandma's cooking lingered in every cranny of the place. The smell made me feel safe. Although she was getting older, she still cooked regularly and anytime she was cooking, I was eating those simple, but amazing, culinary delights. There was nothing more delicious than Grandma's homemade gravy between two pieces of white Wonder bread, no more intoxicating smell than her homemade marinara sauce I had grown up enjoying.

Each and every morning of my senior year, when I came downstairs before school, I found Grandma Giuliano at the table having tea and toast and looking at the newspaper. I am not certain she knew how to read very well, because she only went to a few years of school, but she surely spent a lot of time with the newspaper.

"Do you want breakfast?" she would say.

"No thanks, I don't eat breakfast."

"Okay, be careful."

That last year—my senior year of high school and the year I spent as the New Jersey Key Club district treasurer—was the year I finally started to mature and feel more confident. I was good at something now, and had responsibility too, and friends. I still didn't connect with people very well socially, but my efforts were good enough. Besides, staying so busy with Key Club was the perfect excuse for not having a social life or dating any girls. The district board was a collection of pretty cool guys, some jocks, and, of course, the really nerdy guys. I always went out of my way to be nice to the nerdy guys and interact with them as well as the other, cooler guys. Since I was one of the four state officers, I felt I should try to get along with as many guys as possible. And as the treasurer, I had to rely on all of them to help me collect dues and get the bills paid with the right paperwork and receipts. Cool or not, most of the guys were like me: neither studs nor total nerds. We were all just guys wanting to be involved in something.

After months of hanging out with people I liked, including some from other high schools due to my Key Club involvement, I finally got up enough nerve to ask a girl to my senior prom. Kiffy went to Cedar Grove High School in another town, but we had always hit it off and had fun. Of course, we were never alone, but that did not matter to me. She initially said, "yes" but four days before the prom, she called and said she couldn't go. I don't remember the reason, but it was something in the absurd category of "I think I am going to have homework."

Being dumped, however, brought a strange mix of disappointment and relief. I was forever a square peg trying to fit into a round hole, so I was relieved I didn't have to deal with taking a girl to the prom and all the requisite social protocol; but at the same time, being rejected never feels particularly good.

Right before high school graduation, in June 1974, I went into downtown Bloomfield to the five-and-dime. In addition to *Playboy*, the store now carried *Playgirl*. Pictures of naked women had been around in one form of the other since the first cameras, but finding a magazine full of naked men at the Bloomfield five-and-dime was groundbreaking stuff in the mid-'70s. I purchased one copy of each. I guess I thought that having both that would somehow erase any questions about my sexuality in the mind of the store clerk or anyone else who might later stumble upon the magazines. When I graduated and moved to Arizona to be with my family, both magazines came along. Rather than a major fascination, I considered both magazines objectively, occasionally glancing through each like a detective observing a suspect and searching for clues to unravel my own personal mystery. It didn't take long to realize that *Playgirl* was much more interesting to me, but I kept the *Playboy* as a hedge against my own confusion and as a decoy against the suspicions of others. To me, this "decoy strategy" made perfect sense. I wasn't ready to acknowledge my own truth, and I was far from acting on any impulses I might have had anyway.

My brothers and sister returned to New Jersey from Arizona for my high school graduation. A few weeks before, Dad had another heart attack followed by quadruple bypass heart surgery, so whatever other issues were involved in my family's sudden move to Arizona, his health had really been an issue, too. In 1974, bypass surgery was far from commonplace. We had prepared ourselves for the worst, given the nature of the surgery and expected him to die either during the operation or shortly after it. He survived.

The graduation ceremony mirrored my high school years: predictable, dull, and unremarkable. Even with my Key Club successes, I was just another face in a graduating class of 727 kids. I closed out my high school career as I'd begun it: an average student, with some nice friends, feeling okay about what I had accomplished in high school, but pretty unsure about the future. I never became one of the super popular kids, but I took some solace in the fact that many of my Key Club peers were very cool and went on to have notable careers. Ted Kinghorn from Point Pleasant Boro was the Key Club governor while I was district treasurer and would eventually work for Senator Strom Thurmond of South Carolina and is now a respected lobbyist in Washington, D.C. Dan Gecker, then-district secretary, went on to Princeton University, got a law degree, and was Kathleen Willey's attorney during one of President Clinton's scandals. He is now an elected County Supervisor in Chesterfield County, Virginia. Ted Paszek came out of the closet sometime after high school and was an entertainment attorney in New York and Los Angeles with high-flying clients like Bruce Willis. Roger Brown, Key Club International President from Georgia, did missionary work in Africa for a while and went on to become CEO of Bright Horizons, a multi-million dollar chain of day-care centers. They are all super smart folks whom I was proud to call my friends.

Of course, being young, we also occasionally got into trouble together, too.

I was never much of a trouble-maker; being the councilman's kid early in life taught me it was important to stay out of trouble, but I have certainly done my share of stupid things as a young person. At the 1974 Key Club International Convention in Houston, Texas, for example, I got into a bit of trouble. Having just graduated from high school, and as a former New Jersey District Officer, I thought the rules didn't apply. The convention was at a huge Holiday Inn hotel, and I just so happened to have had a short-term, part-time job at a Holiday Inn, and still had an official employee name badge. For no purpose other than we could do it, a few of us grabbed some beers and started walking around the hotel hallways, after curfew. Naturally, real hotel employees—of the security kind—nabbed us. It was two o'clock in the morning, and we were marched to the room of our advisor, Mr. Briggs, for a scolding and the "you have let me down" speech. It was deserved; I had let him down, and others, too. I knew better.

We were good kids, for the most part. I didn't realize that I wasn't the only one living with a secret.

Decades later, in the summer of 2000, on one of my many trips to Washington, D.C., I saw a picture of a Key Club alum from Bloomfield High School on the cover of the local gay newspaper, *The Blade*. Anthony Falzarano and I definitely knew each other in high school. I contacted him via his organization's website, and we met for lunch.

I told Anthony my story: that after I left Bloomfield High and moved to Arizona in 1974, I'd had only the vaguest notion about my sexual orientation and absolutely no inclination to do anything about it or explore it any further. After high school, Anthony, on the other hand, came out of the closet with abandon; he moved to New York City and, as he told me, became one of Roy Cohn's boys. A federal prosecutor from the McCarthy era, Cohn was a kingpin in New York City's gay underground prostitution circles in the early 1980s until he died of AIDS in 1986. For more than a decade, Anthony lived a high-flying gay life —while I suppressed and denied my true self. When I sat down with him, another decade and a half had passed since his Roy Cohn years and our truths had flipped once again.

Anthony had become a devout, born-again Christian and leader in the ex-gay movement. Sweet Jesus. He tells his story in his book *And Such Were Some of You! One Man's Walk Out of the Gay Lifestyle*.

He told me that one day, as he was walking the crowded streets of Manhattan, God spoke to him and told him to clean up his life. The reward for doing so, as Anthony told it, was that God would spare him from contracting AIDS. Anthony took the deal and eventually became the national executive director of Exodus International, the largest Christian ministry for gays and lesbians who want to go straight. Anthony swore it had worked for him: in his newfound heterosexuality, he had married and had children.

I told Anthony over my Caesar salad that I was now the mayor of my city and openly gay.

"I'm so sorry," he said, shaking his head sadly.

I laughed out loud. "Don't be sorry. I'm happy and being honest, finally."

Our conversation turned to the old days at Bloomfield High. I was fascinated by Anthony's stories of the underground gay scene at our high school, which I had had no idea even existed. He told me stories: guys servicing the football team and things like that. To say I was shocked would be an understatement. I just had no idea. And maybe he was making it all up to add drama to his own story, I don't know.

"Neil, you can turn your life around. You don't have to stay in that lifestyle," he said earnestly before we parted.

"Anthony, it's not a choice. My experience is vastly different from yours. This is who I am, how I was made to be. And I'm finally happy, not hiding." Very interesting how one high school class in suburban New Jersey would one day claim both a national gay leader and a leader of the ex-gay movement.

Forty-eight hours after I graduated high school in June 1974, I moved to Arizona. Getting off the plane, I felt that blast of hot air, somewhat like opening an oven that had been set on 500 degrees for an hour, and I wondered how people actually lived in the desert.

I would never have imagined that Tempe, where I was soon to be a student at Arizona State University, would be my adopted hometown for the rest of my adult life and twenty years later, by June 1994, I would be elected mayor of the city.

In fact, my plan was the opposite: As soon as my father got stronger following his heart surgery, I would head back to New Jersey. I had no intention of staying. I was going to give Arizona exactly one year.

CHAPTER FOUR

Accepting Destiny

On the television in front of us, an Olympic athlete was swimming his way to a gold medal, his tanned body rippling through the water. I admired him silently, but my friend was far more vocal.

"He's beautiful, huh, Neil?" Ed Miller asked me. He was one of my best friends from high school—close enough of a friend that I had flown from Phoenix to Philadelphia to visit him that summer of 1976; twenty years prior to that exhausting and defining night I flew the red-eye to Atlanta to actually attend the Olympics.

We had first met three years before as high school juniors, having both been elected to the New Jersey District of Key Club International Board of Directors; he was the editor of the New Jersey Key Club District Bulletin, *The Jersey Key*, and I was district treasurer. When I graduated from high school and went west to Arizona State University, Ed went south from New Jersey, to attend Murray State University in Kentucky.

Distance breaks up many high school friendships, but Ed

and I had managed to stay close, although we no longer saw each other regularly. And while for many young people, college is an opportunity to expand their horizons, experiment, and come into an enhanced self-knowledge, Ed and I were living our newfound freedom very differently. While I stayed deep in the closet, Ed came out early, some might say with abandon, certainly without shame. Determined to help me face my own truth, he sent me rambling cassette tapes and letters about all he was doing, learning and experiencing as he embraced his sexual orientation enthusiastically.

I kept the tapes. For a long time those tapes provided a window into a world I longed for in some ways and deeply feared in others.

While a part of me was desperately scared about confronting the truth of my sexual orientation, there was another part of me that was irrepressibly curious. The two halves of my personality had already begun sparring with each other. On the one hand, I had a few awkward experiences with girls, but I was technically still a virgin. On the other, I had begun to acknowledge my attraction to men, though I had never acted on that desire. The pressures of college had brought the campaign within to a simmering boil inside me.

Ed's openness both fascinated and shocked me. I was envious of him, but it wasn't anything I would ever have said out loud. He assumed that I was gay, too—which was fine because he was a close friend—but allowing him to make that assumption was as far as I willing to go. Until that summer of 1976, we never discussed it. We never said the words aloud. I didn't see myself as being like Ed. He had an air of total social confidence that I lacked. And he wasn't like the people I heard about and read about while much younger either. When he invited me to come see him, I knew he had something particular in mind. Ed's invitation arrived at a time when I was I found myself willing to take a peek—just a tiny one—into how the part of me like Ed might live.

"I want you to meet some of my friends," he said on the phone. "Don't worry, it will be fun."

Meet some friends. I knew what *that* meant. He added the "don't worry" because he knew I *would* worry. He knew I was terrified of facing what we both knew I had not yet dealt with in my own life.

"Okay, yeah, that would be great," was my response, as anxious as it was tepid.

That I followed through and actually showed up at his doorstep surprised us both.

Ed was spending the summer with his family in Riverside, New Jersey, a suburb of Philadelphia just across the New Jersey state line. I was welcomed there. The weather was hot and muggy and the house was, too—there was no air conditioning. The days were slow and warm and the nights were slower and even warmer. We spent both lounging around, watching the Olympics on TV and talking about mutual acquaintances now attending colleges all over the country.

"Do you think he's a buddy?" Ed asked me, referring to one of our Key Club friends.

He never used the word "gay," but I knew what "buddy" meant.

"I don't know. You know him better than I do," I responded. It was the truth; I didn't know. I tried not to think hard about who else in our circle might be gay—just as I tried not to think about whether I was. It was interesting to listen to Ed guess and surmise about this guy and that one, to wonder if there might be other popular, successful guys who were gay, but that was as far as I was willing to go.

Ed's attention shifted back to the flickering television. High jumper Dwight Stone was on the screen, beginning his warm-up as he readied himself for competition.

"That Dwight Stone is so damn good-looking," Ed declared, his voice thick with admiration.

I didn't want to agree and even the lukewarm "I suppose

so" that I offered up in reply made me tense. I knew where this was going. Ed had never officially said the words "I'm gay," and he'd never actually asked me point-blank if I were. But from the things he'd said, I knew Ed was gay—*way* gay, in fact, from what he had been sharing the last couple of years. Ed was light years ahead of me and ahead of many others of our age at that time. In 1976, at just twenty years old, he had fully accepted himself. He was comfortable with who he was, at ease, confident and matter-of-fact about his sexual orientation. He discussed it openly with anyone around him. How was it that one Jersey kid moves so quickly to self-acceptance, and one stays frozen in time with no sexuality or expressed interest in either sex?

"Tonight, Neil, we're meeting some of my friends," Ed continued, still studying Dwight Stone's toned, athletic body on the TV screen. "We're going to take you to the Limelight Bar in New York City. It's a huge gay club. It'll be a lot of fun."

I'm not ready for this, I won't fit in there, what should I say?

"Oh, okay." It wasn't much of a response, neither enthusiastic approval or firmly resistant. I can still remember it now, and I voiced the ambivalence that was the summation of most of my life: a neither definitive "yes" nor a declarative "no" on this topic was standard response. I was floating uncertainly through my experiences, unwilling to commit.

I allowed myself to be led. And just like that, Ed took us from "buddies" to Dwight Stone to planning a night out at a gay bar.

"Oh, okay," might have been all I verbalized, but on the inside, the fight against acknowledging my true feelings kicked up again in earnest.

I didn't tell Ed that the excursion he planned for me would be my first time going to such a place; I didn't need to, he knew it. That was at least part of the reason why he proposed the trip in the first place. I am sure he felt I needed more "gay" in my life—more exposure to men who lived openly with their sexual orientation—and he was determined to make sure I got that exposure in one way or the other.

That evening, before heading up the highway to New York City, we picked up Ed's friends. They were very cool, good looking, and fun guys—the kind of guys I had always wished to be like but had never managed to become. If I had met them around Philadelphia or on the campus of Arizona State, I would have assumed them to be completely straight, but here we were, in a car together, speeding toward a gay bar as if it were a typical weekend thing to do, which for them it was. Considering that I was Ed's socially awkward, not-so-hot, gay-but-not-dealing-with-it friend from out West, they were very nice to me. They all seemed so all-American, confident, that, by comparison, I was the nerdy guy. They talked of college life, drinking, getting laid, and going to concerts. They were so far out of my league that I hardly knew what to say to them. I could tell them all about my newfound collegiate activities, joining clubs and starting a chapter of Circle K International, but these guys wouldn't care about things like that. They studied hard and partied hard. They had no interest in campus clubs. I sat in the back, wedged between two of these young Adonises, wondering what the hell I was doing there, wishing I could make Ed stop the car and drop me off.

But of course it was much too late for that. Before too long, the New York skyline filled the night sky ahead of us.

There was no turning back.

We circled and passed the Limelight for what felt like an hour while looking for a parking space, and the whole time I leaned toward the window, drinking in a slice of life I had barely known existed. We were in Chelsea, a neighborhood of Manhattan known for its high concentration of gay men even then. To me, it was like landing on Mars and being greeted by friendly Martians: men everywhere. Men walking in small groups. Men alone; men of all types, shapes, and sizes. Hot men and plenty of not-so-hot looking ones. We stopped at a traffic light, and I found my eyes drawn to a short, built, Latino-looking guy in a tight, white tank top on the curb. I leaned forward from the middle hump of the back seat to get a better look just as he glanced over at the car and caught me gawking at him. But instead of bristling at my attentions, he offered me a huge smile and nod of acknowledgement. It may sound silly, but that smile and nod was the validation I had been seeking. As the light changed and the car started to move again, I felt a strange sense of confidence rising inside me. As we finally parked and walked toward the Limelight, I was sure I would find Mr. Latin in his white tank top in the club, waiting for me, but of course he wasn't. His gift to me was that smile and the confidence it gave me, but I never saw him again.

From my first moment inside, Limelight was sensory overload. Flamingly flamboyant and feminine queens in bright pink short-shorts flirted with muscular macho guys wearing Levi's jackets over their broad bare chests. These were the halcyon days of disco, complete with swirling lights and thumping bass, and the place was rocking from the rafters to the cellar. It seemed like there were thousands of men there: dancing and gyrating as the lights flashed and the beat thumped like the life force in my chest had somehow found a home outside of my body. A few weeks later, back in Arizona, I would buy my first disco 12" album, The Tramps' "Where the Happy People Go" as a memento of the experience of being at the Limelight. I still have it.

Ed knew a lot of people—a *lot* of people. Like everyone, or so it seemed.

"This is Neil, my friend from ASU." He must have said that two dozen times as we moved along the crowds of men along the bar. His introduction was always met by a smile and greeting, and some of the men even offered me a hug of welcome. I hadn't expected that: to be received so positively. I hadn't expected to feel so welcome. Something inside me shifted. This was a place filled with guys—gay guys—and I actually felt myself becoming comfortable very quickly.

I had expected to feel unsure. I had expected my eternal campaign with myself to kick in at high gear. I expected to sit back, as I had many times with my friend Ed, and say to myself, *I'm different…but I'm just not meant to be like you.*

But those feelings and judgments never materialized. Instead, I felt good. I was still nervous, because it was all so new and I wasn't sure what to expect or what else might happen. But my nervousness was mingled with more excitement than fear. For the first time in a social setting, I felt like I belonged, even though I lacked the confidence that Ed and his friends so readily displayed. For the first time in a social setting, I wasn't pretending to have a good time; I really *was* having a good time.

Near the bar, a guy who said his name was Billy asked me if I wanted a drink.

"Sure," I said.

He bought me a Tequila Sunrise—the first drink a man had ever bought me. I hadn't been much of a drinker and the only other mixed drink I'd ever had in my life was a Screwdriver. I know, pretty lame. But drinking a Screwdriver didn't seem to be hip or sophisticated enough for the Limelight. I ordered a Tequila Sunrise because I thought it sounded like something one of the cool guys would drink.

"You're good looking," Billy yelled over the music and into my ear. "You're a nice guy." Then he gave me a quick kiss on the cheek and touched my arm.

It was innocent enough, more flirtatious than sexual. But it was the first time I had been kissed by a man, and it triggered a response I was unable to control. Warmth spread through me, and a rush of excitement I had never experienced before swelled. In that instant, I understood what had been missing in my brief encounters with girls: there had never been this odd cocktail of thrill and embarrassment. There had never been that rush of adrenaline that made everything inside me come alive. I had kissed girls on the lips but never had I felt the kind of excitement as when Billy simply brushed his lips against my cheek. I was tongue-tied by everything I was thinking and feeling.

He was waiting for me to say something.

"Thanks, you too," I sputtered. Until then, I only saw myself through my own eyes: a very skinny kid with semi-long hair, without much to offer in the style department. In today's parlance, I was a very thin young "twink." Billy, on the other hand, was older and wearing a tight, orange tank top on his muscular body, white shorts, and stylish round glasses.

This guy's very cool, I thought to myself as we sipped our drinks and talked some more. *He's handsome, nice, and he likes me.*

The tequila lowered my inhibitions a bit more. I let Billy coax me out onto the dance floor. We danced a bit, and I surrendered myself to the beat. The thudding bass took control of me, and for the first time in my life I let myself go and had fun. A semi-slow dance came on and he put both arms around me and pulled me close to him as we swayed to the music. It's probably something every gay man experiences: that first time you're in the full embrace of another man, and for the first time, everything seems right and natural—because it finally is. During a break in the music while standing around, I saw him talking with Ed and I had the feeling that I was a part of their conversation. I knew it was getting late, but I didn't want the night to end.

"We have to get going," Ed announced to our little group a short while later.

"Neil can stay," Billy offered out loud, "I'll make sure he gets over to Jersey tomorrow."

I didn't say anything, but it sounded like a pretty good idea to me. But then, I was clueless. I didn't fully understand exactly what Billy was suggesting. I didn't have enough experience to know how Billy hoped the night would end. I looked at Ed like a teenager hoping to persuade an overprotective parent.

"No, I don't think so. We're all leaving now. Neil too." Ed burst my balloon in a big way, but I kept my mouth shut.

Billy smiled at me. "Okay, you guys take care," he said, leaning in to give me another sweet kiss on the cheek and a quick hug. Then he turned and disappeared into the crowd.

It was two A.M. when we left New York. Once again, I ended up in the middle of the back seat of the mammoth 1970s sedan. The guys on either side of me were slumped against their windows sleeping. In the front passenger seat, Ed was sleeping, too. I, on the other hand, was bright-eyed and fully alert. If I had known the driver, I might have talked to him about all the thoughts and feelings swirling inside me, but we had just met that evening for the first time so I didn't say a word to him about what was happening inside me. Instead, I sat with my feet bouncing on the hump between the seats, smiling, as I relived every moment of the past four hours. There hadn't been a single second of my time at Limelight that hadn't felt natural, good, and right. I was exhilarated and elated—and yet terrified about what it meant for my future.

But after that great time—no, that *amazing* time—I just went back to Arizona State and resumed my hard-working, overly-involved and desperately closeted life. It was all I knew. By then I was serving as District Governor in Circle K International; in my mind, I had come pretty far already. I was use to with living in a constant state of internal confusion and would leave well enough alone.

Two years before, I had squeezed through a red-faced crowd of freshmen waiting for their dorm room assignments toward a corner of the air-conditioned lobby where I could survey the scene. It was August 1974, Nixon has just resigned the presidency, and I was about to start college. Not a small state college in New Jersey like the one my sister had attended. And not even the state's prestigious Rutgers University, which I'd long figured I would be attending. I was now enrolled at

Arizona State University, in the middle of the growing Phoenix metropolitan area, in a city called Tempe, joining more than 20,000 other students gearing up for fun, sun, and some classes. From my metal folding chair, I noticed the overstrained swamp cooler was blowing tepid air across the lobby. In here, it was cooler than the 110-degree inferno outside, but it was far from comfortable.

"God, it's hot," was the most commonly heard introductory comment, beating out "Where are you from?" and "Which floor are you on?"

ASU's Best Hall was a fairly typical 1970s all-male dorm. I was assigned to the second floor. My first roommate dropped out after about five weeks. After a week alone, my new roommate moved in. Jeff hailed from southern New Jersey, was a total stud athlete, and, as it turned out, was as much of a Type-A neat freak as I was. But, where I was more shy, insecure, and reserved, he was friendly and outgoing and the kind of guy who was always introducing me to other people when we hung out together. Although I was years from really understanding my sexual orientation, and still a couple from the visit to the Limelight, I knew having a hot, athletic, and friendly guy like Jeff for a roommate was quite a bonus.

Jeff moved on to live off-campus with some other athletes he met that first semester, and by my second semester I had yet another new roommate: a great, low-key, and chill guy, primarily because he was a hardcore member of the Mary Jane fan club—if you know what I mean. He was a gentle smoker and would sprawl on his bed for hours at a stretch, smiling, and plucking randomly on his expensive Martin D-35 acoustic guitar. On the roommate spectrum, in his predominant zonked-out zombie state, he was low-maintenance and actually really pleasant. Decades later, after I was out of the closet as Tempe's mayor, I spoke at a local high school and a girl came up to me and introduced herself as the daughter of that roommate. She showed me her rainbow necklace and announced proudly that she was a lesbian. The combination of her existence and her out and proud LGBT identity provided me with one of those "you sure are getting old" moments.

In the closing months of 1974, I was working at Legend City, an amusement park not far from the ASU campus as the bumper car operator and I started an ASU chapter of Circle K International, the college level service and leadership organization sponsored by Kiwanis International. As with Key Club in high school, being involved with Circle K gave me focus, a safe social outlet and a place to create an identity that diverted everyone's attention—including mine—from the question of whether I was straight, gay, bisexual, asexual or something else.

I had vowed after high school that I wouldn't get wrapped up in clubs again, especially the college version of Key Club. But there I was, organizing the group, getting the charter, cajoling other students into joining, and being elected charter president. The club became my purpose, my social life, and my identity. Connecting to others in a detached, organizational way afforded me social contact without the risk of any real intimacy or vulnerability. Relating to others in that context became a pattern in my life. I know I should have dealt with all my doubts and insecurities in better ways, but I also could have done much worse, and almost did, considering how isolated and disconnected I often felt.

In college, I decided that my life was exactly the way I wanted it. I wasn't like everyone else in the social department, I told myself. I didn't fit in. For me, it was a choice between getting involved with people in this organization or becoming a *real* loner without any connection to a living soul, and that unknown scared me even more than the lack of truly intimate relationships in my life. I dove into my school activities with abandon.

Beneath the mask of leadership and a whirlwind of activities, my sexual confusion was deeper than ever. More and more, I felt my attraction to men and my desire for intimacy with them.

More and more, I knew I had no place in the "drinking and drugs and dating girls" scene going on around me. I wasn't a gay man like those activists who sat at a table on the campus mall handing out information about their cause. I couldn't imagine ever being so open and up front about that part of me. I wasn't raised that way at all. One didn't talk about sex, private things like that. It just wasn't done.

Did anyone really need to know that about me anyway?

No, I decided, no one needed to know. I didn't want anyone to know. My family and friends weren't interested in that kind of revelation. Being gay meant embracing a whole realm of liberal issues that didn't resonate with me, or so I thought. It meant being an in-your-face activist and everyone I knew rejected them and their causes. Surely, they would reject me as well. I was a more moderate guy, not one to challenge the status quo or rock the boat. Those belief and skills would come later in life.

But these beliefs and decisions also left me adrift. I was never wholly comfortable in either world—gay or straight. Surely there were other guys like me. Surely on a campus of 20,000 students, there had to be others. Where were they? Why didn't I know them?

I focused on school, on Circle K, on success. This path of over-achievement, I've learned, is a common one for social outcasts and loners. The strange and interesting part of my personal journey is that my greatest weakness became the solid path for building my leadership abilities, for finding a place where I could excel, make a difference for good, and serve others.

If I couldn't resolve the issues that plagued my own life, at least I could channel that energy toward other productive channels.

One of the real highlights of my socially isolated freshman year took place four days before my eighteenth birthday, on October 22, 1974: meeting Barry Goldwater and Ted Kennedy when they spoke on campus. The next day, there was a photograph on the front page of the campus newspaper of me getting Ted Kennedy's autograph. It's framed in my home office, nearly thirty-eight years later, a moment captured forever that I get to re-live every time I glance at it. The morning before, I had arrived early to select my seat to see Barry Goldwater speak in the Memorial Union's largest room. Goldwater's politics were to the right of my own, and Kennedy's to the left, and I admired each. I chose a seat on the right, next to the aisle, so that as the senator was brought in, I might get a chance to meet him. I had learned all about staging events while attending and planning large conventions for Key Club, and I knew that was the best spot to get a handshake. It worked. After Goldwater's speech, he was hustled right past my seat and I got the chance to shake his hand.

Years and years later, as ASU's Director of Federal Relations and while mayor of Tempe, I would have many opportunities to chat with Senator Goldwater, including when the drama surrounding my sexuality was being played out in the local newspapers.

"Hello, Mayor," he said at an ASU-sponsored Barry Goldwater Night in 1996. "I've been reading about you."

"Yes, Senator, some interesting things going on."

Barry Goldwater's grandson Ty was openly gay even back then and no doubt helped Barry better understand these issues in the later years of his life. The senator nodded and then added, "Don't let those bastards get you down, Neil."

"No, Senator," I said, "I won't," and the conversation shifted to other subjects. That would be the last time I spoke with him.

A couple years later, in June of 1998, while still the mayor and director of federal relations at ASU, I was one of the lead staff in charge of coordinating Barry Goldwater's funeral at Grady Gammage Auditorium on the ASU campus. Among the political attendees were former Vice President Dan Quayle, former First Lady Nancy Reagan, and seventy members of the U.S. Congress who arrived from the airport in the nicest buses in Arizona. The event, to be broadcast live on C-Span, had to be perfect, and in addition to the funeral itself, I wanted the visual to be as patriotic and respectful a tribute as possible. I checked with city staff and we installed brackets on every street pole along Mill Avenue in downtown Tempe, so that the streets where people gathered to watch the motorcade could be lined with American flags. Barry's widow Susan Goldwater later told me that when their limo crossed over the Mill Avenue Bridge and she saw all the flags and people, her eyes filled with tears. She sent me a personal note of thanks following it all that touched me deeply.

Of course, I didn't know that I would have that opportunity when I first shook Barry Goldwater's hand in 1974. I just knew that being involved with activities on campus provided me with an opportunity to make a difference, and as a result offered the distraction I needed from my own confusion.

During my sophomore year at ASU, I was in a communication class of more than 200 students, which also included weekly breakout groups of fifteen. One day we did an exercise requiring us to be blindfolded one at a time while other students gave instructions. It was an exercise in using one's other senses. When my turn came, I put on the blindfold and waited. The blindfold wasn't tight, and I could still see a bit through it. I caught two guys in the class who had that macho confidence and style to which I secretly aspired pointing at me. Neither of them could see my eyes, but I saw one of them mouth the word repeatedly, "Fag. Fag. Fag."

The other one raised his pinkie finger and flicked his hand back and forth. My classmates were smiling and suppressing their laughter. My ears started ringing immediately, and a burning heat flashed through my body. I could barley breathe.

What had I done? What did I say? How could they possibly know anything about me? I'm not a fag. I'm never going to be a fag. I'm not anything. Just leave me alone in that department.

I was terrified. The professor said something about ending

the exercise, and I handed the blindfold to the next person. The two guys were now standing innocently in the circle, as if nothing had happened. A part of me was angry, but I knew I would never confront either of them. I stood silent in my humiliation. What a coward.

I walked home that afternoon with the same questions rolling through my mind: *What had I done? What did I say? How could they possibly know?*

That was the first public ridiculing I had received. How painful that it happened that way—blindfolded and surrounded by classmates I thought were nice enough, if not friends. The numb feeling lasted the rest of the day. The burn of humiliation lasted longer. Whenever I recall that moment, the feeling returns as strong as ever, unabated by the years that have passed since then. I was angry, but I didn't know how to confront the guys. The anger had nowhere to go but inward, back on my own feelings of self-hate and uncertainty. The confusion and depression and unresolved anxiety gradually worsened, festering inside me.

Today, of course, I am armed with the knowledge and information to fight back against such prejudice and small-minded behavior. An entire generation of young people, and adults too, are standing up with and for each other against bullying, anti-gay language and harassment. A big part of my emergence as a visible and vocal gay advocate, locally, nationally, and even professionally fighting for full equality, is due to having not had the courage to do so when I was young. I stood silent on the sidelines as a young person, tentative, insecure, and afraid to fight for my own rights and those of my tribe.

Back then, instead of fighting back, I redoubled my efforts. I poured my energy into Circle K International and school and church just to survive the tumult inside me. Despair continued to wash over me, but my activities, at least, gave me a life raft that I gripped tightly. It was easier for me to commit to an organization or a group rather than having close individual friendships and relationships. No one could ever really know me.

On weekends when I wasn't traveling around the state for Circle K, I would make the forty-minute drive up to north Phoenix and see my parents and brothers. I did it mostly for my mother, and for the ritual of bringing home laundry on weekends and having a couple good meals. While it was always nice to catch up with everyone, I couldn't really open up and share what was going on in my life beyond the surface. We just didn't have that kind of relationship. It was all nice, fun, and cheerful, nothing deep or challenging would ever become a topic. On many of those Sundays as I said goodbye to drive back to campus, I felt an overwhelming sadness. While happy and enjoying an active college experience on the outside, it was becoming more and more apparent to me that I was pretty messed up on the inside. I hated that I was never going to fall in love, get married, and have a family, as everyone kept asking about and expecting I would. They had no idea how wrong they were, and they couldn't know; I couldn't let them ever know.

By the time I reached the freeway to take me back to Tempe, I would be in tears, grieving the loss of a future, lamenting the pathetic state of the present, sad that I was so distant from my family, but lacking the strength or direction to do anything about it.

Another Friday night came and started like so many others. I went to yet another campus party with guys and girls drinking and playing out that scene while I drifted around on the perimeter, feeling like an alien who knew neither the language nor customs I was witnessing. The stress was cutting into my sleep, and I had lost my appetite. I simply didn't have the energy for this night. I left the party and headed toward my apartment. Then, without warning, the tears started to roll down my cheeks.

I would never fit in either world. Straight people would never accept my sexual orientation and gay people would never accept a gay guy like me who was not an out and loud activist like they all appeared to be. I was sick and screwed up. I wanted to be like the straight guys, but I wasn't. I didn't want to be different, but I was. My pace slowed the more I cried, until I stopped moving completely at an intersection and let the tears comes.

I would be like this my entire life.

My friends in Circle K and in church would never accept the real me. And why should they? What was I anyway?

I would never amount to much. I would only disappoint family and friends.

These were the thoughts running through my mind. It suddenly didn't make sense to continue a life with nothing ahead of me but emptiness and loneliness. If I died, people could remember me for the good I had done up to that point. No one had to know I was gay. The burden of being different would be forever lifted. The bad things I had done would be erased, too. Those other kids from my youth. Were they as messed up as me? Because of what I had done? I understood and believed in forgiveness, I truly felt God loved me, but I doubted I could meet the expectations of God and the people in my life for long. My path was becoming clearer, and it wasn't one I could alter.

I felt the rush of air as cars flashed through the intersection at forty to fifty miles an hour. A pick-up truck rumbled by, then a smaller import car. The walk sign changed green for me to cross, but I just stood there, alive but vacant inside. The walk sign flashed red. Then stayed solid red. Cars began whizzing by me again, and I inched closer to the curb. The light changed again; I could cross the street. But I didn't.

I was ready to do this thing. I had only thought about it a few times, in the dark of night as I fell asleep wondering if I would ever feel right and fit in. The light changed again, and the cars started up. I was standing so close to the street that half of each foot hovered off the curb. Cars were visibly moving left to avoid what, I'm sure they thought, was another drunken college student, too wasted to realize he was crossing against the light.

A delivery truck whizzed toward me. I started counting in my head.

Seven, six, five...

When I reached one, I would step off the curb in front of the truck and this miserable life would be over. I shifted my weight.

Four, three, two...

The truck closed in. Everyone would think it was an accident

One.

I started to step off the curb. I was ready to spring into the truck's path. In an instant, the pain and confusion would finally stop. Just a white space of calm where that voice would no longer have any relevance or power to ever torment me again. All would be peaceful.

Something stopped me. I froze, and the truck barreled past, blasting its horn and whipping wind across my face in its diesel wake. I started shaking, no longer able to control my body as the realization of what I had almost done filled my mind.

When the intersection cleared, I darted across and ran all the way back to my apartment making sounds that were equal parts sobs and screams. I got to my apartment safely, and thankfully my roommates weren't home. The last time I had run home, scared and sobbing like a child, I indeed was a child, and my dad had greeted me at the front door those many years ago.

The rest of the evening is a complete blank.

The next morning, I caught my face in the mirror just as I had a thousand times in my life.

I looked like crap.

I stared into the eyes in the mirror—my own eyes—and said it for the first time out loud.

"This is the way it is. I'm gay. "

I remember feeling resigned to the admission, but hardly liberated or relieved. I found speaking the truth about myself an unavoidable fact.

A week or so later, I called a Circle K friend who I was particularly close to and who lived out of state and told him about being on the brink of suicide. I was just completely lost, and he was the only person I knew who might understand. He was one of the very few people who knew about me, for I had fallen in love with him, even from a distance, the year prior. Our friendship had been as close as it could be without a physical expression, and he knew I wanted that to occur as well. I would find out later in life that he was, in fact, gay.

"How could you do that?" he yelled into the phone.

"I don't want to live this way," I said, on the verge of tears. "I don't want to be this way."

Silence. And then he said: "I love you."

His friendship would be a source of great strength for me over time. No one had ever said that to me, aside from a parent or relative. I would lean on him again from time to time, but we drifted apart as he built and maintained a straight life for a few decades, and I continued to work on accepting myself as a gay man and creating a public life.

That look in the mirror, that acknowledgement, should have been the turning point for my coming out and living openly, accepting who I was and then having the courage to live honestly. But while I acknowledged my reality and allowed myself some peace, it did not make me ready to have everyone else know about me. I was no longer unsure, I knew the truth, and knew I was not going to change, but I still did not view myself as I viewed those gay guys on campus, the activists who wanted everyone to know they were gay, who were intent on getting others to accept them, not look down upon them, not discriminate against them, not treat them as lesser people. That was how society looked at gay people, for the most part, in the mid-1970s and it was a burden I wanted no part of.

My world thus far had not provided any understanding of what it meant to fight for social justice, to stand up for something you know is right and be counted for a cause, even if it meant some would not accept you. I learned about serving others from Dad, at his side during those early political years, but the lessons about fighting for others, or even standing up for your beliefs and working to convince others about the wrongs you see, was never a significant part of the purpose.

Today, the scared and fearful college kid I was is a distant but vivid memory. My memory of that version of myself is also an important one because it reminds me that it took me far too long to join the struggle. When I speak to groups now about the cause of social justice for gay people and I am asked about what motivates me and keeps me engaged, I share two stories that remain constantly in my mind.

The first is a scene that played over and over during those early college years: the group of gay guys at the table on the main campus walkway, the "Free Spirit" clubs' gathering place, and how I convinced myself that I was not like them, that I wouldn't want to be like them.

I walked right by that table hundreds of times and it is cause for great shame to me now. Those men were my true family, my tribe, and I did not have the courage to stand up and fight with them; instead, I walked by. I remember some of the names of those early gay activists on campus. Very sadly, many of them are dead. A generation of gay activists my age, lost to AIDS. The worst part is I didn't fully ignore them; I watched, and even admired them at times, yet always from a distance. I was just so afraid of what people would think if I was open and honest, so I never stood among them when it might have made a difference.

One of those guys was Greg Carmack. He had a mop of curly blond hair and I remember seeing him in a light blue T-shirt time and time again at that table on the mall. He wrote a guest editorial for the local alternative newspaper about his own activism, what motivated him to fight for gay rights titled "Moving Toward Commitment." I cut it out and saved it in a manila folder. While I am ashamed I never did what I should have back in those days, I did take inspiration and strength from their work and much of what I have done over the last sixteen years since I have lived openly is on their behalf, and for those who are gone, in their memory.

I honor them and thank them for paving the way. Without their efforts and courage, my own opportunities would not have unfolded as they did and my accomplishments would not have been realized. The people I have helped might have gone without, too.

The other situation took place years later, but helped me accept that my own personal destiny as a public servant was to be out, to be proud, open and honest, and gave me hope that I would be okay, maybe even stronger, when that came to pass.

Ed Miller and I had kept in loose contact after our college years, exchanging notes at holidays and maybe a phone call or two during the year. I knew he had become a special education teacher in the Philadelphia area, and was quite an out gay activist. He knew I was still closeted, living in Arizona with hopes of maybe getting elected to office and a public life. He would share with me details about his work and his life, the fact that he had a partner and he was very happy. I told him about my work and career; there was nothing personal to share. It was a respectful friendship, but we clearly had chosen different paths. Ed's attempt to free me from my own oppression back in 1976 had been a kind and warm gesture, fun too, but I didn't take that opportunity, and he never berated me or gave me grief about my lack of evolvement in that department. In some ways I wish he had, but I guess the how and why of the journeys we travel must be what they must be.

In October 1991, I boarded the plane to Philadelphia without telling anyone in Arizona that my old high school friend Ed, one of the people who knew me best, had succumbed to AIDS. I had not known he was sick, and hearing the news shook me deep in my soul. Listening to some of Ed's tapes and reading his letters that night took me to a very emotional place. I never admitted to myself the real crush I had on Ed, how proud of him I was, even if I couldn't accept myself as he accepted me. I had loved him. I don't remember who, but someone called me to tell me of Ed's passing and that the service would be that coming weekend. I knew I needed to go, that I wanted to be there. Our history meant a great deal to me.

I told everyone an old friend had died, and I was going to his funeral. That was the truth, but it was also a lie of omission about the nature of the friendship and the fact that both of us were gay. I was on the Tempe City Council and continued to live the way I always had: with one foot planted in the straight world, asexual as it was, and one tentatively placed in the gay world, but only outside of Tempe.

The service was in a large, old church, and it was nearly full. I didn't know anyone but looked for Ed's mom, who I remembered from that visit back in 1976 when he took me to the Limelight. I stood among all these openly gay men who were also there to show their support and to grieve. In muted voices and stillness as people gathered and waited for the service to start, I looked around and noticed the closeness and friendship these men shared. AIDS was ravaging the gay community then, and it was clear these men were there for each other, supporting each other in very profound ways.

I didn't yet see that I could share in that community, their sense of family or belonging. I wasn't "out." I couldn't have that level of intimacy with straight friends either because they did not really know who I was. I could not open up and be honest; I was stuck in some in-between state in neither world. I was a fake and a fraud, dancing between the two without ever fully revealing myself to either.

Where is my honor? I asked myself. *Where is my pride? Why am I living this way? And, what's the alternative? Could I possibly come out in conservative Arizona while a city councilman and survive politically?* That was an easy one: no.

These questions tormented me throughout Ed's funeral.

I cried with everyone when the vocalist sang "Bring Him Home" from *Les Miserables*, and I felt like a lousy friend thinking of my own pathetic situation, even as I mourned Ed and thought of the pain he must have endured as he died of AIDS.

It was Halloween weekend, and an "after-party" was planned as a celebration of Ed's life, costumes and all, some fun drag, too. I had not known about the party ahead of time, but a few of Ed's friends gave me a map and I went. And the guys were great, making sure I met people and introducing me.

"This is Ed's high school friend who is a councilman in Arizona."

"Oh, Ed had mentioned you" was the most frequent response. I could guess what Ed had said, to the point that I wanted to respond, "Yes, I am the closeted guy in public office."

I left the after-party thinking to myself how lucky Ed was to have had such a great group of friends. Someone told me once that your close friends are the family you get to choose in life. I thought of that amazing night at the Limelight fifteen years earlier and cried again. Ed only lived to his mid-thirties, but he lived it to the fullest.

I accepted that night that my own future would not find me hiding in the closet forever, that I would have to summon up the courage and strength to live openly and honestly. I had to use whatever opportunities I might have as a public leader to make a difference for people like me, like Ed and all his friends. I did not know how or when, and I knew I was still terrified of crossing toward that unknown, but I accepted that it would have to happen.

Someday, somehow, I would make Ed proud of me.

CHAPTER FIVE

Connecting

I don't remember much about the last time I saw my father alive, but I know that even after he died, he was with me as I struggled to find self-acceptance. His death came at a pivotal point in my life, and while such a devastating loss might have caused some to wander, for me, losing him brought me an enhanced focus and a motivation to succeed that had been sporadic in the past.

My dad was just fifty years old when he died on October 15, 1978. His heart by-pass surgery, while successful, would only keep him around four more years. The day before he passed away, Mom called me in Tempe from their home in northwest Phoenix. My successful collegiate activities, especially Circle K International, had kept me at ASU in Tempe, my thoughts of returning to New Jersey long gone.

"Come up," she urged me. "Come tonight."

It was a Friday afternoon and although I knew I would visit my family at some point over the weekend—my younger brother John's birthday was on Saturday— I wasn't feeling like making the drive that evening. It had been a busy week in the first semester of my fifth and final year at Arizona State. The previous year was spent traveling the country as International President for Circle K International, with a light course load that necessitated a fifth year of college.

Like my experience with Key Club in high school, my student leadership years with Circle K International in college were powerful and life-altering. Originally, I had not even wanted to start a chapter of Circle K at ASU, but in spring 1976, while the founding President of the ASU chapter, I was elected District Governor. A year later I ran for International President. I didn't think I had much of a chance: my district was among the smallest in the organization and two other governors from large districts in the south were already planning to run. But even though I didn't hail from a large home district, I had made some great friends throughout the organization, had a positive reputation and connected with people on a leadership and service level. I decided to go for it.

With campaign leadership from districts in Florida and Ohio, we built a strong network of support across the country. I shared my message of "Dedication-Ability-Desire" at the national convention that was attended by nearly a thousand people in Kansas City that year. My message resonated; even with two other candidates, I was elected on the first ballot at the House of Delegates in August of 1977. Two years before that at the international convention in Toronto, I had been a nobody from a brand new chapter of the organization in one of the smallest districts with little to no political influence.

Being elected International President just two years later changed both my reputation and that of my district. The size of the district has not changed much since 1977, but since then there have been numerous other international officers from ASU and three other international presidents, including two consecutively, something that has only happened once before at the dawn of the organization in the 1950s.

My term as international president helped to shape my

leadership abilities and skills beyond where they had been and I grew outwardly confidant, even while I was socially locked in a place without much confidence at all. My closeted year as international president was made even more challenging by the presence of an openly gay guy on my International Board. He ultimately became a dear friend, along with others from that time, who would come to know the real me long before my political campaigns and summer of 1996. And we had great success together, too. We built over seventy new chapters of the organization in a year, hosted an international convention of over 1,000 students, started a club in the Bahamas, and even forged a strong relationship with the Muscular Dystrophy Association that would land me on the national broadcast of the telethon presenting a check to Jerry Lewis. In a strange twist, over thirty years later I would end up publicly admonishing Jerry for using a gay slur during his telethon.

My mom and dad traveled to Orlando, Florida in August 1978 to watch me step down as president of Circle K International. They were very proud, and I was thrilled they attended the convention, to see me being honored and appreciated by my peers at the close of an important chapter in my life. Little did I know that just two months later my father would die suddenly, closing yet another chapter of my life forever.

Yes, the last thing I wanted to do that fateful Friday night was drive across the ever-sprawling city of Phoenix to spend the evening with my family. They didn't know my truth—or at least I didn't think they did. Even though I had no specific reason to suspect that they would be anything less than fully supportive of me if I came out, I couldn't do it. My secret therefore put stress on our time together; visiting them would mean having to answer questions about how I was and what I was doing that I really couldn't answer. Their questions were innocent, but I didn't have any answers I felt I could share and I didn't want to lie.

I didn't feel like going to my parents' home and dealing

with the emotions that surfaced in me when I was around them. Instead, I was feeling lazy. I wanted to hang at my place, do some stuff around the apartment, and relax a bit.

"I'll be there sometime tomorrow, Mom," I told her, never thinking that the next day would be too late. Why can't we all have a little window into the future and some advance knowledge when things are about to go tragic? Just a little peek.

I should have gone on Friday night. Oh, how I wish I had.

Although he'd been a heart surgery patient, my father got up that Saturday morning to do a 10K race at Metro Center Mall in Phoenix. No one in the family liked the fact he exercised more than he should have, but he was a cocky heart surgery survivor. When I got the call later that morning, I somehow knew that my father was already dead.

"Your father's been taken to the hospital. Come to the house."

That's what my mother told me, and I immediately got in my car and sped toward north Phoenix. But why was she home and not at the hospital? Instead of going straight to the house as instructed, I drove to St. Joseph's Hospital where I was sure he would have been taken.

He wasn't there. He hadn't been admitted at all.

At that moment, I knew my worst fear was true. So I raced to my parents' house where Father Dale Fushek, then a young priest at St. Jerome's Parish where my family attended Mass, solemnly greeted me at the door.

"He's dead, isn't he?" I said.

Father Dale nodded.

I walked past him into the house and found my mother sitting at that same big wooden kitchen table. A few close family friends were with her. My younger brothers were seated on the couch in the family room.

"Oh, Neil, he's dead," she cried, "your father's gone." She had been at the 10K race, and later said she had a weird feeling when she saw the paramedics rush from their station by the finish line onto the race route. She knew then.

"I know, I know," was all I could say.

We hugged and all I could think of was that I should have come home the day before like she had asked me to. Because I decided not to come, the last time I saw my father had been two or three weeks before, when I stopped by on a Sunday to eat and do laundry. Absolutely nothing significant stands out from that visit: there's no special visual or mental image that springs to my mind. I don't remember the last time we were together or the last thing he said to me and that remains a hard thing for me to accept.

I do remember, however, an exchange between him and my fourteen-year-old brother. John was angry that Dad had planned to run that 10K in a few weeks, considering his heart condition. John had flippantly said, "Oh sure, go run and drop dead on my birthday and miss the party."

That was exactly what happened.

For years, John struggled to accept the fact that his father had died on his birthday—and that he had jokingly predicted that very event.

A light drizzle began to fall as we walked from the church to the limousine and continued to rain over us at the cemetery. I didn't know how I felt. A bit numb of course, but as usual, my emotions were on lockdown. Standing there in the cemetery, just a few feet from the grave opening, saying my last "goodbye," I didn't cry. I kept my feelings under control. As was my habit, I focused on what needed to be done. Funerals are filled with details, and I was involved with all of them. I knew I would confront my own emotions later, in the privacy of my apartment, but for the moment, I did what I'd always done: act first and feel later-if at all.

I thought about what my life would be like without my father. I thought about what my mom would do as such a young widow. At the time, I figured she would move back to New Jersey, where she had a supportive group of friends and in-laws to help her. In the end, however, she stayed in Phoenix. She got a job as a claims adjuster for Safeco Insurance and worked there for nearly twenty years until she retired, raising my two younger brothers, who were fourteen and sixteen when Dad died, on her own. She didn't remarry: she never even dated or sought out any male companionship. Once she retired twenty years later, she went to live with my sister to help care for her newest granddaughter. Being a full-time grandma gave her a renewed sense of purpose and joy, which was wonderful to watch, and I was happy for her.

How many Catholic funerals include the song "Tomorrow," from the musical *Annie?* It was a favorite of Dad's and an upbeat, positive message for all of us—and traditional or not, we played it.

"Remember all the good times you had and those you have to look forward to in your life," well-meaning relatives and family friends kept telling me, during the wake at the funeral parlor and before and after the Mass at St. Jerome's church. "Like when you get married and have your own kids."

"Great, thanks, but that's never going to happen," I wanted to say. But, of course, I didn't.

More than anything, Dad's death made me determined to do something with my life. I sat in the front pew of the church talking to him during the Mass, so many thoughts running through my head, his body in the casket just a few feet in front of me.

So now you know I am gay, maybe you already suspected, and I hope you're not disappointed. I will do some good along the way, I promise. I won't be a screw-up, I want to do good things and make you proud even though you won't be here for it.

I meant it. That very sad semester, fall of 1978, was my best academically as an undergraduate.

Our family dynamic had changed dramatically when my parents moved from New Jersey to Arizona, and I stayed behind. My sister had taken a job with the government and moved on;

she worked as a civilian on Army bases around the world for the next fifteen years and only visited once or twice a year. We left our extended family back in New Jersey: there would be no more long Sunday dinners around Grandma's table. My two younger brothers were growing up without me around.

The splintering between my siblings and me had already begun, but Dad's death signaled the end of the solidarity that we had had growing up together as children. We began drifting even further apart, tackling our adulthood separately, each on our own. There's sadness in our separateness for me, even though we were never the super tight family to begin with. In our family, one didn't share emotions, deep thoughts, or intensely personal information. Perhaps the emotional limitations of my parents, between each other and with their children, created this unusual norm for us. Perhaps they intended to raise us this way, I don't know. We were there for each other in formal ways, in times of tragedy and great need, because that's what family meant and that's what family did.

My mom played the role of the central touchstone, however, and for many years we kept track of each other through news from her. I often wonder if things would have been different if my father had lived, and I am convinced it would have made a significant difference. Even though she lost her husband young—she was only forty-seven when he died—my mom held everything together as best she could. We'd never be a tight, close-knit TV-series family of siblings, but each of us would grow to become successful, independent people. We have our own lives, live in different cities and are following our own dreams. We were all together for my swearing-in as mayor of Tempe in 1994 and it meant the world to me that they all showed up. I remember feeling my siblings' pride in me that day. Only another tragedy would bring us all together at the same place and time, twelve years later. We are a closer family now in many ways and recently were together again for the first time in many years. We're all still growing and learning. Still family.

Whatever the shortcomings my parents may have had, in creating family or between themselves, they loved each other and they did their best. This letter from my father to my mother, hand-written and dated October 3, 1973, is an indication of how they tried to work through it all.

Dear Jackie,
This pad paper is not very fancy but then again neither am I. I know there are times when you must doubt me with regard to my getting things done over the years. Like painting, carpentry, etc. There is one thing, however, that you should never doubt and that is my feeling and love for you. All the other items are superficial. The past twenty years you have put up with me and my shenanigans. I am sure we'll make the next twenty a little easier. I promise to do my best for you—my only goal in life is to make you happy. So whatever may be in store please remember that the most important facts are you and me. I apologize for not making life easier for you on this our 20th anniversary. May God bless you.
Your loving husband, Neil

In relationships, what more is there we can ask of each other than that we love each other and try our best to show it?

When I think about my family, I know there are a lot of gay people who are like I was at that point in my life: we want to come out, but we worry about the changes that decision will bring. We worry about the losses that might result. These fears are valid: family rejection, job issues, and other humiliation do happen. Because every individual has a unique set of issues and challenges, I don't believe in outing people. Encouraging people to step over the line is helpful and important to do, but each person crosses when he or she is ready.

While these things are true, living in the closet ultimately has another cost. We deny a crucial fact: that people around us often already *know* we're gay—and the only person we're fooling is ourselves. Now when I meet people who are still in the closet I think: *Was I that lost and out of touch with reality?* The answer is *yes*—and then some. Since coming out, I've realized that the fears I had about being honest with myself and others were overwhelmingly outweighed by the tremendous support and liberty I felt by finally being able to be completely myself. To be honest.

I might have had an easier time admitting my sexual orientation to my family and to myself if there had been someone to talk to: a mentor, an older friend, someone who understood what I was facing and had the wisdom and experience to guide me through it. Someone else who had struggled. There was no one like that for me. The only gay men I saw or knew were the men who never seemed to doubt their truth at all. And that wasn't my experience. They surely wouldn't understand my predicament; I was nowhere near the same league as them. So, I internalized all my emotions and cut myself off from the love and acceptance of the people around me: family, the out and proud gay people I saw who seemed to have no issues, the straight folks I knew but would never be.

I count myself lucky. I created a pretty screwed up place for myself, but it didn't win the day for my entire life. That would have been an extremely sad thing. But on the other hand, I've seen many guys who come out in a blaze of glory at a young age, and they go wild, sow their oats, as it were. They've been holding back all that pent-up emotion and desire for so long. It's a bit of a gay adolescence when men come out: sometimes their whole life revolves around the gay subculture of going out to bars and nightclubs, hooking up a lot, sometimes getting pulled in to experimenting with drugs. Under the best circumstances, managing one's emotions is difficult for any very young adult. Add the pressure of being gay and managing the emotional burden can be overwhelming.

For me, it was different. I didn't manage the emotional

journey of being gay at that young age. I'm not sure how my life would have turned out had I tried. Instead, I focused on work and achieved professionally and politically. As a result, however, a long period of my life slipped away with hardly any personal or emotional development at all. In some ways, I stayed locked at the moment when my father died and I drifted away from my family to do my own thing and discover what my place might be.

*　*　*

My father lived a typical paycheck-to-paycheck, middle-class life. So there was no estate, no inheritance of any kind, no windfall headed my way. By the time my mom used the small insurance policy to pay off bills, there was little left. I realized I was truly on my own financially. I was only a semester away from graduating from ASU, and I didn't have a clue what to do next. I would start to focus. Law school maybe? The Circle K friend I had been in love with and with whom I shared my near-suicide experience was encouraging me to consider that path. And I almost chose it, just to be close to him. It was the wrong reason to go to law school, of course, and fortunately I didn't take that route.

Doug Wasson stepped into this void for me with the offer of a summer job.

Doug was a Kiwanis International Trustee, a high-level position in the organization, and I had come to know him well in his capacity as an advisor to the Circle K organization. He was also an ordained ecumenical minister who led a congregation outside of Colorado Springs called the Church at Woodmoor. The Church described itself as "celebrating life in the evangelical, Catholic and Reformed traditions." I had spoken at some of Doug's services and led devotional services at Doug's annual Conference on Voluntary Action (CONOVACT), which gathered leaders from Kiwanis, Circle K and Key Club each

November at the amazing Camp La Foret to discuss community service.

Doug saw the emotional and spiritual side of me just below the surface and provided me tremendous opportunities to better know, explore and create a real relationship with God, not merely through church attendance, but through a connection to something deeper and more personal. He was the first to tell me that I had the gift of being able to talk to people in a way that connected with them emotionally. He was the first to suggest that I should develop that gift and pray about for what purpose I might use it.

No one had ever told me I had a gift. Sure, the rabbi had said I was "special" when I was a kid and "would do good things." And sure, I had held leadership roles and been a successful organizer and speaker, but Doug was talking about something deeper, something bigger. In his mind, it was something important.

On several occasions over those years, he assigned me to leading an evening devotional service at CONOVACT. These were designed as a way to connect the community service activities of the participants to their personal spiritual journey and to hopefully strengthen both.

I would spend hours finding stories, quotes, and scripture that I could use to craft a service that would move the participants, touch them in a meaningful way and encourage them to give an ear to the presence of a higher being in their work and their life. And as a result, I started to find an inner peace and comfort, even as I struggled to be open and honest with others about my own secret.

One time for CONOVACT I read from a Calvin Miller book titled *The Singer*. I spoke in front of a blazing fire in the huge fireplace, with only candles elsewhere in the room. About 200 high school and college student leaders sat huddled on the floor that cold November night. In the chairs around the perimeter on the rustic room sat the Kiwanis advisors. I chose a section about unconditional love.

"Are you betrothed?" she asked.

"No, only loved," he answered.

"And do you pay for love?"

"No, but I owe it everything."

It was a retelling of the classic scripture, when Jesus interacts with the prostitute. I spoke about reaching out to the less fortunate, the people who needed our community service the most, and related it all to the opportunity living within each of us to serve as we are called. And after telling the rest of the story as Miller tells it, I closed in a powerful way, using his words:

"He left her in the street and walked away, and as He left He heard her singing His new song. And when He turned to wave a final time He saw her shaking her head to a friendship buyer. She would not take his money. And from a little distance, the Singer heard her use his very words:

"Are you betrothed?" the buyer asked.

"No, only loved," she answered.

"And do you pay for love?"

"No, but I owe it everything."

Communicating and leading in such a deep way helped me connect and build very close friendships, far beyond any I had held in my life up to that point, and helped me connect to myself as well. It helped me become vulnerable and open up in ways I had not been able to before. These interactions and opportunities helped me better understand, if not yet accept, who I was and how I might serve others. Those Circle K relationships, some of which still exist today though at a different level, strengthened and inspired me. They gave me a sense of confidence that overrode my own struggles. These friends, too numerous to identify but they know who they are, are sacred to me: they believed in me when I doubted myself, and it made all the difference, though they likely had no idea at the time of just how critical their role was in my life. In fact, I am sure they had no idea, perhaps until now. Mostly, I understand now, because I failed to let them in.

I had no idea that all of this growth awaited me when Doug offered me a summer position as youth minister for his congregation. I just knew I needed a job.

"Come up to Colorado," he suggested, embracing the role of father figure and spiritual mentor. "Bring a friend, if you want, and get out of Arizona for a while. We'll keep you busy." I'm not sure what Doug meant by "bring a friend," but I am convinced he knew me better than I knew myself.

Doug reached out to his congregation and other contacts and cobbled together a series of house-sitting gigs that kept me in free lodging for the parts of the summer when I wouldn't be off in the poorest parts of Colorado with the young people from the church doing community service projects.

I invited Len to go with me.

He was a close friend from Circle K and from my many activities at ASU's Newman Center, the organizational base for Catholic students on campus. He was also a great guy, quite good-looking, and I had a huge crush on him. I decided I needed to tell him I was gay before the summer, and I did. Fearing rejection, I told him and gave him a small paperback book about being gay to help him understand where I was coming from. Later, I learned his mom found the book in his room and reached a conclusion he had a hard time explaining, but he said he still wanted to come with me for the summer. He didn't offer any information about himself at the time, so I couldn't tell whether he was straight and just didn't care about my orientation or if he was gay and interested—though I hoped for the latter, of course. Whatever his reasons, he'd agreed to go with me and I was ecstatic.

Off we went to Colorado Springs. Within a few weeks, Len made it clear that he was most definitely *not* gay, and I quickly found myself alone a lot of the time. So much for that summer of first love I had hoped for.

One Friday night I went alone to a club in downtown Colorado Springs. Away from the confines of my life in Arizona,

I felt adventurous and ready to explore. I wondered if I could find an experience like that night at the Limelight in Manhattan on my own, only I had no idea where to find anything gay other than the Yellow Pages, which were not too helpful.

The place definitely had an alternative vibe, although not a gay bar. There wasn't much of a crowd. For a long time, I sat at the bar and drank several rum and cokes without really talking to anyone. Then a couple people nearby started buying me drinks—and I drank them. We chatted away the hours and put away more drinks, until the place closed and I was plastered.

Long before the "don't let friends drive drunk" messages, I somehow stumbled to my car in the lot next to the building and fumbled to put the key in the door. Once inside and seated, I remember starting the car. And that's it.

The only other thing I remember was walking into the house where Len and I were house-sitting. I don't remember anything about the thirty-minute-plus highway drive to get there.

"What the hell are you doing?" Len demanded.

He could tell I was wasted. I was lurching and falling through the house, knocking things over as I headed for the bedroom door. I didn't even answer him; I just walked past him, tumbled into the master bedroom of our $500,000, two-week home and passed out.

That's the first, last, and only time I ever drove drunk.

I will always believe that some unseen force protected me that night. Maybe it was my father, I don't know. What I *do* know is that when I awoke the next afternoon, I had an overwhelming feeling that I was still alive for a reason. I knew that I probably shouldn't have lived through that night, driving as totally drunk as I was in a strange city, then up and around winding roads in a mountain town. Every day since then has been a precious bonus gift.

It left me with another weird thought, too: the visual memory of the mysterious Jewish man rubbing my head in front of the local movie theater so many years ago. My journal from that

Saturday afternoon in Colorado includes an emotional note about destiny. How I had tempted my own with my behavior the night prior. What was I thinking? I did have a future, unsure as it still was, and needed to pull my act together.

At the end of the summer of 1979, I had no more crystal clear idea about my future than I had had at the start of the summer, but I was feeling better. Len had not turned out to be the boyfriend of my dreams, not by a long shot, but he was an okay guy who knew me and hadn't run totally in the other direction, not immediately anyway.

When I returned to Arizona, I briefly worked as a counselor and community education specialist for the Center Against Sexual Assault (CASA) and then accepted my first full-time position at Arizona State, as student advisor/counselor in the Office of Disabled Students. Campus life and work was appealing, and I thought a career in higher education would be a great one for me. I imagined myself becoming a dean of students, maybe even a university president one day. With goals, like those, however, it was obvious I needed to chart an academic path that could take me there. I looked at both the Master of Counseling and Master of Higher Education Administration degree programs and talked with the man who was then Dean of Students, Leon Shell, and the Vice-President of Student Affairs, George Hamm, about the options. They knew me as the student who had been International President of Circle K and who now worked in one of their departments, and they were both gracious with their assistance. I took the graduate school entrance tests and did okay, but not stellar, which to be honest was always my academic place. I worked hard, learned a lot, but was not a natural academic. In the fall of 1980, likely with the help of supportive recommendations from Shell and Hamm, I was accepted into the ASU Masters of Higher Education program, going to school part-time while keeping my job at the Disabled Students Office.

Helping students with varying sensory disabilities—blind

and deaf students mostly, and even some quadriplegics and paraplegics—made my caseload interesting, challenging and rewarding. Many of those sessions were quite emotional, and I found myself being able to provide the right balance of empathy and motivation to help my differently-abled students get to class and get the best education possible. I was on my way in a career path and it felt really good.

This was also the time I turned to even greater intensity and relationship with the Newman Center and some of the students there. It would lead to a growing sense that maybe I could, in fact, push aside the feelings I had about other guys, and live a straight life. With the little bit of cash we had received when Dad died, my mom and I bought a small house in Tempe for me to live in, an investment for her retirement. To help pay the bills I found a few roommates from the Newman Center to move in with me. Soon, that house became as close to a seminary or a rectory as it could without a priest living under the roof. We ate together, prayed together; priests came by and said mass in our living room. My roommates were very involved at the Center, a few led the music liturgies each week, and our house was full of the life and music of Christ.

This experience was a far cry from the religion I experienced growing up. That strict Catholic upbringing never moved me close to God, never gave me a sense of connecting or even the desire to connect to God. It was Sunday ritual and obligatory participation at every turn.

You may think that being devoutly Catholic and gay would be contradictory, but it wasn't. The fellowship and piety in the house was very real for me, too. I was like those guys and close to them in spite of being gay. I didn't feel conflicted about having my deepest feelings so inconsistent with the church's tenets, and I still don't. I knew my sexual orientation was not going to change. The issue had become would I choose to ignore it? Would I consciously choose a life I knew was not real to me, but would be real for society standards and allow me to have a greater career, family, life? Would I close down my sexual orientation for my friends and family? Did I have the capacity to choose to be straight and never look back? I was seriously thinking that maybe I could. Maybe I would. I had locked away the reality of my feelings I experienced dancing that night at the Limelight. I locked away the memory of the electricity and comfort I felt in the presence of so many other men. I convinced myself I could be happy in other ways.

But then something happened that revived the deep core of my true sexuality and brought new questions, too.

My office was in the Student Health Services building on the north side of campus. One sun-splashed afternoon in April, 1981, as I was walking to lunch down Palm Walk—so named because it is a long sidewalk with towering, skinny palm trees on each side—a muscular guy with reddish-brown hair walked by in shorts, a tank top, and flip-flops. He was really good looking, and so I turned and looked back after he passed me. To my surprise, he was looking back at me, too. I turned back around and kept walking, but I couldn't stop myself from looking over my shoulder one more time.

He had reversed course and was following me. My heart raced.

"What are you doing?" he asked, smiling, when he caught up with me.

"Nothing. Just going to lunch."

Wow, what a great smile, I remember thinking.

"You work in there?" He gestured to the Student Health Services building without taking his eyes off me.

"Yeah," I replied. "And, um, I'm in grad school here, too."

His name was Pete and we ended up sitting at the same fountain where I had once sat with Father Tom from the Newman Center, discussing the priesthood as an option for my socially empty yet service-filled life. With Pete, however, it was a nervous, short-sentence, question-and-answer conversation at first, and before we parted, we exchanged phone numbers.

I never expected he would call; I knew I would never have the guts to call him. But I wanted him to call. And he did. Two days later, we went out to eat. He was the total package in my eyes. He was at ASU on a track scholarship and lived with his track team buddies. Where I was unsure how much I wanted to act on what I knew was my true orientation, Pete knew exactly what he wanted, and it wasn't a life with a woman. He was very confident. Ours wasn't an emotional connection, not for him anyway, just an intense mutual attraction. For me, there was more to it and for a first experience, I can't imagine it being better. That's always the way it goes, right? The person for whom it is "the first" gets attached emotionally and unrealistic expectations occur. No denying that was my case.

Pete was patient with me and funny. He often laughed at my inexperience, especially since I was five years older. His three roommates, who were all pretty damn hot-looking, knew his story—and consequently mine—and didn't seem fazed a single bit. For athletes in the competitive sports world, they were far ahead of their time.

We hung out together all summer until Pete transferred and headed back to northern California. After he moved, we exchanged a few letters, but lost touch over time. That was the first time I ever got picked up by a guy, not the last, and Pete taught me more than a few things, about myself and about being gay. That *Everything You Always Wanted to Know About Sex** book was very wrong indeed.

From 1981 to 1983, I continued graduate school at ASU. My connection through the Newman Center and housemates evolved and a group of us became active in student government. I ran the campaign for a roommate, Bob Mulhern, who was elected vice-president and was then appointed parliamentarian of the student senate. The following year I ran the campaign of Clarissa Davis, an African American student senator running for student body president who lost. I sat in the student government offices one afternoon around the time people were starting to jockey to run for the various positions and gave some thought to what I wanted to do for my final year of my graduate program. I looked down at the closed door to the student body president's office in the corner, and imagined myself working on the other side of it. I'm a believer in the art of visualization; literally visualizing the people, places, activities, and desired outcomes before they are even underway. While I had run the campaign of her opponent, she was sharp, successful, and a class act as president. We have remained in touch over all the years since student government days; Denise Resnik is one of those true pillars of the community in Phoenix, and I have called on her wise counsel over the years, and highly value her encouragement and support.

I was studying Higher Education Administration, so it sounded to me like a good idea to get some experience working with a university administration, up close and personal. Why not run for student government president?

I knew I could do a bang-up job as president and offer solid leadership for the many activities of the office. I also considered seeking the student post on the Arizona Board of Regents, but a friend, Chris Spinella, decided to seek the regent spot and I decided to run for president rather than compete with him. I won my campaign; he was not selected student regent, but remains a friend and loyal ASU alumnus. The young man who was selected student regent, Vada Manager, would also go on to a great career of public and private sector service, as an advisor and press secretary for both Arizona Governor Rose Mofford and Mayor Sharon Pratt Kelly of Washington, D.C. and is a friend I always enjoy catching up with when our busy lives align in the same city.

When you don't have a social life—no girlfriend (or boyfriend) or any relationships or friendships of any depth—you work. I was the classic over-achiever. If I got involved with something, before long I was looking for ways to make it better. I channeled all my energy and focus into service. Of course, it wasn't enough to just be active in student government; I had to be student body president. And so I was. It was a fun campaign, and I had great support from friends at the Newman Center and friends from the fraternity system, especially Sigma Nu. My fellow past president of Circle K International Greg Faulkner even flew in from New York City to help campaign. We won handily.

I was alone and lonely personally, and that brought back the familiar and successful pattern from my Circle K International days: work, excel, enjoy making a difference for other people, and meet some great friends through that engagement; it was a great fit for me, despite the loneliness.

It wasn't all sacrifice by any means: I truly loved helping people and making things happen. I didn't mind being in charge, either. I was learning valuable lessons, making mistakes, growing, and leading other people who were committed to a united purpose. These were all things that would serve me very well down the road. I was good at it.

As lonely and frustrated as I often felt, I know things could have been worse. Many men in my situation have turned to alcohol to shut down their feelings. Others have turned to drugs. In fact, there are probably dozens of destructive outlets I could have pursued, but I became a workaholic and honed my leadership skills. The pattern that started when I joined the Key Club in high school continued. I channeled my angst over not "fitting in" into serving organizations and helping people.

The difference was now I *knew* I was gay, but since I still felt I could never be fully open about it, my reality changed nothing in my behavior. There were no openly gay leaders that I knew of, and as natural as I had felt about being with Pete, that was mostly a secret. I wasn't about to proclaim my sexual orientation for everybody else to know. While I was student body president, I knew that there was a group of gay guys on campus who had heard the rumors about me, but they left me alone. These were the pre-Internet days, when one's personal life, especially on the down-low, could pretty much stay on the down low. They respected my privacy, and I was happy to stay closeted. I wasn't going to be an "out" gay guy. My gay experiences were genuine for me, but that wouldn't be my "lifestyle."

Only much later would I realize how stupid the "lifestyle" tag is for one's sexual orientation. The "style" of my life was not about my sexuality, then nor now. It was and remains about being of service to others, making a difference, treating people with respect, doing good work.

Self-respect, however, was hard for me. I was sure I would have to marry a woman and maintain a straight life, even though I knew it to be a falsehood. That knowledge gnawed at me constantly, but I just didn't see another way to live.

After being in Key Club and Circle K—both youth organizations sponsored by the Kiwanis Club of Tempe— it was natural that now that I was an adult, I would join that organization. I joined February, 12,1981 while still in graduate school, even before running for student body president, and in doing so, began to make my first forays into becoming involved with the wider Tempe community.

Around the same time, I also had a secret fling with a student so smart he was getting a double degree in engineering and business. His name was Michel and he was tall, dark-haired, quiet, and handsome. I was student body president and he was in the student senate, so we ended up working on student government issues together regularly. Think about it: the president and a student senator carrying on a "gay affair" in secret. A scandal in the making for certain.

"You want to catch a movie Saturday night?" he asked me over a quick lunch between meetings one day.

"Sure," I said. At the time I had no idea that he was gay—not the first clue in the world. I thought we'd just hang out together; I didn't realize it was actually a date. Sort of.

We went to the drive-in theater on McKellips and Hayden in south Scottsdale. He had a huge Chevy Impala with a bench front seat, without the barrier console between the passenger and the driver that bucket seats have. As the movie unfolded, his hand slowly inched my way.

I thought it was strange for him to have his hand stretched out like that.

Clueless, that's what I was. I was twenty-six years old, in graduate school but an emotional adolescent when it came to relationships. I had had no real lasting personal relationships, with either sex. I had dated Sabra while an undergraduate, a fellow Circle K club leader, but she figured me out and moved on, which saved us both additional drama.

Nothing much happened between us that night at the drive-in, but we did become physically involved later. Not only was Michel super smart, sexy, and had a killer smile, he was the kind of guy that no one would have ever guessed was gay. Perfect for a closeted guy like myself. A pattern was emerging already for me—a masculine guy with a great smile and smarts will win me over every time.

How did he know I was gay? How did he know to make the moves on me? I don't think I ever said or did anything "gay" around him. But he knew and he sought me out. I was sending a signal, without even realizing I was sending it: my complete lack of a personal life and the dizzying array of student activities that comprised my life screamed loudly that I must be trying to ignore or avoid something. Today I see that my "smoke screen" was more like a smoke signal. But back then, I didn't see it at all.

We only went out a few times. After the third time, and a fun evening, he said, "I don't think we should get together anymore."

"Why not?"

"I'm just really not comfortable with this anymore."

I was confused. My thoughts circled around and around everything that had happened between us, trying to understand what was happening. I wondered, *Is he gay but just doesn't want to see me? Is it me? He pursued me and started this, now he's just ending it?*

It felt like Michel was ripping away the little confidence I had gained around my sexual identity. In my exuberance over the fling with Michel and the earlier experience with Pete, I'd taken a few small steps toward becoming more honest with some of the people around me. I'd told one of my roommates, Tim Smith, that I was gay—and that I was sure about it, even though I hadn't figured out whether I would live as a gay man or a straight one. Poor Tim must have been more confused than I was, listening to my blabber. We sat out on the diving board of the backyard pool one night and talked about it for a couple hours. To my surprise, he took the news in stride. Remember, my house was full of deeply Catholic men to whom homosexuality was not cool. To my housemates, "those people" were to be avoided. Yet Tim neither condemned me nor rejected me. I never felt his knowledge of my secret changed how he treated me at all.

Along with Tim's reaction and my experiences with Michel and Pete, another encounter had my mind reeling over the signals I must have been sending unconsciously.

Tim's sister got married that spring, and I was invited to attend the wedding. Using my office as student body president, I had helped them reserve a room in the Memorial Union building for the rehearsal dinner. At that event I met the groom's brother, Stanley, an Army soldier who had a chiseled handsome look and was wearing a pair of snug white pants. He could have been on a U.S. Army recruiting poster. Stanley and I hit it off immediately.

"I'm in town for a few days after the wedding," he told me. "If you have some time, maybe you can show me around."

I was sure that Stanley was straight. *He was just being nice*, I told myself. I agreed to play host. Nothing bad could come from spending time with a hot Army man, I figured.

Stanley and I arranged to have dinner at the Black Angus Steakhouse, on Broadway Road in Tempe. He was quite a man: blond hair in a close-cropped military cut, athletically built, and very proud of being a soldier in our Army. We talked about our lives, families, things we cared about, and went on and on. During dinner Stanley pushed himself away from the table and stood up.

"I've got to go to the restroom," he said, his voice clipped and military. He took a step away from the table, then stopped, turned back and leaned toward me. "By the way, the answer is 'yes.'" Then he smiled, turned, and threaded his way through the restaurant toward the restroom.

The answer is *yes*. Wow. Had I even asked a question? It did not matter that I hadn't asked: we both knew what the question was.

Because the answer was "yes," Stanley and I had a fantastic three-day date, touring the town and each other in his hotel room. We had long, deep philosophical talks into the night, and once again, I felt completely comfortable, completely at peace.

Pete, Michel, and Stanley were three unique guys who had very little in common, if you were to sit them down together and compare their looks, their interests, or their goals. Their common traits included their smarts, their intense smiles, and yes, the fact that they carried themselves in a very confident manner when it came to their sexuality, a characteristic that was deeply lacking in me.

However, Stanley's story has a sad ending.

Seven years later, in early 1990, my close friend, Circle K colleague and former roommate Mike McAuly called.

"I have some bad news, Neil. Remember Stanley, the Army guy from the Smith wedding years ago?" he asked.

"Of course." I had told Mike about our few days together. "He's awesome. I'll never forget Stanley. What happened?"

"He's dead."

I was stunned.

"Was it some Army accident or something? Where was he stationed now?"

"No," Mike said, dispelling my notions of some training

mission gone badly. "He caught some strange virus and died within a couple weeks. Mrs. Smith called to tell me."

I could vividly recall Stanley's face. I remembered how we held each other the last night he was in Phoenix and how much he loved being in the army. He was honored to be a soldier, and I'm glad he had the chance to do what he loved.

"I don't think anyone in his family would say it," Mike continued, "but don't you think it sounds like it could be the AIDS virus?"

"I suppose so. I don't know. Did his family know he was gay?"

"I don't think so," said Mike.

For all his confidence, Stanley had had his closets, too, both personally and professionally. Him being in the Army, I shouldn't have been surprised. And I know that, had he lived, he would have been among the first to serve as an openly gay serviceman. But in the 1980s, pre-"Don't Ask, Don't Tell," when he was in the Army, that wasn't possible.

I remembered him fondly, feeling both sad to hear of his passing and warmth at the memory of the brief happiness we shared. Rest in peace, Stanley.

I never regained contact with Pete, and I think about him from time to time, as we all remember those first experiences. Michel the student senator briefly returned to my life a couple years after I learned of Stanley's death. I was having lunch with a colleague from ASU at the Corcoran Art Gallery in Washington, D.C., when I looked up and there was Michel, looking at hot as ever. Our eyes connected across the short distance of the restaurant, and my heart started racing. He came over and handed me his business card.

"It's good to see you again," he said with perfect professional coolness and that same smile. "Give me a call when you get a chance."

I couldn't wait to end that lunch and get the rest of the day behind me, so I could call him. This was 1990—before everyone had smart phones in their pockets at all times—and I had to wait until I was back in my hotel to call.

That brief affair, our secret three-week fling eight years earlier, had left an indelible mark on me. I was eager to know what he had been doing and whether he was gay after all. I was now much more emotionally mature, a new city councilman with significant professional and political responsibilities. And while my personal life had not evolved very much, I at least understood myself now, both the strengths and underlying challenges that were a part of who I was, and was still becoming. Yes, I understood enough to look back and know I had the biggest crush on Michel when I was twenty-six going on sixteen.

Today, we're friends on Facebook.

CHAPTER SIX

My Dinner With Chip

May 1983 marked the end of an amazing and successful year as student body president—and I earned my master's degree in Higher Education Administration. Academically, I had hit my stride, knew how to learn, and was applying for entry-level student affairs jobs at colleges and universities all over the US. I thought it would be valuable to experience another campus environment, and it was clear that experience at various campuses was the profile of nearly all high-level university administrators.

In June, one of my mentors on campus, Betty Asher, the Vice-President of Student Affairs, asked me to stop by her office. She told me they were going to create a full-time position out of the graduate associate role I had held from 1981-82, the year before I was student body president. They would look for someone familiar with the leadership scholarship program and who could further develop a leadership course for the students.

"Think about it, Neil," she said. "We'd love for you to consider staying here at ASU."

I had been excited about moving to a new place, to a new environment, but I did think about it, and decided to apply. The decision forever altered my adult professional life, and unbeknownst to me at the time, my political and personal life as well. It wouldn't be the last time that Better Asher would have a profound influence on the path of my life. Like joining Key Club as a high school sophomore had been at the time, that conversation with her stands out as a one of the few truly defining decisions of my life's journey.

In August, I started my first professional role as ASU's program coordinator of student leadership and development. Actually, it was my second professional role, since I had worked in the Disabled Students Office before and during part of my graduate schoolwork. But it was my first since completing my advanced degree, so I felt differently about it. There is something about having your academic credentials: this time I felt like I belonged in the job in a way I hadn't before.

It was a great position, working with incredibly smart and talented students, many of whom I had known since they had arrived on campus. I revamped the curriculum for the leadership class and made it my own. My network of friends and supporters on campus had grown large, and included many of the guys from Sigma Nu who had worked hard to get me elected student body president. I became the academic advisor for the fraternity, and a general mentor to many of the men who were involved in campus activities.

After I returned from the Key Club International convention in August of 1984, I had a dream that I was on the ASU campus and all the people with me were friends from Key Club and Circle K International. That same week I had lunch with June Malos. June was the scholarship officer for the financial aid office and had been of tremendous support to me over the years. June found me a couple small scholarships that I applied for and received. Once, after I had been elected student body president, she called me to her office and gave me a $300 check.

"A clothing scholarship," she said. "Go buy a blue sport coat, some khaki pants, and a pair of nice shoes for the official meetings you'll be attending as student body president."

This lunch with June was different and would lead to the creation of a program that has changed and altered the futures of many lives since 1985. That may sound trite and over-stated, but in this instance, it really is true. June mentioned she had some out-of-state tuition and fee waivers available.

"Do you know any really great students around the country we might try to recruit?"

I had stayed in close touch with the Key Club organization and its leaders since I had graduated high school. Most years I still went back to volunteer on the convention staff, and eventually, I became a part of the core group of five people who assisted Pete Tinsley in running the convention sessions. From my perspective, I knew the very sharpest high school student leaders in the country and it would be awesome to bring some of them to the ASU campus.

With June's support I created the ASU-Key Club International Leadership Scholarship Program. The first of the scholarships recipients came to ASU in fall of 1985 and between two and four students have attended each year ever since.

These students are part of the larger Leadership Scholarship Program (LSP) for graduating high school seniors in Arizona. The students and alumni from this small component of the larger group have added a great deal to the program and today they are some of the university's most engaged and successful alumni. It is a wonderful program with exceptional people and I am so proud to have been involved in a meaningful way.

After a year and a half running the Leadership Scholarship Program—and almost ten years after I had first come to the university campus as a freshman—I pledged Sigma Nu Fraternity at the ripe old age of twenty-eight, even though I had not been looking to join a fraternity.

I was asked to pledge by Bob Venberg and Walter Batt, two of the more respected guys in the fraternity; Bob was Eminent

Commander, or President, of the fraternity. Walter had run my campaign for student body president and when I won, I appointed him my executive assistant and then he followed me as president the next year. In fact, Tom Ajamie, also a Sigma Nu, had been president two years before me, and another Sigma Nu followed Walter. Four out of five years in a row, once I was initiated, there was a Sigma Nu as student body president. I don't think that kind of hold on campus politics would be possible today, but it was back then.

Walter and Bob invited me to pledge as a way to know more about the fraternity from the inside and to get to know the guys better. It made sense, and was quite an honor, so I said yes. They indicated I could be inducted into the fraternity in a somewhat "honorary" capacity, since I was also a university employee, teaching a leadership course, and a bit older than most pledges. But while they thought that would be what I would prefer, they were wrong. If I was going to do it, I explained, I would do it the way everyone else did it. I would work just as hard and participate just as the others had participated. I wanted to take on the full experience. They agreed.

I know a twenty-eight-year-old "pledge" sounds odd, but from the fraternity photo, I fit right in. In fact, I don't think anyone could look at that photograph and single me out as the "old guy" or say I looked out of place in the slightest. I look the same age as my pledge brothers.

The spring 1984 pledge class of Sigma Nu—may it live forever—included some very smart and savvy guys, many of whom have gone on to great success and leadership roles in life while raising wonderful families. I count many of them as tremendous allies and friends.

In the spring of 1985, the alumni leadership of the fraternity asked me to consider becoming the live-in resident advisor for the fraternity. I saw this as the opportunity I needed to truly help me discover that I could and would straighten out my personal life.

Perhaps you think that moving into the fraternity house would be a closeted gay man's dream. I'd spend my days surrounded by some incredibly attractive men who I could admire all day and night. But that wasn't my strategy at all. In fact, it was the exact opposite. To my mind, being rooted in a fraternity—the bedrock of masculinity where "beer-girls-sports" was the sole mantra—would somehow alter my gay-ness. Maybe, just maybe, if I hung around them long enough, I could become like these cool guys and function straight, if not become straight. Surrounded by a cadre of beer-drinking college studs, how could I not become more heterosexual myself? Their hardcore heterosexuality would wear off on me. It was all about whom you chose to associate with, I told myself. I had decided long ago not to count myself as one of those activist gays, as though denying those men would make me "less gay."

What an idiot.

There was only one problem with my strategy—and it took me years to accept its truth: a tiger living with a pride of lions never loses its stripes. At a time when I should have stood up and been counted as an openly gay student leader, like so many are doing today on campuses around the nation, I stayed closeted and seeking to figure out how I could ignore my orientation enough to live a straight life.

Just a couple years ago, a young student at ASU contacted me via Facebook and asked if I could meet with him to provide some advice. We met for coffee in the Memorial Union building, where twenty-eight years prior I paced the corridors and meeting rooms as the leader of the campus. We met, and I learned he was very involved on campus and was going to run for student body president. And, he added, he was gay, but not out. After acknowledging the immense change in culture since 1982, I expressed that he should do what I had not had the courage to do: be authentic, be open, be himself. People would respect him more, and his opportunity to lead would be enhanced by virtue of his candor and willingness to be honest.

I could tell he was really struggling with the notion of being openly gay. But I knew he hadn't reached out to me for the message "Stay hidden and lie." He didn't need to meet me for that kind of encouragement. That we were meeting at all was the evidence that he was ready to be true to himself. All I needed to do was assure him he would be fine; in fact, he would thrive with the liberation of living openly.

Brendan did publicly acknowledge that he was gay as his campaign started, and I was so proud of him for doing so. He lost the election, but it taught him much and he won the potential of a balanced and open life in all respects. He's now in law school and can create whatever future he desires.

His campaign within had lasted maybe a year or so. Mine had lasted a good twenty.

Someday, and for some people this is already the case, gay people won't have to "come out" because we will have a society that doesn't force one to hide who they really are in the first place. We're not quite there yet.

Although I hid my sexual orientation from my fraternity brothers, every now and then something would happen and my closet door would pop open, revealing a glimpse of my truth that would just not go away.

Over spring break in 1985, on a glorious, sunny March day, I was driving near campus in my green 1977 Volvo. While I was stopped at a light, a white VW GTI with a sunroof pulled alongside me. A blond, muscle-bound young guy was driving it, and the car looked like it had just rolled out of the showroom. A keyboard-heavy '80s track thumped out a steady beat. I couldn't help but stare, and he stared back. The mutual staring went on through several traffic lights. I headed east on Fifth Street and turned into the parking lot at Sigma Nu, where I was now an initiated brother of the fraternity, and soon to be moving in as the live-in resident advisor. As I was getting out of my comparatively unspectacular Volvo, the young blond pulled in behind me.

"Hey, what's going on?" he asked.

In spite of all the staring we'd been doing, I was surprised. I looked around me and shrugged. "Nothing? No one is around. Spring break."

"Yeah, I know. Hey, just wanted to see if you're doing anything later on."

"Uh, no. Why?"

I thought I knew where he was going with this conversation, but I wasn't sure I wanted to play. I was going straight, damn it, and now here was this random stud asking me out. The parking lot was scattered with a few cars, but almost all of the fraternity guys were off on beaches, drinking beer, and getting turned-on from staring at girls in tiny bikinis. I, on the other hand, was staring at a total stud with military-short, blond hair and chiseled looks.

"I just thought we could go do something," he said.

Do something? Yes, we could do something alright.

"Why would we do that?"

He reached up and turned down the music and smiled right at me. "I don't know. Just to hang out. I saw you back at the stoplight there."

So this is how it happens? I attempt to ignore my true self and hot guys just randomly follow me? Do I just scream gay or what?

"Yeah…I…saw…you, too."

This was weird. No, this was more than weird; it was becoming a pattern.

Yes, I was attracted to guys, but I had sworn I wasn't going to act on my attraction. And overwhelmingly, though not entirely, I hadn't. Still, somehow, guys just kept seeking me out, inviting me into the very situations I'd sworn not to be a participant in. First, Pete followed me on the campus mall, then Michel wanted to go to a movie, and Stanley said "yes" before I asked anything. Now this hot guy in his sexy car had followed me back to my soon-to-be home at the fraternity house, where I had hoped to bury my sexual orientation issues forever.

Well, so much for that plan. He told me his name was David and I don't recall how but that night we ended up sitting across from each other at Minder Binder's, a long-standing local college hangout, eating hamburgers. David told me all about his big Mormon family, how he told them he was gay when he recently returned from his church-obligated mission to grow the Mormon faith on the planet. According to David, the folks weren't dealing with his news too well.

I shared that I was working and teaching on campus, and not out. After dinner, we drove around in his VW GTI, which was very cool at the time. Nothing happened until he dropped me off at the house where I still lived with all the Catholic guys from the Newman Center.

"Thanks. I had a nice time," I said and moved to get out of the car.

He put his arm on my shoulder and held me there, making my quick exit impossible. Then he leaned over and kissed me.

There I was, kissing a guy, right in front of a house full of religious men, my roommates. I had thought when I moved in with those men that their pious example and prayerful environment would straighten me out, but they and the boss, the big "JC," hadn't done the job. Not that I hadn't done my share—I prayed. Often. I asked for guidance and strength and focus and signs that would help make me become the person God wanted me to be; that would make my father proud. Increasingly, however, the house was so absent of anything sexual, as far as I knew anyway, that there was no influence at all on my own sexuality or any expression thereof. In one way, it was as it should be: full of love and acceptance without regard or discussion about sexuality. But my truth was that I needed the discussion and emphasis, of the straight kind, to help become focused and determined to live a straight life and reject my true self.

If only I had understood much earlier that my prayers were being answered, and I was being shown the way—the honest way, the way that was *my* truth, the truth I was born with. But society had never understood my truth well; in fact, our entire culture clung to a misunderstood religious framing of a natural human condition. Because of that misunderstanding, generations of people like me led unhappy lives filled with lies, emotional pain and suffering. If only I had understood that denying my truth made me yet another one of those sad people. But back then, I didn't.

Instead, I pinned my hopes on Sigma Nu. The fraternity house's testosterone and borderline misogyny would have to succeed where Catholic rituals and wrong expectations had, predictably, failed. I was ready to leave the religious household. I hated living a lie of omission with all my housemates except Tim, who was the only one knew the truth. I wanted to have integrity and be honest, but I clung to the notion that if only I could find the right surroundings—in this case the fraternity instead of a religious household- I could transform myself and truly be a straight man.

I hoped, and yes, even prayed from time to time, that the fascination with men that I'd felt since a teenage boy rode by on his Schwinn Sting-Ray would somehow dissolve away. I hoped that if I spent enough time in a hyper-masculine world, women— and everything about them physically—would take on the same great magic and appeal to me the way they did to straight men. It hadn't helped that in my undergraduate Human Sexuality course at ASU, the lecture on Sexual Deviancy included the topic of "homosexuality" and even included a real "homosexual" as a guest speaker. I sat there listening and observing closely. I was nothing like him. Why did he need to talk about what he did in private with other men? But of course, I was like him, and in future years would speak publicly about my own journey and gay issues.

I took up residence at the Sigma Nu fraternity house in late May 1985, and David and I continued our secret romance over the summer and into the fall. I was completely infatuated with him, I felt more confident and strong around him and our physical relationship over that sustained period of time, which was new for me, certified my sexual orientation was certainly not straight. We hung out all the time and even double-dated women, as a way to conceal the true nature of our relationship. That was actually very seductive and great fun for us: winking at each other over dinner and a movie, knowing the real date would begin later, after we dropped off the girls.

But it didn't last. David moved to Seattle in the fall of that year to create distance from his family's resistance and our relationship ended. To say that I missed him would be an understatement. His departure put me back in my awkward self-imposed sexual quandary. Ours was the longest and most satisfying of any of my encounters with other men up till that point, and twelve long, lonely years would go by before I found that same level of intense physical and emotional attraction again.

By the time David moved, my life as a live-in fraternity adviser was in full swing. Added to that were the pressures and responsibilities of my full-time job as coordinator of student development and leadership. My schedule could best be described in a single word: insane. I worked at least eighteen hours a day and sometimes much more than that, as situations at the fraternity house sometimes awakened me at all hours of the night.

I would get up in the morning at 5:15 and help the fraternity pledges set up for breakfast at the house. I had breakfast often with Rob Weinman, a scholarly and athletic guy who was in ROTC. He was up early to go to drill formation or to work out. Every day he would say "Morning, Gerard," and I would respond "Morning, Gerard." We shared "Gerard" as our middle name. He was a local Tempe kid, soon to graduate and be on his way to a long military career, had fate not stepped in. On October 4, 1989, the tanker jet that Captain Robert Gerard Weinman was piloting exploded over Canada, killing all four crew. A tragic loss, he was just twenty-seven. After breakfast with Rob and others I would go to my full-time job on campus until midday when I'd take a lunch break back at the Sigma Nu house. After checking on what was new with the brothers, I'd go back to my "day job" and work until five or six P.M. After work, it was back to the fraternity where my adviser duties would begin in earnest: Greek life meetings, counseling students, officer meetings, social planning committees, and so on. Those meetings and activities would go on most nights until at least 11 P.M. every night of the week. For three years, that was my life and I thrived on being the go-to person, not an elected leader, but clearly one who was needed and valued by most of the men. I would like to think I made a positive difference and added to what many consider some of the very best years of Sigma Nu at Arizona State.

In my one-on-one advising sessions, students came to me with every conceivable problem:

I'm failing every single class: would you call my father and tell him?

I think I got this girl pregnant; what should I do?

Yeah, we got into this fight and think maybe we really hurt this guy. Should we, like, go back and find out if he's dead?

Kelly's in the hospital with alcohol poisoning, and you have to call his mother.

In 1985, Arizona raised the drinking age to twenty-one, and soon after Sigma Nu National implemented a new alcohol policy for its chapters. For liability reasons the fraternity adopted a policy stipulating that no fraternity funds could be used to purchase alcohol and consumption at large parties would be monitored. Major buzz kill.

Not surprisingly, that news was not well received by the eighteen-, nineteen-, and twenty-year olds in the prime of their drinking lives. And as their adult adviser, my role shifted. Instead of the "big brother" role I'd enjoyed, I became the rule enforcer, the authority figure on the premises. Resentment against the policy turned into disdain for me, because it was now a part of my job to make sure the fraternity policy—and the law—was complied with. Usually the anger was general and directed mainly at the new rules, but occasionally, the attacks became personal. Once one of my "brothers" took a hose, ran it down the hallway, and stuck it under the door to my tiny one-bedroom apartment near the cafeteria. Then he turned the water on full blast.

The party crowd of the sixty-man residence and the party contingent of the additional forty or so brothers who did not live in the house saw me as the problem. They truly believed that if only I were gone, the kegs could return and the beer would flow freely again. They would rail against me at informal fraternity meetings, sometimes getting close to the truth.

"Why do we need a chapter adviser living here anyway?" a big, muscle-bound kid from Newport Beach who was an officer of the fraternity said in one of those meetings. "He's older than us. He doesn't need to be here." He jabbed a finger in my direction, sending every eye in the room toward me.

Oh shit, I thought, bracing myself. *Here it comes.*

"Why is he even here? What is he? Some kind of homosexual or something?"

Not some kind, just one kind. Remember that blond athletic kid named David?

By the time the meeting ended, the guy's words were almost forgotten and other topics had stolen everyone's attention. Still, I was shaken. No one had ever said something like that about me out loud. Not since the guys in that communication class who had pointed and pantomimed about me when I was blindfolded and they believed I couldn't see them had I ever been so painfully aware that people talked about whether I was gay behind my back.

There must have been some murmurs, but for the most part that kid's remarks—and any others like them—went nowhere and no one raised it with me privately. The majority of the guys liked having me around. Most of them understood that I was a big help to many of the brothers, in a lot of ways. They knew that getting rid of me would make their lives worse, not better. They might have remained silent while some brothers challenged me, but their support was real.

Much later, many of those same Sigma Nu brothers would turn out to support me when I needed it most—when a recall election threatened my tenure as mayor of Tempe. That kind of mutual support and relationship embodies the real life-long value of fraternity membership and is an example of true brotherhood. It means a great deal to me

To my great dismay at first, and later, my joy, my fraternity years did not make me straight. After David, I had no relationships or significant experiences while at Sigma Nu. I did meet a newly-graduated doctor through a personal ad service in a local alternative newspaper, and we became great friends. Later, he would contribute the absolute maximum amount of money allowed by law to every campaign I ever ran for public office. He was always there to patiently listen to my medical inquiries, as well.

Although there were rumors from time to time about guys in the fraternity house being gay, or at least fooling around with guys (or each other), nothing like that ever happened to me in the entire three years I lived in the Sigma Nu house. I did my best to avoid even being involved in any conversations about who might be gay—let alone anything more overt.

My fraternity involvement and the close relationships I formed through them led to one of the most powerful and profound experiences of my life.

On the Friday night of homecoming weekend in 1988, just after I had moved out of the house, fraternity brother Chuck Hopkins was killed in a car crash in Tempe. He was one of my closest friends from Sigma Nu, an outstanding and outgoing student leader on campus and had run for student body president. At the time of his death he was the vice-president of the student alumni association, the group I advised, and he was one of the most popular and decent students I had ever come across. He was killed when another car didn't yield and slammed into his while he was making a left turn. His death came too near the ten-year anniversary of my dad's.

The whole experience—Chuck's death, and for me its proximity to the anniversary of my father's, the unexpectedness of it all—shook all of us to the core. I didn't know how to handle it emotionally, but I knew what I *could* do: I planned and coordinated the memorial service, bringing 800 students together to grieve and pay their respects. Everyone knew and loved Chuck.

Chuck's mother was a Hollywood insider and actress. She had played one of Ricky Nelson's girlfriends on *Ozzie and Harriet* years ago. She also co-founded Childhelp USA, the nation's largest child abuse and prevention organization. Being painfully close to a family when they lose a child in a horrible accident, or in any manner, requires a calm and steady focus on the details that need attention.

She asked me to speak at Chuck's Los Angeles funeral service and I agreed to do so, even knowing that the other speaker was the famous actor Efrem Zimbalist, Jr. who had starred in the series *The FBI* that I had watched as a kid. I know I wasn't as eloquent as the actor, but my feelings of loss were sincere as I spoke of Chuck's life and the impact he had on so many other lives at ASU. About thirty-five fraternity brothers from ASU made the trip to LA to pay their respects, as well. The reception following was a star-studded gathering but still extremely sad.

Back in Tempe, my feelings were very unsettled and I was a wreck. The night after returning from the funeral in LA, I woke up in the middle of the night. My eyes and face were wet. How does one cry when asleep? I felt warm and calm but I couldn't move. It was as though I was frozen in place, staring into the darkness in front of me.

My father was standing at the edge of my bed by the door

looking at me.

"Things are okay, Neil," he said. "Things are fine. And you are going to be okay, too."

I know: you're thinking I was dreaming. Or delirious. Or drunk. Or even slightly crazy. Emotion and pain distort our realities; they can make things seem real that aren't. I know that. But I also know I wasn't dreaming. I was wide-awake. And I don't think I was, or am, delirious or crazy. He was there. He was there because I was really struggling with Chuck's death. Here was a kid with truly great promise, and he was gone.

I was feeling uncertain about my life and my next move. In January of 1988, I had accepted a new job at ASU, as Director for Constituent Relations at the Alumni Association, a promotion and great opportunity. I had decided to move out of the fraternity house and grow up. Personally, however, I was as confused as ever.

Dad was there because I needed him to accept and reassure me. While he was alive, I had tried not to think about how he would feel if he knew I were gay—I'd barely been willing to confront that in my own heart and mind.

But when he came and stood at the edge of my bed and told me I was "okay," it was clear: I was okay and always had been.

Real or not, it was a turning point for me.

I wasn't ready to come out fully, but I would not choose to live a dishonest, straight life. The games of dating women and trying to convince myself I could deny my reality for some potential political career or to satisfy others would cease. I would navigate it another way, but I would not become that person. I had come close to thinking otherwise, dating a great woman in the community who was a chamber of commerce executive. Everyone thought Kathy and I would be the perfect political couple. Only they didn't know what I knew, and thankfully, for Kathy as well as for me, I finally had the clarity to choose another path.

I moved out the fraternity house at last. Even more

significantly, I began to think seriously about running for my first office beyond a student leadership role.

In addition to having been president of the Kiwanis Club, and a member of Class 1 of Tempe Leadership, I was now serving on the board of directors for the Tempe Community Council, Tempe Leadership, the Valley Big Brothers-Big Sisters, and the Data Network for Human Services organization. My commitment to community work was evident, I had a solid reputation and I was asked more and more often to consider running for city council or the state legislature.

As has always been the case, I had tremendous support and encouragement from others for all these roles. It was Betty Asher who gave me the application for the Tempe Leadership program and Virginia Tinsley who pointed me toward serving on the board of the Tempe Community Council and my first run for office. While I was still in the Tempe Leadership program, Virginia was the very first person to suggest I should seek elected office.

"So when will you run for the legislature?" she said to me one morning during a break between the educational sessions at the Fiesta Inn.

"I have no idea," was my initial response. By this time I knew I was capable of taking on a leadership role in the broader community, and I knew it was something I wanted to do, but was unsure of when and how to make it all come together. But Virginia was persistent and she, along with a couple other friends, became my lead support group for seeking a public office.

By late spring of 1989 I had decided on running for city council in the spring 1990 election and began lining up support. It was an uphill political situation: all three council incumbents were planning on seeking re-election, and there were only three seats on the ballot. I would be a true challenger. The many community leaders I knew from Kiwanis and other groups assured me that I wouldn't win this time, but I should run to set myself up for the following election in 1992. They were happy to help me and support me with that understanding between us; we'll make a go of this, but against incumbents, we have to be realistic so let's make it a measured run. That all sounded fine to me: the experience would be helpful, and I would learn what I needed to know and build a strong base for the future.

Funny things happen in politics, however.

By September 1989, one of the incumbents was in the midst of a messy divorce and ended up resigning from the city council. His appointed replacement, a former council member, had committed not to run at the close of the term. There would be only two incumbents in a race for three council seats.

By that point, I had been building a campaign and getting commitments for a couple months. Seven other non-incumbents joined the race once there was an open seat, but I had already lined up a lot of community support, albeit originally that support had been intended for a casual campaign that would be a practice run for 1992.

We had a lot of fun on the campaign trail. Walking neighborhoods, attending events of all sizes, talking into the night about the issues, candidates, which candidate was doing what and how we would position our campaign and my public response. It was exciting to be a candidate, like my father had been some twenty years prior in New Jersey. John Fees, Guy Roll, and many other former current students and friends got involved. Things got a bit feisty when my opponents came after me on a couple of issues in an attempt to get attention and to take me down a notch or two in the public's eyes.

The first effort exposed the fact that I had never voted in a city election prior to 1988. It was a fair shot—and true. When it was raised at one of the candidate forums, my response was to the point.

"That's absolutely correct. My community service and involvement were focused on campus up until a few years ago. I regret that, but people involved with the city have not done a very good job of coming onto the campus and reaching out to those of us who lived and worked there. That will change if I am elected."

No one ever raised the issue again, and the press never even reported on it.

The second issue was even easier to dispatch. After the first campaign contributor filing deadline, when my report indicated a lot of donations from people who lived all over the country, many more than from residents of Tempe, one of my opponents claimed I was being supported by "outside special interests."

The alleged "outside special interests" were simply my friends from all over, who were rallying to support my first bid for public office. So I met with a local reporter, who had called to ask about the charge, and took a copy of the report with me. Then I proceeded to go person-by-person, amount-by-amount, and explained the relationship I had with the donor.

"This person served with me as a Key Club officer in 1974. This person is a member of Sigma Nu from ASU. This person served on the Circle K International board with me. This person is an ASU alumnus and volunteers with the Alumni Association. This person is a former student of mine from my leadership class at ASU." And so it went, page by page.

The reporter told me later that he informed his editor of the meeting and concluded that based on my contributions, the "outside special interest" they could expect if I was elected was a panty raid on City Hall by fraternity men!

My former ASU students and my brothers at Sigma Nu played a crucial role as campaign volunteers. The fraternity house on campus was turned into something of a campaign headquarters. I had only moved out of the house about eighteen months before so I still knew everyone. We wrote a "please vote for Neil for City Council" script and planned two weeks of making phone calls from the house, each night after the formal house dinner. Imagine thirty guys each making thirty to forty calls a night, from each of the thirty rooms of the house. We did the math and realized we could reach a huge number of voters, and we did. As dinner ended, the guys would leave the dining hall with a list of voter names and numbers, all public information of course, and the script. We probably called every Tempe voter who was going to vote in the election at least once. It was tremendous outreach that presented my campaign in a professional and responsible manner. I don't think anyone ever knew those calls were made by a bunch of fraternity men.

Sigma Nu alumni who were living in Tempe helped a great deal, too. Many were active in the community and knew all the local political players, and they used their connections to vouch for me to people they knew in the community. My election night party was held at the home of one of those alums, John Thoren.

The competition was stiff, and included the current mayor's campaign manager, a candidate heavily supported by the local firefighter's union, and the incumbents: Carol Smith and Frank Plencner. In the primary election, Carol Smith received more than 50% of the votes cast and was re-elected outright. Five other candidates got too few votes to continue and were eliminated. The remaining four of us moved on to the general election, where two of us would be elected. I now had a 50-50 shot at winning a seat on the city council. Maybe because I was young and there were so many candidates, or maybe it was just the climate of the times in this university community, but sexual orientation, mine in particular, was never even a side issue in the campaign that I was aware.

The campaign pressed into full gear. I worked extremely hard to reach voters, remain positive and upbeat, and offer myself as a candidate who would serve Tempe well—I honestly did not campaign on the issues of the day. My focus was on being a good council member, serving the community and doing my best. Others tried to find support based on this issue or that topic, but at the end of the day my message of being a solid community servant resonated very well.

1990 General Election Results
Neil G. Giuliano   3,652
Frank Plencner   3,494
Dennis Cahill   2, 945
Chuck Malpede   2,868

Not only did I win, I surprised everyone, including myself, and came in first. I had even beaten an incumbent; though Plencher was elected as well, he wasn't thrilled about being beaten by a total novice. It was a non-partisan election, but in the end the two of us who were elected were registered Republicans and the two who were not were registered Democrats. At this time in Tempe's history, it was still a majority Republican city and the rise of those registering as Independents was still a decade or more in the future.

I was thirty-three and about to become a member of the Tempe City Council. It was humbling, exhilarating, and overwhelming. I knew I was up to the task; by that point I had been observing council meetings for over a year. During those meetings I would listen intently to the discussion, debate and content of the issues before the council. Before the council voted I would think about how I would vote on the issue, and most of the time my silent votes from the audience mirrored those of the actual majority.

When I got home on that first election night, I sat down at my kitchen table. It was the same large wooden table that I grew up with, that my family had sat around for all my life. No one from my family was there this time, but I had a little chat with Dad, the former Bloomfield council member. I recalled the chat we had at his funeral, not quite twelve years prior, when I promised him I would make him proud. I was a little emotional, a little scared, and very proud to have made good on my promise. I would serve and do my very best.

In addition to being proud to be a Tempe city council member, I was proud that I had moved beyond thinking I would force myself into a straight relationship just for appearance's sake. Interestingly, it was the campaign itself that made me absolutely realize I could not and would not lead that life. Early in the campaign, with the warmest and best of intentions, my mentor and campaign co-chair, Virginia Tinsley, had suggested I might take Monica Hermon, the daughter of a former city council member and current state representative, to some of the campaign events. "Just for someone to go with you. It looks better," she said.

I knew what she meant, but I couldn't take her advice. Fortunately, I didn't lose her support. Virginia, along with former mayor Rudy Campbell, would become my campaign co-chairs for every election I sought in Tempe.

I had thankfully moved beyond the thought that I could and would lead a life of lies by marrying a woman and conforming to society's expectations. There had been more than a few women with whom I thought I could pull that off, and I am so grateful and thankful that I found the strength to not do so, even if I was not yet ready to live openly as a gay man. We've heard too many stories about those politicians who chose that path—a certain Senator with a "wide-stance" for one. The saying "There, but for the grace of God, go I" comes to mind.

Once seated as a council member, I began attending all the city events of course, including the annual Police Department Awards Banquet, which in 1990 was held at the Tempe Public Library. I was the new guy, so a lot of people wanted to say hello and meet me for the first time.

I was at the bar ordering a Coke when I heard a man say, "Congratulations on being elected to council." I turned around and thanked him. He introduced himself as John Greco. He was a former San Francisco cop who was then working in Tempe as a budget and administration officer for the police department. He fit the tough cop stereotype: burly, shaved head, a strong, in-your-face assertiveness. He continued, "We just want you to know there are a whole lot of us who are proud of you, and we're just happy you got elected."

I politely thanked him, although at the time I did not pick up on what he was really saying. Then, stepping toward me, he said something I'll never forget: "If you ever find yourself in a situation where you desperately need some help, just give me a call because there are people who care and will help you." Then he joked a bit and added, "You know, if you're in a bar surrounded by a crowd of people or something like that."

"Okay, I'll remember that, but I don't really go to many bars," I responded. I didn't in any way acknowledge or ask why he was offering unsolicited bodyguard and protection services. I wasn't taking women to events and pretending to be straight, but I was so deep in the closet that I was sure he couldn't possibly suspect I was gay.

John, however, wasn't deceived. In fact, few were deceived. I was just deceiving myself.

Over the years, as we developed a casual friendship, I began to realize John knew about me. We'd get together, maybe once a year for coffee or lunch, and though no words were spoken on that topic one way or the other, it was a situation of "I know you know, and I know you know I know." I left it at that.

Our personal and political fates would collide in September 2000 as my biggest political challenge unfolded while he served as interim city manager.

Then, in 1991, Ed Miller died.

I've already written about the impact his death had on me. When he passed, I was seriously contemplating a future move to Washington, D.C., where I often traveled as director of federal relations. That was where I had my gay life and a circle of friends with whom I could be open and honest. I could walk from Dupont Circle to 17th Street—the gay section of the city—and find more people I knew than if I walked down the main drag in Tempe. That's how I came by the nickname "Mayor of 17th Street": my friends often joked that I knew more people in D.C. than those who lived in the area. I liked that status and it gave me cause to walk tall and be proud. If only I could feel that way, for the same reasons, back in Tempe, too.

On one of those trips to Washington, on the night before the first Clinton inauguration in January 1993, I met Chris Crain, an attorney in Washington, D.C., at JR's, a gay bar, on 17th Street. Chris is a six-foot-six, Harvard Law graduate who thought I looked like George Stephanopoulos. We struck up a conversation that led to a friendship. That summer he took me to Rehoboth Beach in Delaware, about three hours from D.C., for a weekend at the beach house he was sharing with about ten guys. I shared a room with Vince, a hot, "short and tight" Italian guy. We became friends and he even came to Tempe in the final days of my first mayoral campaign in '94 to wish me luck and volunteer. I'll never forget the experience we had while we were at the beach, though. We were hanging out at a club when this greasy, balding, round guy in a horizontal, red-and-white striped shirt made us an indecent proposal. "I'll give you each $500 if you come back to my place right now," this stranger said. "I want you guys to do it in front of me; I just want to be in the room." We laughed it off and said we weren't even dating. In the end, the weekend was a fun, low-key time of great dinners, dancing, and just hanging out at the beach.

Indecent proposals aside, that's what I loved about my D.C. time. I felt freer to be myself than I ever felt in Tempe up to that point. At the same time, I loved Tempe and felt that what I was doing there was important and worthwhile. I was a new young voice on the city council, and people were expressing support for my ideas for improving both the process and content of the conversations among the council. I was having some influence, even as a new member, and that was motivating. I was torn between the city council and the ASU work I loved, and the happiness I had created for myself twenty five hundred miles away. I couldn't choose—and I couldn't yet imagine a world in which I could have both.

Through Chris I met Rod Seymore, a smart and sexy

African-American guy who went to law school in Boston. He, too, would become a dear friend, visit in Tempe, and be there for my first mayoral re-election as an openly gay candidate. Years later in Washington, on the night of the second Clinton inauguration, I would meet Zac Mathews, a young Coast Guard officer, who would become a friend for life. In June of 2012, I officiated at his wedding to a former Air Force officer in Provincetown, Massachusetts. For many of my mayoral years, Zac would fly to Arizona on New Years Eve, as soon as he was off-duty, and accompany me to the many Fiesta Bowl event and activities. There is something about a man in uniform.

Meanwhile, my work in Washington was introducing me to many high-profile lobbyists and Washington power brokers. George Ramonas was one of those people and would eventually be a key operative on Bob Dole's 1996 presidential campaign. ASU had George on retainer to be our lobbyist in Washington, D.C., and he had worked on the staff of conservative Republican Senator Pete Domenici of New Mexico. My job as director of federal relations for ASU was to communicate and share information with the Arizona congressional delegation and staff members, and we were working with then-Arizona Senator Dennis DeConcini's staff.

"You need to go see Chip Walgren on this," George said about some issue we were dealing with. "He's the appropriations staff member, Chip's been with the senator for years. He's very highly regarded."

I nodded. I didn't think the Senator would have any chumps on his staff. I wasn't sure where this was heading and why George felt the need to go into such detail, but it seemed wise to just let him talk.

"Just so you know some background, Chip went through an issue of scrutiny when the senator had applied on his behalf for his top security clearance," George continued. "Everyone knows Chip's gay, and Senator DeConcini supports and trusts him."

I stiffened. *Why is George telling me this? What does he know and why does he think I need to know this piece of information?*

I made my face a mask, doing my best not to acknowledge any particular interest or emotion regarding this information and allow the conversation to move on.

When I met Chip for the first time, I already knew his basic story, but we had business to take care of and our personal statuses were irrelevant.

"Hey," he said as we were finishing our brief meeting and shaking hands, "next time you're in Washington, let's have dinner."

Once again, I felt myself locking up. *What did I just do? Did I somehow send out a signal that I'm gay and needed a date? Did George give Chip some similar "background" information on me prior to the meeting?*

"Okay," I heard myself saying. "Sure, sounds great."

I felt uncomfortable, but we made plans anyway. On my next trip to Washington, I walked from the Barcelo Hotel near Dupont Circle to 17th Street where I was going to meet Chip for dinner. It was a defining moment. I was going to have dinner with an openly gay political peer who knew everyone else who worked for the Arizona delegation. He knew the members of Congress, he knew a lot of gay people I knew in Washington, D.C., and he was probably already, at that moment, connecting all the dots. They say that there are six degrees of separation between every two strangers in the world—but in the gay world there are only three degrees of separation. The community is smaller than you might think, and when you start talking to someone for the first time you quickly find out you know people in common. In sitting down with Chip, I was consciously narrowing that gap to one degree, bridging the connection between my straight professional world and my gay social life. I'd had plenty of dinners with gay men in Washington, but having dinner with Chip represented the first time I would dine with a gay man I knew professionally, and not purely socially.

And it made me very nervous.

It doesn't seem such a big deal to me now, but then, I felt as though I was blurring and erasing that carefully drawn, thick line I had in place for so long. It worried me a lot. Chip would talk about it and a broader circle of professional and political people would draw conclusions that I wasn't sure I wanted them to draw yet.

I had dinner with Neil Giuliano.

Oh really. Where'd you eat?

This great little place on 17th Street.

Translation: 17th Street. Gay Area. Chip's gay. Interesting. So Neil's gay, too.

Was I ready for this? Yes, I knew it was coming, had accepted that fact while at Ed's funeral, but that reality did not ease or eliminate my fear.

That's what I thought about as I walked toward the designated restaurant. My hands were sweating, but I wiped them on my trousers and kept walking.

I knew that if I turned around and went back to the hotel, and make up some excuse about needing to cancel dinner, I could maintain the separation between my professional/political hat and the personal one... but I was still walking. There was a part of me that knew I had to keep moving toward coming out of the closet, no matter how afraid I was of who might talk and what they might say. I knew this was my destiny and I would face it, but not being in full control was very difficult for me.

I arrived at the restaurant.

It was a vibrant, bustling place with chatter wafting out to the street each time the double-doors swung open. The place was packed with professional gay men. I took a deep breath and saw myself in the reflection of the glass door. My face showed all the anxiety I felt. I imagined the conversations others in my professional and political life would have about me, but I took a deep breath and made a quick decision.

OK, I thought, throwing caution to the winds. *I'm having dinner with Chip right now.*

It was much more than having dinner with a professional colleague and I knew it.

I'm going to let this all play out. People are not stupid. Some people must already assume the Tempe councilman is gay anyway, so what am I afraid of?

I pulled on the restaurant door and knew, deep inside, my closet door had swung open, too.

CHAPTER SEVEN

Campaign from the Closet

I'd enjoyed being on the city council, but much of the challenge and excitement of those responsibilities was gone a few years into my four-year term. I suppose I was ambitious in one way: I wanted to sit at the end of the table and lead the conversation and agenda in a more obvious manner. And I knew I could offer a lot and be darn good at it. But in another way, I saw running for mayor as a possible escape route. Before I even entered the contest, I had decided that if I lost, I would become a private citizen again, regain my personal freedom, and perhaps move to Washington, D.C., where I could more easily integrate my personal and public lives. And that would be a win, too.

In short, if I didn't become mayor of Tempe, I'd give myself permission to come out fully as a gay man.

No one expected me to throw my hat into the ring, and certainly no one expected me to get beyond the primary. An early poll in the fall of 1993 found me in dead last place—behind my one-time council colleagues Don Cassano and Barbara Sherman. Both of my opponents' supporters tried to convince me that now wasn't the time. "Wait your turn," they counseled. "You're young. You'll be mayor, but not yet. Run for a second term on the city council. Wait."

Their logic was sound. I could wait. I could run for council again. By waiting I probably was ensuring my victory down the line. But what the other candidates and their supporters didn't know was that I was perfectly fine with losing the mayor's race. Sure, I planned to give it my best and run a solid campaign, but I viewed it as an experience. If Tempeans would have me, I would serve. If not, well, the door was open for all kinds of new possibilities.

I quickly discovered that while some of Tempe would support me, there was another contingent that would be quite vocal in its opposition to me: my friends on the religious right of the political spectrum. By early 1994, with the mayoral primary election only a couple of months away, I was ready to drop out.

It wasn't the campaign that was getting to me. I had filed all my nominating petitions to be on the ballot and was able to withstand the normal campaign stress—the constant strategy sessions and endless rounds at fund-raisers, events, and functions. I handled those pressures easily.

No, it wasn't the campaign that was making me lose sleep, grinding my nerves down to raw tendrils, and making me question the wisdom of getting involved with local politics in the first place. It was the letters and calls: the threatening letters that arrived in my mailbox and the messages on my phone almost daily.

"We know about you," they said. "We know about your lifestyle."

This was three years before Fritz Tuffli would stand up in a council meeting and make insinuations that would change the trajectory of my political career—his speech had a much earlier foundation, beginning with my 1993 campaign. The letters and calls were pointed and nasty. Whoever was behind them knew what they were doing; they knew they were picking at the padlock of a secret I had no intention of revealing. The possibility of being "outed" had me on the edge. I felt like I was about to crack. And yet, I had allowed, even invited, such chatter and speculation by stepping further and further out of the closet while in Washington D.C. For the most part, I remained extremely discreet and private in Tempe. But people talk. And I knew they would.

Unsure what to do, I called a friend in law enforcement. I asked whether we could meet for a drink because there was something I needed to ask him. I was vague over the phone, simply asking him if we could meet. I had begun to feel paranoid, wondering if I were being watched or if my phone was being tapped. Later, when I told my old friend and campaign strategist Mike McAuly about the threats, he said without hesitation, "Have your phones checked for wiretaps."

I didn't heed his advice, though in hindsight, it was definitely sound.

I met my police department contact at the Paradise Bar and Grill in downtown Tempe. I showed him a letter I received at my home address and told him about the voicemail messages I'd received in which a woman said: "You shouldn't be running for mayor. We have a file folder on you, more than an inch thick, and we're going to make it public. We know your lifestyle."

The one page, hand-printed letter included the following warning: "We're going to come to all your events and speaking engagements and tell everyone about you and what you're all about."

I told my cop friend, "I'm thinking of getting out of the race and wanted your law enforcement take on all this." I suspected he was gay, too, but it wasn't something we discussed or acknowledged. Whether he was or wasn't didn't matter: I felt safe confiding in him. He promised to do some research and get back to me.

A day or two later, he called me.

"They are real. And they do a lot of threatening and

intimidating," he said. "But they never take anybody out."

Those were his exact words: *They never take anybody out.* Well, that was reassuring. What the hell were we talking about here—murder? Political murder, perhaps.

He added, "I can't tell you what to do, but I can tell you this is what they do. It's what they're all about."

We didn't even know if it was a large organization or just a few crazies lobbing random grenades, but either way, they had the potential to do my career and my campaign great harm.

The following Sunday night, I convened a meeting at my house. I invited my close friends who were involved with the campaign in some way: my friend Malena Albo; my roommate and fraternity brother Rick LaManna; Jeff Lowe, a former LSP student of mine, now a public relations professional; and Mike McAuly. The guest list was small for the single reason that these were the only people involved who also knew I was gay. They weren't the people managing my day-to-day campaign operations: Manjula Vaz, who worked for a Republican county supervisor, Charles Huellmantel, who worked for a Democratic Congressman, Rob Kubasko, another former LSP student and Kristen Rubach, the daughter of the mayor of Mesa, Arizona. I felt terrible about it, but at that time even my closest campaign advisors were not officially privy to who I *really* was. In all our discussions about all aspects of our campaign strategy and the issues at stake, we had never once discussed my sexual orientation.

I told Malena, Rick, Mike, and Jeff what was going on.

"I can still get out of this whole mess," I told them earnestly. ""I'm going to the debate tomorrow night and withdrawing from the race," I said. "I'll say it's because my mother's ill and thank everyone for a great four years on the city council."

I wanted them to support my surrender. I wanted them to encourage me to quit. But at first no one said anything. No one knew what to say.

I had never considered running as an openly gay candidate. That wasn't an option. I knew the temperature of the community very well; it was a moderate and tolerant community, but I was convinced Tempe was not ready for an openly gay elected official. My real concern was simply that if I stayed in the race, I would be outed. Winning or losing the mayor race wasn't important. Avoiding being outed was absolutely crucial. That would happen when I was ready for it to occur, not in the throngs of a political campaign. In fact, most everyone, including me, assumed we were in an uphill race anyway. It wasn't likely I was going to win. Why stay in a race I can't win and get publicly outed in the process?

In the end, however, I stayed in the race. And more importantly, I resolved to stand proud and answer honestly when I was asked about my sexual orientation.

As scared and unsure as I was, there was something in me that wouldn't let me quit and walk away. Somewhere deep within, an ember of "fight" was burning. Deep inside, I was furious that someone else felt they had the right to commandeer one of my most personal revelations. It wasn't their business or their place. However uncomfortable I might have been with making my sexual orientation public, the how and why and when of doing it was a decision that belonged solely to me. Dropping out would give these crackpots more power over me than they deserved— and I wouldn't let that happen.

"I'm staying in," I said, after we had talked for well more than an hour. "I don't know what's going to happen, but what the hell." I thought it through and decided that, if the worst happened, it could still be good: I wouldn't win, and as a bonus I'd get my life back. If I were outed, then all of the fears that had kept me in the closet would become meaningless anyway. There would be no more hiding or pretending and having two lives. I could go out and be myself without all that fear of being discovered. So in my analysis, it went from a lose-lose situation, to one that offered a win-win. That did not make me comfortable with the decision, but it made the decision clear and firm.

On debate night, March 1, 1994, I stood at the front of the

small room in the Pyle Adult Recreation center before a full house of maybe 150 people. I was sweating so much that my cotton T-shirt, my white dress shirt, and my black pinstripe suit pants were soaked and the debate hadn't even begun. At the back of the room, Malena pushed the corners of her mouth up as a signal that I should smile. I forced my lips to curve upwards but inside I was terrified. The room was full of faces I didn't know. Were the people who sent the letters there, waiting, ready to humiliate me? Where they going to say something? When would the attack come? Would it be the first query out of the gate? The last? Two of my campaign strategists, Rob and Charles, were there as well, they but didn't know of the threats that had me sweating and shaking. They thought it was just a debate. They couldn't offer the same support. Only Malena knew.

It was the first debate forum and all three mayoral candidates—Barbara Sherman, Don Cassano and myself—were in attendance. I braced myself. Tonight might come the moment when finally someone asked me directly, "Are you gay?" My life strategy on that subject had been anchored in avoiding it altogether at all costs. But the night prior I had confronted and resolved an inner fear that had been brewing for a lifetime; I had decided that if I were asked directly, I would speak my truth. It gave me some measure of pride to know that if confronted, I would seize the moment for myself rather than let anyone else do it for me. That would be what my dad would do, too, I reasoned.

The debate began. Each of us made an opening statement. Other than noticing the sweat soaking through my clothes, I was oddly calm. No heart palpitations or nervous stomach. That had become the template for my life: cool outside, tormented inside, but on this night, with my silent resolve, I was nervous, but not tormented. Then the moderator began asking us questions. I participated, I responded, but over and over, I repeated my mantra in my mind: *It's almost over, it's almost over. Just make it through this night, and if those wackos aren't here, maybe I'll be in the clear.*

With each passing minute, I got closer to making it through the horrible ordeal. All of a sudden, an hour had passed, no public accusations had come, and the audience was asking questions. The question-and-answer portion was the last segment, but also the most likely time for some fanatic to launch a political direct hit. I just had to get to 8:00 P.M. and the debate would be over. The questions were about the concerns of the day: zoning issues, city budget considerations, the Rio Salado project (a redevelopment project to convert a dried riverbed into parks and other public space), and downtown redevelopment.

And just like that, after our respective closing statements, mine being particularly brief as I rushed to the finish line, I picked up my notes and caught Malena's eye. We smiled at each other; I had survived. I made my way to the door, and as we walked out, she patted me on the back and said, "See, that wasn't so bad."

Easy for her to say.

At home that night, I talked briefly with Rick, Malena, and Manjula. Because Manjula was there, we weren't talking openly about the victory within the victory—that I hadn't been asked to reveal my sexuality—but the relief we all felt was palpable. After the women were gone, Rick asked, "So how'd it *really* go?"

"Fine. I think I did really well. I would be a good mayor. My ideas are better, my approach is better, far less political than the others, and I know I can be a strong leader for the community. I know I can do the job and do it well. "

"That's all good, but you know you don't *have* to do this," he said.

"I know I don't have to, but I'm going to. I'm going to stay in this race. Who knows, maybe I can pull it off? Maybe I can somehow win. I'll be able to do a lot of good things. I think it might really be something significant if I can get elected and serve."

"Okay, but you don't *have* to."

Rick always had a confident detachment about my political life that I truly admired. His ability to put situations in a wider perspective gave me strength.

"Thanks," I told him.

I took a shower and went to bed, emotionally drained but with a great sense of relief.

In the after-debate assessments, it was clear that I was the also-ran candidate. Barbara and Don used the forum to square off against each other. They had been on opposite sides of most political issues while serving on the council together. Don, the Republican former Chamber of Commerce president and Barbara, the Democrat self-proclaimed community activist, just never got along. Neither could stand the other and that, it would turn out, would give me a completely unanticipated opportunity. Maybe my path to victory was stronger than the conventional wisdom of the day.

After the debate and in the few weeks leading up to the primary election, my fear of the right-wing group outing me faded. I focused on running a strong, upbeat, positive, ethical campaign. My campaign message was "Bridging to the Future." I had taken the better part of a weekend listing and thinking through all the issues and challenges facing the community and what vision and direction I would offer for each. After I narrowed and refined the list, we published a twenty-page booklet highlighting my position on ten key issues: transportation, the Rio Salado development, neighborhood services, city council operations, regional cooperation, creating a human relations commission, the arts, engaging young people, public safety, and university relations. I talked about solid issues and had a plan for addressing each. It was broad enough for everyone to find something they could agree with, yet specific enough to not be just another list from yet another politician. No one had ever been as specific, focused, and positive about Tempe's future, at least not in a political campaign of this magnitude. This would become my agenda for the community over the next decade that I would speak about publicly up until the day I left office. Quite intense message control, before we knew enough to call it such. It had been sixteen years since Tempe had an open race for a new mayor; it was a defining moment for the community. The *Tempe Tribune* newspaper endorsed my campaign, and cited my "Bridging to the Future" booklet, which was a bit of a surprise, and we raised about $60,000 to finance the effort. Somehow, things were clicking, and I was starting to feel confident. And I was having a blast as a mayoral candidate. Could we actually win? This wasn't a race for a city council seat, like my previous election. This race required I grow into the role as the campaign evolved, I had to become more than I was, as a leader and as a candidate. And I did evolve, and I believe that is what caught the attention of the voters as much as any of the issues. They began to visualize me as their new mayor, as I had visualized it for myself.

The other two candidates still weren't worried about me. Only two of us would face off in the general election and I had far less support than either of them. With time and resources limited, they didn't bother to take shots at me. They were probably thinking, *Why bother with that guy? He's not a threat.* And so, at each public forum the three of us attended, I happily took the neutral seat as Barbara and Don bloodied themselves with attacks on each other. My neutrality was what first cast me as an attractive alternative for voters, and then when they looked closer, they learned I was fully prepared and up for the role.

Before the primary election, both Barbara and Don sent me their pledge of support if—for some unexpected reason—they failed to win one of the top two spots and did not move forward to the general election campaign. That was easy for them to say; few expected me to place any higher than third. I was outwardly very optimistic, as a candidate must be, but privately just as doubtful that I would place above third.

Wrong.

In the third week of March 1994, I finished second in the primary election—ahead of Barbara Sherman—and surprisingly just 127 votes behind primary winner Don Cassano. That meant Don and I would square off for the Mayor's job in the general election.

1994 Primary Election Results
Don Cassano   4,475 (35.6%)
Neil G. Giuliano   4,348 (34.6%)
Barbara Sherman   3,569 (28.4%)

The results were monumental. I was in the general election, and I had a legitimate shot at winning. Most voters who had supported Barbara Sherman would now support me simply because they were not at all fond of Cassano. Don's strength, so long identified as a Chamber of Commerce Republican, was just unacceptable to Barbara's core base of support. And that's putting it mildly.

As expected, Sherman would later meet with me, at a diner on Scottsdale Road, to offer her support. I was grateful. Before doing so, however, during our conversation she slid a hand-written page of paper across the table: it was her list of what she wanted should I be elected mayor. She called them items she was "strongly suggesting" I implement if elected. I slid her list back across the table and said if she wanted to support me, fine, but that I would not guarantee or promise anything except to always be willing to listen. I don't think she liked that answer, but I certainly wasn't going to start off as mayor beholden to anyone else's agenda. I had crafted my own.

My placing into the general election set off a fresh round of rumors, whispers, threats, and innuendoes.

There was a "push poll" conducted in mid-April asking people about the primary election and the candidates. A push poll is a questioning technique that leads the person responding by presenting specific information within the question. The line of questions went like this:

"Who did you vote for in the primary—Barbara, Don, or Neil?" If they answered "Neil" then they were asked: "Are you aware that he's single and does not have a family?"

And then: "It's likely there will be an initiative on the ballot this fall supporting the civil rights of homosexuals. Would you support that initiative?"

No one has ever admitted responsibility for conducting the poll, and who was responsible for it no longer matters, although I have a pretty good idea who was behind it. At least forty friends and supporters called me during the next three days, outraged that someone was asking these kinds of questions. At the time, I thought it was interesting that no one in my camp ever connected all the dots—and if they did, they never felt the need to come to me to ask: "So are you gay, Neil?" To their credit, it didn't matter to them, but it was still surprising.

I understand now that there was a very good reason why none of my supporters ever asked me directly whether I was gay or not: they already knew the answer. Because I was not being open and honest, I assumed that everyone else was deceived. They weren't, but without my ever discussing it with them or asking for their help on my behalf, many came to my defense privately and publicly.

The push poll backfired. I obviously couldn't attack it or defend myself against it without making my situation worse, so I chose to ignore it rather than bring more attention to it.

One night, a journalist from a local newspaper called me. I answered the wall phone while standing in my kitchen. "Have you heard about this poll?" he asked. "And do you know who's doing it?"

A cold sweat broke out across my body. The next question, I was sure, would be, "So, are you gay?"

As willing as I had been to state so publicly at that first forum, I was terrified of having to answer that question. So much more was now at stake. I was now closer to winning than when the campaign began, and that brought added pressure to ensure I managed this well while remaining true to my internal commitment to be honest if asked directly about my sexual orientation. I hesitated.

"Well, yeah. We've heard a little bit about it." I wanted my pace and tone to be both respectful and dismissive.

He said rather quickly, "I just want you to know we'll report on it if you want to comment for the record. But we're inclined to ignore it."

I couldn't believe what I had just heard. He wasn't going to ask me whether I was gay. He wasn't going to ask me anything about it. He was sounding like he had to call and inquire, but wanted off the phone quicker than me.

"We're just ignoring it, too" I said, trying to sound nonchalant and very busy to signal the end of the conversation.

"Okay. Fine."

To date, it's one of the shortest conversations I've ever had with a reporter. The push poll was never reported in the press. But behind the scenes, in political circles around town, the buzz about it was loud. There was much speculation over its impact on the voters, and fresh speculation over me. Here is where my then-status as a registered Republican played to my advantage in the non-partisan race. Had I been a Democrat at the time, the Republicans would have been free to come after me more directly, or have their right-wing voices do so, perhaps forcing the issue into a much more public conversation. And that would not have bode well for my campaign. I am convinced I would have lost if that had happened. It would have been too much for the community at that time.

Meanwhile, my fellow registered-Republican Don Cassano's campaign was struggling. Once in the general election, his team suddenly added a new campaign slogan: "Foundation for the Future." Shifting major messaging usually means panic, especially a couple months before the election. But they knew what we knew at the time: my campaign was gaining strength.

My positive message of "Bridging to the Future" was catching on and attracting supporters who saw me as a fresh, young candidate who might actually represent a new future for Tempe. In the final weeks prior to the election, we sent targeted mailings to voters based on information from the phone calls we were making every night. We would categorize each response by issue and print a personal letter that addressed those particular concerns. I personally signed each letter. I credit my campaign team with organizing and conducting that logistics-heavy process. It made all the difference.

We also solidified endorsements. My mom even got involved at a grassroots level by calling all the residents at Friendship Village, a large retirement community, where Don Cassano had come in first in the primary. We didn't take any voter for granted. We also sent letters signed by long-time Tempe residents and respected senior community leaders Rudy Campbell and Kathryn Gammage, the widow of the former university president for which Gammage Auditorium is named. They helped a great deal and gave me added credibility with long-time residents.

On the day of the election, I got up at 4:00 A.M. to go to the various polling places and put up yard signs. That was my Election Day ritual, something I had done in every campaign I had been involved in, dating all the way back to my campaign for student body president in 1983. There was something very peaceful and calm about driving around town by myself before the polls opened. Once voting had begun, I had different responsibilities, including visiting certain polling places and making phone calls from my house.

All day, I was just glad it was going to be over. If I won, it would be historic and a new journey would begin. I would be the youngest mayor in the history of the city, although not much younger than the outgoing mayor when he was first elected. My team had worked so hard, I was very proud of everyone involved, and proud of the campaign we planned and ran together.

But losing would be okay, too. In its way, it would be a huge relief for me personally. Election day for the candidate is always a combination of greeting people as they come to vote at various locations, making phone calls to likely voters, checking-in with staff while they do all they can to calm the nerves and implement the "get out the vote" plan to the fullest.

By early evening I had made my way home, stopping along the way to pull up yard signs on street corners and toss them in the back of my jeep. And by 7:30 P.M. a hundred or more friends and supporters had already arrived at the house, packing the kitchen, living room and yard area and helping themselves to drinks and the food that had been brought in, waiting for the results to be phoned in from City Hall. This was before the Tempe cable channel broadcast the results *live* on TV. In between chatting with the volunteers and well-wishers in the house, thanking them, and trying to appear calm and ready for any result, I would make my way to the back bedroom/campaign office where Manjula, who was on and off the phone with Rob, who was at City Hall, was keeping a running tab on how we were doing.

"You're pretty dead even in south Tempe," she said. "That's not bad considering it's where he should have whipped you."

I silently nodded and shrugged my shoulders. She was right, but "pretty dead even" was a nice way of saying "you're losing" and I knew she would be annoyed if I asked for the actual vote totals, so I just stood there, awaiting more information.

"Go talk with your people, it's going to be another ten minutes before we have more numbers," she said.

I was being kicked out of my own campaign office, but I knew it was the smart thing to not have me hovering, so I returned to the party and casually told my mom and the folks standing with her: "It's close in south Tempe, we'll know more soon." "Close in south Tempe" spread through the house like a gasoline fire and a smattering of cheers erupted.

A few minutes passed and I ducked back in to the office and shut the door. It was loud in the house by this point and Manjula was on the phone, writing on a yellow legal pad. I stood by the door and listened to her responses to the information that was being relayed:

"Uh-huh. Okay. What precinct was that? What percentage of vote is in? Uh-huh. Okay. Hmmm. Okay. What did she say? Who is all there?"

Do we really need to know who is there? We need to know the numbers.

"Okay then, thanks, Robbo. See you soon."

She hung up the phone and turned to face me, still seated.

"Well," she said slowly, "it's not really crowded at City Hall, you can stay here."

I wasn't planning on going anywhere, but would like to know my future please.

"And you won," she said matter-of-factly.

What? It's over? We really won the election?

"You're going to be the mayor!"

"I won? Seriously? Really? By how much?"

"It doesn't matter, but by a lot. Go tell your mom and everyone. I have a couple calls to make. Congrats, this is so exciting!"

In an instant, what had consumed my life for the last year was over and a new chapter was unfolding. From the moment I walked out into the living room as the mayor-elect, I knew everything was going to be very different. And I fully embraced it all. The self-doubts, second-guessing, the anxiety of winning versus losing, all vanished in that instant. The adrenaline rush was overwhelming, and yes, a bit intoxicating.

I opened the campaign office door and walked out into the living room, the entire room had been watching the door, everyone knowing we should have the results by now. I just smiled widely and nodded, barely getting out "We won" before the entire place erupted in cheers and applause.

Somehow the crowd quieted down a bit, long enough for me to offer some words of thanks.

"Well, everyone, we did it! This was *your* campaign all along, that's what bridging to the future has always been about and will be about for Tempe. We did this together and we will make Tempe better together. It's what we worked so hard for, and it's all a bit overwhelming right now. I am so grateful for your friendship and support. Thank you so much for all you gave to make this happen, for me and for our community. I will do my very best every day. We actually won this!"

As people continued to applaud and cheer, Mom, who was standing next to me, gave me a hug and said, "Your father is so proud of you, and me too."

Even though we had seen indications the campaign was going well, I was stunned; we were all stunned by the size of the victory. I won the 1994 general election by 1,110 votes capturing almost fifty-four percent.

1994 General Election Results
Neil G. Giuliano   6,936 (53.5%)
Don Cassano   5,826 (45.0%)

Thanks to Mom, I even won the precinct that included Friendship Village, which I had lost in the primary. The night was a blur of congratulatory calls, people stopping by and champagne corks popping. The celebration continued into the wee hours of the morning. When everyone had departed, and the place was a mess, I took a moment to just sit still and take it all in. I was elected the mayor of the city. The skinny, unsure kid from New Jersey had been on quite a journey the last twenty years since arriving in Tempe not knowing a soul. And while not always an easy journey, with a great deal of support and help, I had journeyed a long distance. And yet, I knew I still had unfinished business to take care of, too. I was winning, but had not yet won the campaign within.

Unbeknownst to me that night, across the Phoenix metropolitan area, gay community leaders and activists were gathered and celebrating my victory. I only found that out much later and heard it was a pretty fun time, too.

The next day, I went first to my office at ASU, where everyone was very excited, although my election would mean a restructuring of some of my federal relations workload moving forward. Then I went to City Hall and was greeted enthusiastically by all of my fellow city council members and staff. Congratulations calls and notes and even candy were flowing into City Hall. The small city council office I shared with a colleague was packed as folks came by to say hello. Everyone's your "friend" the day after you win an election. Every single person you meet voted for you. Even some of the same people who had once urged me to "wait your turn" were congratulating me. I was excited and scared, too. I was very proud that somehow I had won when, early on, no one outside of my own team gave me a chance. I remember thinking: "There are a lot of people counting on me now."

The following night at my house, my roommate Rick was awakened by a noise. Being a former police officer, he was concerned enough to grab his handgun and leave his room to check all the doors and peek out a few windows. He didn't see anyone and eventually went back to bed.

The next morning, I learned that Mike McAuly had been trying all morning to phone me and kept getting a busy signal. He was concerned. For my part, I remember thinking that given that the election had been only two days before, the phone was oddly quiet. When I finally picked up the phone to make a call, I discovered that the line was dead.

The local phone company responded quickly. I suppose getting a call from City Hall about the mayor-elect's phone may have hastened their response time, because I've never gotten service that quickly before. A few hours later a repairperson was at my door. She checked all the wiring and all the jacks. She couldn't find anything wrong.

"What about that room there?" She pointed to a room she hadn't been in.

"That was the campaign office, but there's no phone in there," I told her.

"Is there a jack?"

"Well, yeah, but there hasn't been a phone in that jack in more than eight months, since our other roommate, Brian, moved out and the campaign started."

"Let me check it anyway," she said.

She found the jack under a card table by the closet.

"Here's your problem, honey," she said, bending down to take a look at it. "The cover's off, and it looks like something was clamped on these wires, and when the clamp was taken off, all these wires got crossed together."

"Clamped? What?" I asked, confused.

"That's why you're getting nothing but a busy signal on your entire phone system."

"That's weird," I said.

"Not so weird. You just had a clamp on your line and your wires got crossed. If that happens on one jack, it will affect your whole system."

Her explanation wasn't totally registering. I hadn't clamped any jack—and I couldn't imagine who would have done such a thing when there wasn't even a phone in the room. What she was saying made it sound like...

Then I made note of the sliding glass door in that room, which opened into the house's side yard. That sliding door had been unlocked all day, every day during the campaign because people were coming over to the house at all hours to work.

"Someone tapped the phone," Rick said later. "And when the election was over, they came back for their equipment." Because the jack was under the table and there was no phone in the room, we had never noticed anything.

We guessed that was the noise he had heard the night before.

Rick's movement around the house had hurried the intruder out, resulting in a poor removal and damaged wiring. How else would a phone jack that wasn't used for eight months have the wires pulled out of the jack and clamp marks on them? Once we put it all together, my first thought was that someone had heard everything. And everything was a lot since the campaign phone line was also my personal phone line. But who would do that?

I thought I knew. Mike McAuly had been right: I should have checked my phones after the first threats early in the campaign.

I didn't call the police because I didn't want any drama or attention. Rick was the only person who knew about that incident. At that point, I figured, the people who tapped the phone had whatever information they had, and there was nothing I could do about it. I was feeling empowered because I had won the mayor's race, so whatever information the perpetrators had didn't have nearly as much leverage now. Or, maybe they actually had more. I would have to wait and see.

On July 14, 1994, at the age of thirty-seven, I took the oath of office. In Arizona, I was the young, up-and-coming, moderate Republican mayor of Tempe. I was also director of federal and community relations for ASU, where I also taught a course in personal leadership development. Between the election and the swearing-in I had several transition meetings with the outgoing mayor of sixteen years, Harry Mitchell. He was helpful, offered good advice and while he had moved out of the mayor's office a few days prior to the actual transition, I kept my office things in the hallway outside my former city council member office until after I was officially the mayor.

On July 16, I threw a huge post-swearing-in party at Rick's business, Harrison Marine Center, just up the street from were we lived on Balboa Drive. Hundreds of people showed up throughout the evening, including a lot of my gay friends, both locally and those who had flown in for the festivities. It was quite the fun evening.

My friends in Washington, D.C., were excited for me, too,

and I was anxious to get there to celebrate with them. These were friends who really knew me, all of me, and whose private support from afar meant a great deal to me. Two weeks after my inauguration, I was in Washington, D.C., with them, celebrating at a dinner in my honor organized by Chris Crain and Rodney Gould.

I was enjoying the attention of those closest to me, and unaware that my victory was the topic of conversation among various national gay support and advocacy organizations, most especially the national Log Cabin Republicans and the Gay and Lesbian Victory Fund. I never got deeply engaged with Log Cabin, but I would get to know the Victory Fund well in my future campaigns and political life that followed that first mayoral election.

After all of the drama surrounding my election, things quickly settled down into a regular routine. I made the decision to keep Randy Gross, the previous mayor's chief advisor, as my new chief of staff. Most would not even consider such a move, but although the outgoing mayor had not been a vocal supporter of mine, he was neither a vocal supporter of Don Cassano, who everyone assumed he was supporting since they had worked together for ten years. I was busy governing, organizing the council, creating the foundation for what would be a decade-long agenda of advancements for the community and Randy helped me with those activities for three years. I was still working and teaching at ASU, and I was still living my dual life.

When I ran for my second two-year term as mayor in March of 1996, I ran completely unopposed.

Life was really good, until July 18, 1996 when the sexuality issue reappeared with a vengeance during that bizarre city council meeting. Although the issue of my sexuality kept popping up from time to time, I continued to anticipate that it would disappear again, after a couple of days, just as it had in the past.

This time, however, the issue wasn't going anywhere. Soon, my back would be against the wall. The day was near when I would choose to speak my own truth, rather than have others speak it for me; I would choose to live openly, I would come out of my too-long-inhabited closet.

CHAPTER EIGHT

Off the Hinges

After that July city council meeting when for the first time someone actually made innuendoes about my sexual orientation to my face and in the presence of others, I spent numerous sleepless nights stretched diagonally across the foot of my bed, staring at the ceiling and out the sliding glass door at the sky. Public policy and my sexuality had collided thanks to the unexpected controversy over the fee waiver granted to Arizona Pride and the shock waves it sent through the political community in Tempe were significant.

When I returned from my trip to the Atlanta Olympics, the issue was still very much alive and well. I hoped it would have faded into the background, as it had in the past, but this time seemed different. Inside, I was torn. I didn't really want to confront the issue, but I was unsure about exactly what I was going to do, because I knew deep down this was the experience and destiny I had committed to at Ed's funeral years earlier, during the first mayoral campaign, and on many other occasions. It was going to play out, and I knew that. It had to.

My campaign within was reaching another important scene. Would I be ready for it? I had to be.

July limped to a close and the blazing heat of August began. I had planned to travel to San Diego for the Republican National Convention from August 12-15, mostly for the parties since I was not a Party activist at all, and while I did make it to the initial events, I wasn't there when the convention nominated Bob Dole as its presidential nominee.

On the second day of the convention, I stepped outside one morning to check my voicemail and got a real shock. A woman had left voicemail messages at both my office and home.

"We're coming to the city council meeting next week," she said. "And this time we're going to ask you straight out if you're a homosexual. We're gonna make sure everyone knows what kind of deviant you are and if there are any more of you, on that council—or anywhere else on the city payroll—that police officer or water department employee—we're going to find out about them, too."

That's when they crossed the line. I might have been living in the closet for twenty years. Maybe my days of hiding were over, but listening to those messages, I resolved I would not let them turn the city council meeting into a witch hunt against public employees who might be lesbian or gay, no matter what it meant for me personally or politically. They could come after me—that die was already cast—but they would go no further under my watch.

The clock was ticking. My mystery caller had vowed to raise the issue at next week's council meeting, which normally would have given me about three days to prepare. Apparently she hadn't known that the coming week's meeting was cancelled and the council wasn't scheduled to meet again for ten days. That provided me precious planning time, and I would need it all.

In a way, the timing was disappointing. I had been enjoying the convention. A highlight for me was spending time with Senator John McCain and his wife, Cindy, and all my other

Arizona friends. After a gathering in his hospitality suite, I had the honor of walking with him and his entourage to the convention floor where thousands of cheering supporters greeted him. It was a nice diversion from what was unfolding for me politically back home.

I have known John McCain since I was student body president at ASU, when he participated in a campus forum during his 1982 U.S. House congressional race, his first campaign. I was asked to be at a Republican primary debate on the ASU campus between the candidates for Congress. On the slate were some local legislators who were running for the federal office as well. They were all worked up about this new "outsider-carpetbagger"—John McCain—running for Congress from Tempe. I remember getting calls from local Republicans trying to discredit McCain because he wasn't a native: in fact, he had rather recently moved to Arizona.

I'll never forget my first impression of him when he arrived for the forum that night: he had a thick shock of white hair and he moved with a presence that, within seconds, had me thinking this guy was a total Navy hero stud and those other candidates should watch out. While the other candidates were all decent people, none had the charisma, verve, and steely determination of John McCain. For the candidates, that event was one of many perfunctory campaign stops. To me, however, it was significant and memorable. I had met a young principled leader who had left a significant and lasting impression on me. For many years, he was a political role model. I admired how he endured the challenges and attacks against his credibility, emerging as one of the possible nominees for president of the United States in 2000. I served as co-chair of Mayors for McCain in that campaign with the mayor of San Diego at the time, Susan Golding. Two pro-choice, moderate republicans, one woman and one gay man, trying to line up Republican primary supporters are probably not the best people for the role. We did what we could, of course, but McCain's opponent was the Governor of Texas, whose father was a former president of the United States. Most of the nations' mayors who were Republican hopped on that bandwagon early. Still, I admired McCain's perseverance and integrity.

When McCain ran for re-election to the U.S. Senate in 1992, I was a young councilman and asked to be a surrogate speaker for his campaign. I would go to events and speak on his behalf, which was a pretty easy duty. McCain had already served two terms in the U.S. House, elected in 1982 and 1984, and one term in the U.S. Senate beginning in 1986. He easily won re-election. Six years later, in 1998, he would be re-elected for a third term, then a fourth and fifth, in 2004 and 2010 respectively. Our views are not often on the same page any longer. But his personal treatment of me cements my loyalty regardless of our political differences. When my crap hit the fan, Senator McCain was doing commentary at the 1996 Democratic National Convention. Some reporter stuck a microphone in his face and said, "The mayor of Tempe has just announced he's homosexual. Do you have any comment?"

"Doesn't make a damn bit of difference to me," McCain said. "He's a good man, a good mayor, and a friend of mine."

I didn't know I'd have that kind of support as I stood outside the Republican convention hall with my cell phone pressed to my ear. I searched my brain for some kind of response. I needed some kind of plan. I was too stunned to go back inside the convention hall. Instead, I went straight to my hotel, packed my bag, and headed to the airport. I waited on standby to get the next flight back to Arizona. Once in the air, although still shaky, I found my inner resolve and decided I was not going to live this way any longer. It was time to take control of this crazy situation—way overdue, in fact.

The showdown my adversaries desired only made me dig my heels in, because there was no way I was going to let them come to a public forum and start asking about the personal lives of city employees. It was my career they wanted on a platter—

and I was prepared to give it to them—but would do it on my terms. I would take back control of the situation by stopping the charade I had played for so many years. It was time to simply be honest and let the chips fall where they may. I began to think about a written statement that I would release to the press, my "coming out" so to speak. But before that statement could be delivered, there were people I needed to talk to. There were people to whom I owed a personal conversation.

I made a list of the people I needed to speak with right away. First, I had the very uncomfortable task of informing Virginia Tinsley and Rudy Campbell, two mentors who had served as my campaign chairs for every one of my campaigns. They were both Republicans and in their seventies. They were two people I respected and admired a great deal. They staked their community credibility on me when I was an unknown and supported me for years. Virginia was the person who first asked me when I was going to run for public office. I had known Rudy even longer, since 1982, when I was student body president at ASU and he was serving as a member of the Arizona Board of Regents. He was also a former mayor of Tempe himself.

They knew me so well, would this revelation really be a surprise to them? Had others in the community, who would have been more likely to hear the gossip and chat about it, protected them from the reality of my sexual orientation? They were both political veterans in the community, surely this would not be a totally unexpected bombshell for them, but I was not sure.

I felt like a child who desperately did not want to disappoint his parents, but it was time to speak the truth. We met at Bob's Big Boy restaurant on Southern Avenue, as we had many times over the years. After a few minutes of catch-up and meaningless banter, I broached the topic.

"I think you know these right-wing people are coming forward and making accusations about my personal life," I said.

They both nodded. They knew what was going on.

Summer vacations on Pelican Island at the Jersey Shore were an annual event for as long back as I remember.

First communion in the Catholic church was a big deal, although I look like I am thinking, "Take the picture so I can get out of this all-white outfit."

Family photo for Dad's campaign for mayor of Bloomfield, NJ. That deer-in-the-headlights look must have been brought on by the double-breasted gold corduroy jacket they made me wear.

As a high school senior at a party, with Key Club friend Ed Miller in the background.

Fall of 1975 as the Charter President of the ASU Circle K Club.

On the night of my election as Circle K International President in Kansas City, MO, August 1977, with Ted Eastmoore, one of my campaign managers. It was a first ballot victory that surprised everyone, including us.

My Farewell Session at the Circle K Convention in Orlando with Rev. Doug Wasson and my parents, August 1978.

With my roommates from All Saints Catholic Newman Center on Verlea Drive, 1981: l. to r., Paul Hillebrand, Tim Smith. John Nemecek, Bob Mulhern, and Mark Keough.

As ASU Student Body President, touring the campus with Arizona Governor Bruce Babbitt: l. to r.: my executive assistant Walter Batt, ASU VP-Student Affairs Betty Turner Asher, Babbitt security, the Governor, and me.

President Gerald Ford came to the ASU campus for a series of appearances while I was coordinator of the ASU Leadership Scholarship Program in the late '80s

Working on the production staff for Key Club and Circle K International conventions for more than twenty years brought knowledge and understanding for planning large scale public events that would be very helpful later in life.

At the summit of Humphrey's Peak in Arizona, with Sigma Nu Fraternity brothers, l. to r.: John Tattersall, me, John Halsey (an Alpha Epsilon Pi member), Bill Halstead, Bob Venberg, and Rich Hoag.

With Arizona Governor Rose Mofford in the ASU Activity Center, as we awaited the arrival of President Reagan, March of 1989. Speaking at ASU was his first trip out of California since leaving the presidency.

Then-ASU Student Body President John Fees and I took an unconventional approach in bringing Reagan to campus: we invited him, got him to say yes, and then told the University President and other officials he was coming. I'm lucky I wasn't fired as a student advisor, but it worked.

Being sworn in as a city councilman in July 1990, with l. to r.: City Clerk Helen Fowler, Carol Smith, and Frank Plencner.

Attending to neighborhood needs was always a priority. This neighborhood needed sidewalks.

The night of my first swearing-in as mayor of Tempe. I could never have predicted the journey that took me to this night, nor the one that followed.

The team that ran my first campaign for mayor, l. to r.: Kristen Rubach Venberg, me, Manjula Vaz, Charles Huellmantel, and Malena Albo. Team member Rob Kubasko was probably taking the photo.

With my family on my first evening as mayor, l. to r.: Greg, Kim, me, Mom, and John, who I guess couldn't afford long pants at the time.

Visiting schools was a part of the regular schedule, even though the city did not have any authority over them. Being a topic of the "what did you do at school today?" conversation in homes throughout the community is never a bad thing.

In 1997, the symbolic start to a transformative project for the community: Tempe Town Lake in Rio Salado, l. to r.: Councilmembers Linda Spears, Joseph Lewis, Carol Smith, me, Deputy City Manager Pat Flynn, Councilmembers Joe Spracale, Ben Arredondo, and Dennis Cahill, and City Manager Gary Brown.

Just days before his re-election in 1996, President Clinton came to ASU for a rally. As ASU Director of Federal Relations, I helped stage the event, and in January of 1997, as mayor, I presented him with a framed picture that included one of when Theodore Roosevelt also spoke on the ASU campus. Before President Obama, they were the only two sitting US Presidents to visit the campus.

My first election night victory as an openly gay candidate. In the background, campaign Co-Chairs Virginia Tinsley and former mayor Rudy Campbell, who stood by me through all my political ordeals. I'm very grateful.

Former President George H. W. Bush came to Tempe and ASU in 1998, and I greeted him as protocol dictates.

Chatting with Vice President Al Gore at a US Conference of Mayors meeting. It was also fun to host him and Tipper when Tennessee played in the Fiesta Bowl in January 1999.

I represented the National League of Cities at the Brazilian League of Cities Conference in Rio de Janeiro, and took some time to play tourist too.

At my last election night victory party, in March 2000, I donated $10,000 for the campaign to build a new performing arts center in Tempe—I wouldn't need campaign funds any longer—but then came the recall election in 2001. Standing l. to r.: Gail Fisher, Diane Cripe, and Joseph Lewis.

The recall campaign began in October 2000, after I questioned funding the Boy Scouts via the city United Way campaign and while I was in China on a Sister Cities trip. It all might have been different if I had been home to manage the issue, but my adversaries' message prevailed in my absence. In hindsight, the recall effort made me stronger, personally and politically.

March Down Mill
September 22, 2001

September 11, 2001: the day our nation was attacked and the day of the recall election. We held a march to bring the community together, and I gave a solemn yet reassuring speech.

So many great friends as family in my life over many years, top, l. to r.: Tim Norris, Zac Mathews and me; below, l. to r., Steve May and Martin Espinoza.

My niece Jia rode with me in my last Fiesta Bowl Parade while mayor. She's a natural with the wave.

Making thank-you calls in my empty office on my last day as mayor, July 2004.

Just minutes into being a former mayor, with my predecessor Harry Mitchell far left and my successor, Hugh Hallman, in center.

Gammage Auditorium on the ASU campus in Tempe, dressed to host the final Presidential Debate, October 13, 2004.

One of my proudest moments came after I left office: co-hosting the final US Presidential debate of 2004, at ASU in Tempe. It was an amazing event and capstone to my career at ASU.

Walking out onstage at the Kodak Theater in Hollywood as GLAAD President for the first time was daunting, but a great deal of fun.

We were all surprised when Kathy Griffin accepted her award from T.R. Knight in a bikini.

The annual GLAAD Media Awards recognize the fair, accurate, and inclusive images of LGBT people in the media, and bring out the stars. Ellen DeGeneres and Portia de Rossi attended when Ellen presented an award to Janet Jackson.

Judith Light has stood with the LGBT community as an outspoken advocate for equality and HIV/AIDS awareness. She's also as wonderful and genuine a person as you'll ever find in the entertainment world.

Rev. Gene Robinson and I were snorkel buddies during a memorable trip to the Galapagos Islands over Thanksgiving, 2010.

Crossing the finish line after the 545-mile AIDS/LifeCycle bike ride from San Francisco to Los Angeles, June 2011. An exhilarating and life-changing physical, professional, and personal accomplishment everyone should experience. www.aidslifecycle.org.

"I'm not going to publicly deny the accusations," I said. "We're just going to have to deal with that reality and then move on as best as possible."

Virginia looked like she was about to cry. "Are you okay?"

"Yes. It's going to be rough though. The media firestorm about this will be hotter than anything we've ever experienced and I am sure you'll get calls, having been so close and supportive of me all these years. I'm not sure how it will all play out, but this is going to happen, it will be a big story and I thought you should hear it from me."

I was grateful that Rudy, as usual, put his positive spin on the whole thing. "Well, you know, Neil, this will be difficult, but we support you. Have you talked with your family?"

I had called my mom the night before, giving her the two-minute version and not really going into much detail. Her reaction was one of concern.

"What do these people want from you? I don't know why you put yourself through all this, Neil," she had said in an exasperated tone. She understood public life—my dad's career as a council member back in Bloomfield had given her plenty of exposure to it—but she resented the nastiness of what was happening to me. After all, I was her son, her child. "Why can't these people just leave you alone?" she had said. "It's politics," I had told her, "and we know they won't just leave me alone."

Next I met with Manjula, Charles, and Kristin, all of whom had been integrally involved with my campaigns. They were also close friends. But as close as we were, we had never discussed the issue of my sexuality. Their response was supportive. They weren't surprised by my revelations. I had been pretty sure they knew the score, and as people close to politic and politicians, they understood fully what was about to ensue. But, like Virginia and Rudy, they were concerned for me.

"I'm okay," I told them. I said it to everyone who asked about how I was doing. I hoped it was true. I wasn't sure. There was a personal aspect to this story playing out, a political side, and a professional side as well, for me and for all those close to me. And that concerned me. I was ready to take the fallout myself, but was concerned for others who had connected themselves to me and my political service and future.

At City Hall, I convened a meeting with Randy, my chief of staff, Nachie Marquez, the public information officer, and city manager Gary Brown. I had been thinking about how to do so in a professional way that respected the fact that they were civil servants, not political staff. They worked for the city organization, not for me personally, although we worked together every day. So I would require their support with the issue management aspects of the situation, but could not require or expect them to "handle it'" or be concerned for my political future following the announcement.

"I've been working on a statement," I said after I told them my truth and how I was going to attempt to control the messaging over the next few days. I was relieved to receive their support and wise counsel.

"When you're ready, go talk to Dan at his office and give it to him personally," Nachie said, referring to Dan McCarthy, editor of the *Tempe Daily News Tribune*.

I told her to expect inquiries from national media and especially the gay press, but to make it clear to them that beyond my written statement, I was not going to be available for interviews, knowing that would make her job tougher. "Congressman Kolbe from Tucson coming out just last month will help buffer this somewhat, but it is still going to be a big story. Sorry for the extra work," I joked. Randy would run interference with outside groups and constituencies like the chamber of commerce and neighborhood groups as necessary. Sharing big media news with key people before they read about it is a critical way of building and maintaining a support base in the community. Having done so over the years would especially help in this situation; my allies would be vocal and hopefully far outnumber my adversaries. Gary would inform city department heads of the pending news late in the day, once the news had been provided to Dan McCarthy at the *Tribune*.

The city council was scheduled to have a dinner meeting at a local hotel restaurant early in the week. After our staff had left, I knew the time had come for me to discuss the topic I had always hoped I would never have to discuss with them. There was no more hiding. We sat at an outdoor patio, gathered around two small cocktail tables.

"I know you all know what's going on," I said, trying as best I could to look directly into their faces. I knew they were extremely uncomfortable, and I was about to make them much more so, but our mutual respect, and the fact I was the mayor, meant they would sit and listen. "I'm taking a statement to the press tomorrow and am going to acknowledge the gossip. I'm not denying anything. It's time. I'm doing this and then we'll move on." I was clearly stating my resolve and intent, I was not soliciting suggestions or input.

Over the course of the previous twenty-four hours, having told my closest political team members and key city staff, and having received their full support and acceptance, I had become emboldened to keep moving forward with my plan. And that assuredness and confidence was important because dealing with the council members would be different. They were each elected in their own right, and each had a unique political brand identity and constituency. I knew them all very well, but would not have been quick to predict how each would handle this prime time political drama. It was critical that my resolve and strength, in what was my most difficult political hour, be obvious and clear. As unsure and nervous as I was, to them I would not appear weak.

Their first reaction was total silence. No one said a word. It felt like half an hour before the silence ended.

Ben Arredondo spoke first: "Neil, you know the people doing this are not Tempe. This is ugly, and it's not Tempe. I don't know about others, but if you're having a press conference and want me to stand with you, I'll go. We'll all go to the press conference and stand behind you." One by one, each council member agreed. Their support meant the world to me and choked me up. I explained I was not doing a press conference, but was just going to provide a written statement for the press.

At City Hall the next day, Joe Spracale, a father figure of sorts, gave me a supportive card signed by him and his wife, Sandy. It included the "Serenity Prayer." You know it: "God grant me the serenity to accept the things I cannot change, the courage to change the things I can, and the wisdom to know the difference."

I would somehow find acceptance, courage, and wisdom, but meanwhile there was still plenty of work to be done. The next two days were a blur. My schedule was full of official duties and I needed to execute them, even though the larger part of me was greatly distracted, and stronger, by the public statement I knew I was about to make.

One event I had to attend was the Arizona Cardinals season kick-off luncheon, back at the Buttes Resort. As I entered the ballroom, I saw a long-time friend and supporter Bill Sheppard, an attorney at a prestigious law firm, arts advocate, and someone who's been open and out as a gay man for as long as I can remember.

"Boy, you sure don't look good, Neil," he said, concerned. "What's going on?"

He's going to hear it soon enough, I might as well clue him in.

"Well, all these issues and pressure from the religious right." I confided in him. "I guess it's taking a toll."

"Everyone is talking about that, what's going to happen?" he said.

"I'm going to acknowledge the truth," I said flatly. "I'm not going to deny it. I'm working on a statement for the press."

Bill is a very expressive person, and his face showed his genuine surprise, and then his positive excitement. "Really? You're going to come out?" he said wide-eyed as if there could be nothing negative at all about doing so. Bill, and most leaders in the gay community, knew I was a closeted member. My openness in Washington, D.C., had led to open speculation and then confirmation among the Phoenix gay community. They respected my political situation, my closet, but they certainly knew the truth.

"Well, I won't lie, I just need to do this and move on. I have to say something first."

Bill could not hide his excitement, which reminded me I was doing the right thing. It would matter to a lot of people that I was going to choose to live openly and not hide any longer. At least someone was excited about what was about to happen. I wasn't sure I was, even though I knew it was the right path.

On Wednesday morning, before the Thursday night city council meeting, I called Dan McCarthy, and asked if he had a few minutes free for me to stop by. This being far from regular, he said yes and I then walked alone a few blocks to his office. I was a nervous wreck. I felt like I was stepping into a political abyss, and it was uncertain if I'd ever emerge from it again.

I met with Dan and reporter John Yantis. Externally, my resolve remained steadfast. After some chit-chat about city issues and the nasty political climate at the time, it was time for the purpose of my unusual visit to the newspaper office. "You'll both want a copy of this, do what you want with it," I said, handing them the statement I'd prepared.

Statement by Mayor Neil Giuliano
August 28, 1996

Recently a number of citizens shared their strong opposition to the unanimous recommendation (8-0) of the City Sponsorship Review Committee and the unanimous City Council acceptance (7-0) of their recommendation to waive a partial amount of the city fees associated with the 1997 Arizona Gay Pride Festival to be held, as it has been since 1991, at Tempe Diablo

Stadium soccer fields. Like other events, this group of citizens met the criteria as a non-profit organization whose event is open to the public, without operational problems and whose proceeds go to other charities. For the rare occurrence when the sexual orientation of event organizers or attendees is known, the City of Tempe does not discriminate based upon this information.

It is unfortunate that some citizens uncomfortable with these decisions have sought to make the issue personal with comments of innuendo and speculation about the personal lives of myself, other Council members, and city employees.

Let me state clearly that my private life, although I happen to be gay, or that of any other Council member or city employee, is not and will not be a topic for discussion at a City Council meeting. Meetings of the Council are to conduct the business of the city, not to discuss the personal and private lives of individuals serving either as elected officials or employees.

While I regret that some people have an interest in my private life, I accept that such is a part of elected public service. Having lived in Tempe for twenty-two years, since I was eighteen years old, and through my commitment and work as a student leader, volunteer, Councilman, Vice-Mayor, and Mayor, I believe the community knows well the quality and content of my public service and leadership for Tempe.

With the end of summer comes a great deal of city activity: advancing the Rio Salado Project, neighborhood enhancement programs, our community policing efforts, downtown redevelopment, and transportation issues are just a few of the current topics under discussion. I remain focused on these important issues and will continue to build bridges to a brighter future for all Tempeans.

As they read over the statement, an eerie calmness came over me. I had just willfully exposed the most vulnerable part of who I was to a newspaper. It would forever change my public life, if not my private one, too.

I stated the truth.

We had a short, polite conversation. Dan indicated he hoped for the time when this was not news, but that time had not yet come. He inquired if they were going to be alone with the story and I shared I had plans the rest of the day and evening and would not be speaking with anyone else about the topic.

I got up and walked back to City Hall. A part of me was scared to death on that walk, and a part of me was freer than I had ever been. Peaceful even. I could not control the headlines and news coverage of what I had just done, but I was glad I had done it. I did not really understand it at the time, but of all the campaigns I had undertaken, this one had been the longest. And I was finally winning the campaign within—an internal war I had been waging since the boy on the Schwinn bicycle caught my eye and captured my imagination.

I went back to my office for a planning meeting with the staff. Ever the great media person, Nachie said she would touch base with Dan later in the day and see if he had any follow-up questions, and try to gauge how the story was going to be written. The city council meeting—the one where the mystery woman had threatened to appear and out me—was the next day and there was still city business to conduct, whatever else might occur. Then, I went home and hit the phones, calling friends and supporters, letting them know what would be in the *Tribune* the next morning—and why. The reality was the story was already being spread like wildfire among the political circles, that dominant coalition of people who are engaged and involved in the life of the community. Fortunately in 1996, we did not have the instantaneous online presentation of news from anyone wanting to blog about any topic, or I am certain by the time I had even made it over to the newspaper office, the speculation about the speculation would have been in the public space. While the news was no doubt being shared via phone and person-to-person conversations, there was still time for me to inform people myself.

I went to bed, but never fell asleep that night. The bedroom window was open and it was a clear night. Moonlight covered the room as I surfed channels trying to take my mind off of the day ahead—my first day as an openly gay elected official.

It was 5:10 AM when I heard the *Tribune* land and slide on the driveway.

Okay, time to see how this is playing out.

I stepped out the front gate of my courtyard to the driveway in just my boxers, it was just a few steps and it was dark, and grabbed the paper as I had many times before. It was folded with a rubber band around it, so the headline was invisible at first. My hands shook a little as I freed the newspaper and unfolded it in one motion. Across the top of the front page, in large bold letters were the words: "Mayor Says He's Gay—Feared Inquisition."

The story was accurate, and I read it a couple times while sitting at my kitchen table. I read it as most politicians read stories about themselves: What will the follow-up story be? What questions are left unanswered, to ensure there would be a follow-up story? What did both my allies and adversaries say for the record, and from that, what will they be saying off the record? What will be the story about the story?

The story's lead sentence made me laugh to myself about the supposedly safe closet I had been hiding in. It read: "Ending years of rumor and speculation…"

McCarthy had written an editorial column on the topic as well, essentially saying I was the same person when I left his office the previous morning as I had been when I walked in. It was interesting that he noted the campaign tactics of that first campaign for mayor:

For years there has been talk and innuendo. For years, some of Giuliano's opponents—even those who should have known better—had attempted to use the gay issue against him. At one point, in a phone survey during an election several years ago, people were outraged when they were asked questions about the issue they felt were improper. The tactics soon ended. For not putting up with that sort of campaign strategy, all of Tempe can be proud. But we have a long way to go.

He closed the piece with a hopeful message:

A half hour after he arrived the mayor left my office, just as he arrived. He was talking about the city and telling me why the transit tax that is up for a vote in Tempe on September 10 would be good for the city and make it the leader of what one day will be a Valley-wide system. Nothing had changed.

Very nice words, deeply appreciated. He was absolutely right on one level, of course. But to me, everything had changed By 7:00 A.M. my home phone was ringing off the hook. My coming out was the story of the day: on morning drive time talk radio, on the television stations in the Phoenix market, and, of course, all over *The Tribune*. I did not answer the phone, but the voicemails ranged from supportive to downright ugly, with many more of the former. After a while, I got tired of listening to them. It was only 7:30 but I decided to go to my office at ASU, which was my usual second stop of the day. My first stop, the ASU recreation center to work out from 6:00 A.M. to 7:30 A.M., would not happen this day.

As the office staff arrived, they came by individually and in groups to offer support and encouragement. By 9:00 I had supportive voicemails from more than a dozen ASU colleagues, including the president, Lattie Coor, and senior provost Milt

Glick. By 10:00 a TV news crew arrived and perched outside in the hallway of my ASU office. Ironically, the reporter sent to cover the story was a closeted gay guy who had known about me and I about him from the gay rumor mill, but I sent word to him that I would not be giving any interviews. He waited nearly three hours for me to emerge for a one-on-one, exclusive interview. But I meant it when I said I was not giving any comment beyond my written statement. He finally gave up and left, and I lost track of him over the years and am not sure if he ever came out or remains in the closet.

I was not aware that, for the previous few days, my campaign support team and my friends had been calling others to encourage them to come to the city council meeting to show support for me personally and as their mayor. I spent most of the day on the phone with friends near and far, just touching base, letting them know what was going on, and that we would take this day by day and see how it would go. Everyone was very supportive, with the exception of one Republican state representative for Tempe, a very conservative Mormon. I remember her saying, "This is a mistake. You didn't need to do this. It will hurt you."

The agenda for the council meeting that night was actually quite brief. It was the Thursday before the Labor Day holiday, and we tried to keep a light agenda before any three-day weekend.

Council meeting chambers are on the garden level of City Hall, and the entrance for council members and staff is actually behind the dais where the council sits during meetings. I rode the elevator down from the third floor with some colleagues and joked, "This ought to be a doozy of a meeting, huh?" I was trying to make light of it all, to try to put people at ease a bit, but no one really knew what to expect. Everyone was nervous.

Were my accusers going to be there? Would someone get up and ask me point blank whether I was gay, now that the truth was the headline in the *Tribune* and had been on TV and talk radio all day? Would one or several of them make a statement during the public appearance part of the meeting? Would they still want to know the sexual orientation of a police commander, public works employee, and other "suspected" homosexuals on the city payroll?

I walked through the door into the council chambers, having decided that I would do so proudly, with my head up, and smiling. But I was totally unprepared for what I saw as I entered.

The room was mobbed. Every seat was filled, and people were standing in the aisles as well. The noise from that many people talking among themselves was as loud as I had ever heard in that room, equal to the night just a little more than two years prior when I was first sworn-in as the twenty-sixth and youngest mayor in the history of the city. A couple of TV news reporters stood with cameras on tripods off in the back left hand corner of the room, a far from common situation. But having first told the local newspaper, I knew the story would still need to be covered in the dominant paper for the state and region, *The Arizona Republic*, and on broadcast news.

I could see people were standing outside in the courtyard of City Hall too, beyond the glass doorways, and was overwhelmed when I recognized almost everyone I saw as my eyes quickly scanned the room. It was packed with my friends, supporters, and even people I had not seen in years. It was a bit like that final scene from *It's a Wonderful Life* when all of George Bailey's friends walk in the house and he's just overwhelmed by their gesture and support.

Mom was sitting in the front row off to my left with Virginia Tinsley and Rudy Campbell, smiling at me as I walked to the mayor's chair in the center of those of the council members. She did one of those tiny waves with her hand held down in front of herself just above her lap.

I sat down, smiled to everyone and no one in particular.

I quickly processed whether I should acknowledge the crowd, the reason for their attendance, and give a quick off the cuff speech about the last few days. I felt choked up and was almost made teary by the tremendous outpouring of support and wanted to thank everyone. Just as fast, however, I changed my mind and decided not to alter the normal flow of the meeting. Nothing had changed with my new status as an openly gay mayor, or so I hoped.

I received the signal from the staff that we were now broadcasting live on our cable television station, Tempe 11, which meant anyone watching was seeing me. I nodded an "okay," punched the button to turn on my microphone, took a deep breath, and called the meeting to order exactly as I had for the last two years on Thursday nights.

"Good evening. Welcome to the Tempe City Council Meeting. Please rise for the Pledge of Allegiance and an invocation."

There would be a non-denominational prayer read by a pre-selected council member. I would bow my head, but I wouldn't hear it.

My mind was racing and my heart was beating hard. One long chapter of my life was clearly over, and another was about to commence.

CHAPTER NINE

Living, Loving, Letting Go

Within a few months and as the holidays approached in fall of 1996, the furor and attention of having come out publicly started to fade. There were only a few catcalls from the crowd when I walked in the annual Veteran's Day parade that year—I heard "queer" and "boo"—as I strode down Mill Avenue. I made sure not to turn my head toward the sound, but to keep walking and smiling. We weren't sure what to expect as my official responsibilities as host mayor for the Fiesta Bowl kicked into gear that year. As was the tradition, I would escort the Fiesta Bowl Queen across the football field at half-time in front of 80,000 people in Sun Devil Stadium. Everyone was terrific and there were no incidents, although I will admit to being a bit nervous about it at first. A mayor who is gay having a hugely visible role in a major sporting event had never happened before.

The most significant activity in 1997 was moving toward construction of the Tempe Town Lake, the focal signature of the Rio Salado Project. I had campaigned on a commitment to make this urban flood control and multi-faceted urban development project a reality, and it was happening.

Summer had arrived and I was expecting a nice lazy Saturday of laundry, errands, and some work around the house. I had no public events on my mayor's schedule, a rarity that was much welcomed.

I was sitting on my couch with my legs and feet up on the cheap coffee table that I regularly abused in such fashion, surfing channels. Rick's bedroom door opened and Rick came out, followed by a guy who was so attractive I actually caught my breath. He had beautiful eyes and a face that you want to see on the pillow next to you every morning for the rest of your life, framed by short, brown hair. His body was tight and compact, maybe five-feet eight-inches of lean muscle beneath tanned, smooth skin. Even without a shower and in yesterday's navy blue cargo shorts and white T-shirt, he had that special something. It was all working. Especially the smile.

Wow. Where did Rick find this one?

Seeing a hot guy walk out of Rick's bedroom was nothing new; Rick is striking in his own right and, unlike me, was comfortably expressing his sexuality, although he was somewhat closeted too and not out at work. The young man with him this particular morning was different

"Hey, what's up?" I said.

"Hey, I'm Jason," he said, stretching out a hand.

"Nice to meet you," I murmured as we shook.

"Yeah, good to meet you."

No, the pleasure is all mine, I assure you.

They walked through the kitchen and he left a minute later.

Rick disappeared back into the kitchen, while I sat there trying to contain my excitement. I wanted to know all about this Jason, but I didn't want Rick to know just how interested I was. I waited, and then called out casually, "So, who was that cute one?"

"We've been hanging out for the last week or so." Rick replied. He wanted to leave it at that, but I wanted to know more. After a few more meager facts, Rick changed the subject.

The following night when I happened to glance out of the kitchen window into the front courtyard, I saw Rick and Jason holding each other in the darkness. A storm was brewing and the wind was blowing hard, ruffling their clothes and hair. They stood motionless, embracing. They weren't kissing; I could tell that this long hug was a goodbye.

Two days later, Rick told me: Jason had ended their short relationship. They had vowed to remain friends, but their three-week fling was over. While Rick was my friend and my roommate—and had been for years—a part of me was glad.

I wanted to see Jason.

A week passed, and then I got my opportunity.

"Me and Jason are going to a movie. You want to come?"

Rick posed the question casually; he had no idea of the conflagration of emotion this simple query had set off inside me. *Did I want to go along?* I tried to contain my enthusiasm, matching his nonchalance syllable for syllable.

"Sure, what are we going to go see?"

The three of us went to the old Valley Art Theatre in downtown Tempe and saw *Love! Valour! Compassion!* I tried not to make my attraction to Jason obvious, but I'm not sure I succeeded. I was very interested in getting to know him.

Another week went by before I got the courage to call him. I had found his phone number on a message pad that Rick left on the kitchen counter. I called him while home for lunch one day, while Rick was at work.

"Hey, I don't know if you remember me. I'm Neil, Rick's roommate."

There was a painful pause that seemed to me to stretch out forever. Finally, he said, "Oh, yeah. What's up?"

"Not much."

That was a lie. There was a lot up on my side of the conversation. What was "up" was that I was a forty-year-old man who felt like a high school freshman having his first crush. My palms were sticky, my throat was dry and my heart was racing. This was the adolescence I never had. I don't even remember what I said or how it came out, but I do remember being completely dumbfounded when he said "Sure" to my casual invitation to grab lunch sometime. At that moment, I was seventeen again.

All men experience a physical adolescence of course. Gay men usually have a second one when they acknowledge their true orientation. Dating someone in the beginning or in the midst of his gay adolescence can be a problem. In my life up to that point, I had had a few brief encounters, but I had never been an initiator of any of them. Romantically, I'm pretty conservative and not particularly aggressive. I know that seems hard to fathom, given my work and political involvements over many years, but it's true. I rarely make the first move. Once someone has expressed an interest and lets that interest be known, I'm more aggressive. My fears of rejection have usually kept me from being a "pursuer," but with Jason that pattern changed. I called him; I pursued.

Jason and I had only gone out together a few times when my heart started to take flight. I was walking in the clouds. My casual dates with Jason had me thrilled to the point of giddiness. Because of my limited experience with relationships, I thought that feeling would last forever. I understand now that those initial weeks and months of being in a new relationship are rare, beautiful, and fleeting.

About a month after we started seeing each other, we shared our first kiss. I saw fireworks—literally and figuratively, just like in the song by Katy Perry. Of course, it helped that it was the Fourth of July.

We had made plans to get together after my official mayoral duties at the Independence Day celebrations were complete. Jason was house-sitting for friends, so I went over to see him at his temporary home. We sat in the lounge chairs in his friends' yard and talked for hours. He asked me so many questions that the conversation felt more like an interview. He asked me all about my past, especially about my "gay" past. I told him everything. I did not hold back. I *wanted* him to know everything about me I can't remember being so honest with anyone, especially someone that I'd known for so short a period of time.

Finally, we were all talked out. It was very late when I got up to leave. My heart was racing again. My palms were wet. It was about to be one of those moments that could go either way: a quick, casual goodbye or something more intense? Jason was hard to read, so I held back my desire for the latter.

"Thanks. See you again," I said.

"Yeah. Thanks," he replied.

Then he looked right into my eyes, stepped toward me, and our lips met, lightly at first, then melted in a kiss so long and passionate that I was left breathless. I had never been very into kissing; I never felt I was very good at it. But I'd never felt this level of intensity and desire for anyone. As I've said, I finally understood why people compared a first kiss to fireworks. The first time I kissed Jason, I saw those brilliant lights firsthand. After that wonderful kiss, I drove home with a smile on my face. Jason called almost as soon as I got there, and we talked for another hour. Then out of nowhere, he said, "I'm going to call my sister and tell her I'm gay." Jason was twenty-five years old at the time; I was fifteen years older. Both of us had been deep in the closet all our lives, which for him had been a lot fewer years. He hadn't told anyone. He drove to his sister's house late that same night, woke her up and spoke his truth. I'm glad to say he received her complete support and acceptance that night.

Our relationship progressed. In late July after I returned from the U.S. Conference of Mayors' summer meeting, we spent a lovely night together at the Hermosa Inn. The chemistry between us was as intense as I had ever experienced. The closeness, the fit, the sense of belonging, and attachment were all a new experience for me. I had waited for that feeling for a very long time.

I had begun the process of coming clean with Rick, but there was still enough left unsaid, requiring Jason to have to slip secretly into my room when Rick was home. I watched as this silhouetted figure crawled into my bed. Sleepy-eyed, I reached up and touched his smooth, shirtless chest. We didn't speak, just embraced, kissed, and fell asleep, spooned together, with me holding Jason from behind, my face pressed up against the back of his neck.

Jason and I continued to see each other over the summer and into the fall. For me it was exclusive, both emotionally and because the sheer logistics of my schedule barely allowed me enough time to see him, much less anyone else. After telling his sister about being gay, he told his other sister and then his mom. They were tremendously supportive and knew about me. They knew he was dating the mayor.

My own self-esteem issues and fears, however, kept me from meeting Jason's family. The age difference between us bothered me: I feared his family would see me as some kind of lecher preying on young, impressionable guys. That idea kept a part of my brain thinking, *Maybe this whole thing is a bad idea*, while the other part of my brain knew that I wanted to be with Jason all of the time. I couldn't stop thinking about him. I felt great when I was with him. I felt like a better version of myself; indeed, I *was* a better version of myself.

In retrospect, I wish I had agreed to meet Jason's family a lot sooner. I could not have been more wrong about how they would receive me, and my reluctance created doubts in his mind about my feelings for him. He was very close to his family and they were very accepting of him and of me. My fears about them were unjust.

After about five months of dating, Jason was falling in love, too. He wanted to move in and for us to live together. He wanted a commitment. He started buying cool pieces of furniture and accent pieces for my house. In one of those pillow-talk conversations that couples share, we discussed having kids.

"I wanna have one with you," Jason told me. "Maybe one of my sisters could have your kid. That would be the best."

Whoa, I remember thinking. *That's a pretty deep conversation for a relationship that was only six months old.*

At the National League of Cities meeting in December 1997, I attended a dinner for the caucus of gay, lesbian, and bisexual elected officials. There were fifteen or so of us from around the country and most had brought their partners with them. I did not. I was one of only two single guys. Over my steak and French fries, I couldn't help staring around the table at the happy couples, all elected folks with their supportive and understanding spouses.

What is wrong with me? I thought. *Why am I holding back? What am I so afraid of?*

When I got back to my hotel room, I called Jason.

"What are you doing tomorrow night when I get back?"

"No plans. What's up?" He sounded surprised.

"Let's get together."

When I got back to Phoenix, I drove straight to Jason's condo in Awatukee, a seemingly endless Phoenix suburb of cookie-cutter stucco and red-tiled roof homes. In nearly six months of dating, I'd never spent a single night at his place. I had told him it was because he had such a tiny bed, which was true. But that was only part of the truth. The other reason was that my re-election campaign was fast approaching. It would be my first campaign as an openly gay elected official, my schedule was insane and it was just easier for me to have him come to my place when I had some time. The National League of Cities Gay, Lesbian, and Bisexual Elected Officials dinner made me see my relationship in a new light. Perhaps I could have both: a political career and a solid, loving relationship.

Once inside his condo, I was feeling playful and free. We were wrestling each other and began rolling around on his floor like two kids. We kissed. I was finally ready to take the next step.

"I have a question for you," I said.

"What?"

"How would you like to be my boyfriend?"

When he smiled, I melted. "Of course."

We kissed again. It was a wonderful moment for me because I had finally let go. Jason was my boyfriend. This was everything I dreamed it could be. It seemed perfect: I was out and happy, in a relationship and winning the campaign within. Unfortunately, there were political challenges mounting around me that would push and test me, and our relationship, to the limit.

* * *

Toward the end of 1997, the strain and pressures of running as an openly gay candidate for my third mayoral term had me frazzled. In my other campaigns, my opponents had operated in the shadows. This time it was different. My adversaries were now visible, vocal and ready to fight. And compared to my first re-election campaign in May of 1996, with no opponent at all, this was going to be a very different race.

The same people who had threatened me, maybe tapped my phone lines, and ultimately forced me into making a public statement acknowledging my sexuality had used those events to gain momentum, including finding a candidate to challenge me. They ran an ugly campaign of attack ads filled with whispered hate speech.

In May 1998, the Christian Coalition published a voter guide highlighting my support of domestic partnership benefits, my decision to establish a hate-crime liaison officer, and my pro-choice stance. The "voter guide" appeared on car windshields in church parking lots across the city on the Sunday before the election. The newspaper reported that over 4,000 phone calls were made to voters, laying out the same "voter guide" positions in the attempt to sway voters against me. They called it a "voter guide," but really it was nothing more than veiled homophobia and anti-gay propaganda.

I am a Christian, a Catholic. I believe the basic tenets of Christianity, that Jesus Christ is the Son of God and that He rose from the dead. When I die, I believe there's life beyond what we experience here. What I *don't* believe in is a literal interpretation of the writings of the men who were around Jesus. They were men writing stories about their world and that had to include, I believe, their individual biases, prejudices, opinions, and human shortcomings. The Bible is a divinely-inspired work that can teach and uplift, but I do not believe that every word written by these ancient storytellers is intended to be accepted at face value. To the religious right, however, a few passages in the Bible are the end of the discussion about gay people. They believe gay people are an aberration, evil sinners doomed to hellfire and brimstone simply because of our sexual orientation. To them, having a closeted gay mayor was bad, but electing an openly gay mayor and giving him legitimate public authority and respect would never be accepted.

During the campaign, I got letters weekly from fanatics urging me to repent and save my soul. I could have walked on the water of the future Tempe Town Lake, and they still would never have accepted me. One morning I woke up to a phone call from a friend telling me to go look at my campaign road sign at the intersection of Priest and Rio Salado Parkway; it had "GAY" spray-painted on it in huge red letters. I called Rob, who had a pick-up truck, and we rode over and took the sign down, but not before word of it spread and soon a newspaper photographer was at my house taking a photo of the sign, now in my garage, with me standing behind it.

Facing these kinds of homophobic slurs, anxiety was my constant companion. My campaign team was carrying most of the weight of the re-election effort because most days I felt politically immobilized. I tried not to let on to friends and supporters who were working so hard on my behalf, but I was struggling. Would people still vote for me now that I was an openly gay man, running for mayor? Did I have the inner fortitude to fight these kinds of attacks, day in and day out? I wasn't sure.

What I was sure of, however, was Jason. He was a tremendous support to me during that time. He got to know my campaign team and got involved with the re-election effort. The team loved Jason, too. "He's good for you," I was often reminded. They were right.

As I had in my first campaign for mayor, I told myself that if I didn't win, it would be okay. I would have more time to spend with Jason and our relationship would finally get the attention it deserved. Jason understood that I was the mayor, but he grew tired of having to deal with me in my stressed-out state. Even worse, I was often too busy to spend time with him at all, thanks to a never-ending litany of events. He tolerated being the boyfriend of a political and public person, but he did not really enjoy it. His support was phenomenal, and he was easily the best thing that had ever happened to me. But with all my duties and the campaign, I wasn't a particularly good boyfriend.

I did the best I could by Jason, but the truth was I was drained by the negativity of the campaign. Right up until the last moment, I felt personally attacked, condemned, and repudiated. On Election Day 1998, I was at the polling place at University Presbyterian Church on College Avenue and Alameda Drive when two elderly ladies came in, each clutching a Christian Coalition voting guide.

"Good morning," I said. "Thanks for coming to vote today."

"Good morning," one of them said. "Who are you?"

"I'm Neil Giuliano," I said. "I'm your mayor."

The way the expressions on their faces immediately turned sour said it all. They hurried inside the building to vote for my opponent.

After the polls closed that Election Day, I headed to our party at Tempe Mission Palms Hotel. Jason was going to come and he was bringing his sister, too. It was already crowded when I arrived with more than 200 people milling around the ballroom. As the hours ticked by, we began to get more and more nervous; it seemed like it was taking longer than usual for the results to be reported. The Mission Palms Hotel was just across the street from City Hall, where the official results would be announced, and finally, I got impatient enough and decided to walk over there. As I headed out of the hotel I saw Manjula and Rob walking slowly toward me. They did not look happy.

"Well, it's good and bad," Manjula said as she approached me.

"Why?" I wanted to know, and fast. Manjula could see I was irritated and not in the mood for any "guessing" games.

"You won. You're still the mayor," she said quickly, reassuring me. "But Linda will be in a tough run-off for her council seat."

Hugh Hallman had been elected to the council in the primary by capturing more than 50% of the votes, forcing my good friend and council member Linda Spears into a general election runoff with fellow incumbents Carol Smith and Ben Arredondo, and challenger Leonard Copple. Only two of the four would get elected in the May election. Hugh had been a Sherman supporter in my first mayoral campaign, and as a show of unity I had appointed him to a prestigious city commission. His campaign had launched extremely aggressive and negative attacks, particularly against Carol and Linda, which helped enable the Copple and Arredondo victories in the general election.

For the sake of all my supporters waiting back at the hotel, we focused on my victory. "Look, they threw it all at you," Rob reminded me. "You kicked ass. Fifty-six percent is not a close election." He was right, of course, but that didn't satisfy me. I had run unopposed in my last election. This time with the support of the Christian Coalition and others, a total unknown had received forty-two percent of the vote. Still, they failed. I would remain the mayor. I survived.

1998 Primary Election Results
Neil G. Giuliano   8,481 (56.0%)
Jay Mansperger   6,452 (42.6%)

When Manjula, Rob, and I walked into the ballroom, the word spread fast that I had won. The cheering started before I went up to the front of the ballroom to make a brief thank you and victory speech, with campaign co-chairs Rudy and Virginia standing at my side. Mom was there, I introduced and thanked her, too, and it was a wonderful night.

It's too bad you can't bottle a moment in time and seal it up to keep forever.

On the surface everything seemed fine, but things between Jason and me were getting more complicated. Our time together was spectacular. We never fought, and we enjoyed each other's company immensely.

We spent the Memorial Day weekend of 1998 in Miami Beach. We stayed a few nights at Walter Batt's —the friend who had run my student body campaign sixteen years earlier and had since come out himself and was enjoying a very successful career in the private sector—then we moved to the Ocean Inn in South Beach, one block from the Versace mansion. One night during that trip, just as we were going to bed, Jason disappeared. It was about midnight. Just as I was starting to become concerned, Jason was back with a vanilla sundae and two spoons. We sat on the bed, in that warm tropical air, and ate ice cream together.

Another moment I wish I could bottle.

More and more, however, cracks in our relationship were beginning to show. I did love Jason, and I was slowly coming around to our living together and committing to him, but he wanted more than the workaholic mayor could offer.

Shortly after my third two-year term began, Jason introduced what I knew would be a touchy subject.

"Are you going to run again in 2000?"

"I think so," I replied. "I always said I'd run four times."

I could tell by the look on his face that I'd just given the wrong answer.

In June 1998, we went to San Francisco Pride together. I was the guest speaker at the California Log Cabin Republican annual dinner. I wanted Jason to see me doing well, making a difference as an openly gay person. I hoped that if he understood the difference I was making, he'd be able to reconcile all the personal sacrifices it meant for our relationship. The trip, however, resulted in a fateful turning point in our relationship.

We went to the dinner, and, afterwards, Jason wanted to go out. We hit a couple spots, had a few drinks, and then I was done.

"You go ahead, wander around some, have fun," I said. "I'm beat."

He grabbed my hand. "No, come on, I want you to come with me."

I squeezed his hand and smiled. "It's okay, you can go; I'm going back to the hotel."

Although I insisted he go enjoy himself, he refused to go without me. We ended up walking back to the room in an uncomfortable silence, each of us lost in our own separate thoughts. In bed, with the lights out, we talked about what had happened. Out of nowhere Jason said, "No matter what, I know you'll never love me as much I love you."

I did not think that was true at all, but I did not want to get into a big discussion about it either. I said nothing, and let the words fester inside me in the darkness. He'd just dropped a bomb on me.

Finally, Jason fell asleep, and although I tried to sleep as well, I couldn't. I was replaying everything we'd said to each other in my mind. Finally, two or three hours later, I slipped out of bed and started quietly packing my bag. My mind was racing.

Where's this relationship going? What am I doing here? He doesn't really want me here. He's already given up on us, so I might as well take off.

I had never thought of myself as a drama queen, but boy, I was going for an Oscar that night. Chalk it up to emotional overload, but those were my thoughts as I threw stuff into my bag and slipped into the bathroom with the pad of paper from the hotel desk. I closed the door and sat down to write a note on the hotel letterhead, and I felt as lost as that adolescent kid being rejected by the cheerleader. I began my note:

Jason, maybe you're right. Maybe I'll never love you as much as you love me. I don't know. Maybe it's better if I just leave. You have a great time. I'm going home.

Tears spilled from my face and hit the paper as I leaned over the sink's counter, writing. I didn't hear him push the door open, but when I turned he was standing in the doorway.

"What are you doing?" he asked, taking in the sight of me all dressed, my packed bag on the floor, and my wet eyes.

"I should just leave," I responded. "If I'm never going to love you as much as you love me, then I should just go."

Silence.

Although I was older than Jason, managing the ups and downs of a relationship wasn't something I had ever learned to do. Avoiding my true sexual identity when I first discovered it those many years ago left me immensely under-equipped for handling personal and intimate relationships. The fact that our culture has changed and young people can find support and encouragement at younger ages is probably one of the very best aspects of the visible and advancing quest for full equality. It makes me so happy to see kids able to be themselves at a young age.

We stood and held each other and cried. The familiar scent of his body and feeling him close was comforting. We went back and sat on the bed.

"Maybe I'm not right for you. I can't be everything you want and need in a boyfriend."

"You can't leave," he said crying and holding me. "I'm not ready to lose you yet."

By late summer 1998, the Tempe city council had grown more contentious. The equation and tenor of the meetings had moved from "create consensus" to "create dysfunction" and I had to adjust how I led the team as a result. The result was a much more stressful period for me as mayor, and it got so bad I was getting migraines. I went to my doctor who, in turn, sent me to specialists who put me through a string of MRIs and tests. Jason was by my side during all the doctor visits. We were spending most nights together and talking three to four times a day. For a while, I dared to hope that the hard words and intense feelings of San Francisco were behind us. It felt good to have him—my boyfriend—with me when I walked into the doctor's office to get the test results. The nurse and doctor seemed completely at ease with us. They never questioned anything or made us feel uncomfortable in any way.

"There's no tumor," the doctor said. "We don't see anything that might be causing the pain and pressure. Are you under intense stress?"

"Yes, he is," said Jason without hesitation.

He was right. It seemed like the council was always fighting. Fighting had become the new "normal."

"Well," the doctor, continued. "That could be it. There's nothing medical going on."

For Labor Day weekend, we went to San Diego and Black's Beach. Things were comfortable and fun, but I could feel something was off. When my birthday came and went without much fanfare, I could sense him pulling away. We had stopped communicating with each other in the ways we had in the past. I didn't know what to do and wasn't sure what I wanted to do.

Politically, I found unending and greater demands, and a much higher profile in the region: I had been selected by my peers from twenty-six other communities to serve as Chair of the Regional Council of Governments and was enjoying my expanded opportunity to lead. I thrived on it, but it was not without a personal price. My major initiatives enjoyed solid majority support. We were driving forward with a new transportation plan and with construction of the Rio Salado Project and Tempe Town Lake, two of my key initiatives. Yet it seemed like every city council meeting had become a major battle, sometimes over a major policy issue, but more often it was just political theater over small issues. The drama and ugliness was unproductive. I carried the burden of those meetings into my relationship.

In an effort to show Jason that I was still committed, I threw him a surprise birthday party in early November. I called about twenty of his friends and invited them to celebrate with us at my house. It was fun, and I know he appreciated it, but the party didn't have the desired effect. Losing the relationship was too painful to think about, so I convinced myself that everything was fine. I went all out for Thanksgiving: I threw a celebration and invited family and friends, including Congressman Jim Kolbe. By early December, I was feeling optimistic. Things between us were turning for the better. I had finally stepped up. I was acting like a good boyfriend, not accepting every invitation to every event in town, available to be with him more often. I was planning things and spending time with my partner. Everything should be fine now.

Was I ever wrong.

On the second Saturday night in December, Jason said, "I think we need to take a little break for a while."

Okay, yeah. Makes sense. Step back and think about where things are. Good idea.

I completely missed his point. I had absolutely no clue that what he just said meant he was breaking up with me. Having never really dated anyone the way we had been dating, I had never really experienced a true break-up either. I didn't know there was no such thing as taking a "little break." I didn't realize that what he was talking about was permanent.

"That's great because I'm busy with ASU work, the Fiesta Bowl season is coming up, and I could use some time," I said.

Exactly one year prior, when he was still mostly in the closet and we had been casually dating for six months, he had been ready to move in with me. It had taken me so long to respond, to start showing that I felt the same way that now, he was ready to move on. It was ironic: I had been the cautious one initially, but now that he had become cautious, I was ready to go to the next level and commit. Send in the clowns, as the song goes.

Of course, things deteriorated naturally after that. When I finally understood we were broken up, I was an emotional mess. I was depressed and losing weight. I wanted to reconnect and I was still pursuing him, but he was done with me. Like a lovesick teenager, I just wasn't getting it.

I purchased nice Christmas gifts for him and his family, including eight tickets for a mid-January performance of *The Phantom of the Opera*. We planned to meet for dinner beforehand at P.F. Chang's in downtown Tempe. Jason showed up late and was polite but not really engaged. It was obvious to even me that he didn't want to be there—and I was acting like the desperate mess I was.

"Us getting back together is not going to happen," he said to me one time after we had a casual meal. "I want to be single. I'm going to be single for a while now."

I was devastated.

Spring came and went. That summer, my career seemed to reach a new high, even though my spirits were at an all-time low. I went to the U.S. Conference of Mayors meeting, which was attended by Vice President Gore and fifty others. While attending that high profile meeting, my mind drifted constantly to Jason.

Later that summer, I went to a three-week Executive Leadership program at Harvard University for state and local officials. It was probably the best program I had ever attended with great case studies and information. While in Cambridge I was visited by the *CBS Sunday Morning* production team; I was going to be featured on a segment about openly gay officials, along with Ambassador Jim Hormel. It was quite an honor and fun to do. They had been in Tempe earlier in the summer for some footage and the piece ended up being well done and well received. It took my visibility as an openly gay mayor to a new level. More and more cards, letters, and now emails were coming my way from people all over the country, adding to the thousand or so that I had received when I first came out in 1996.

Although I was still grieving my break-up, being a part of the national dialogue about sexual orientation helped me realize I did have an obligation to speak out and be visible—especially for young people struggling with their sexual orientation, who might be wondering if there was anyone out there like themselves just as I had done years back while an undergraduate student.

Professionally, I was doing well. Back in Phoenix two weeks later, however, I saw Jason at B.S. West, a gay bar in Scottsdale. It was a Sunday afternoon but the place was filled with the thump of loud music and a dance floor packed with shirtless men. This was the first time I'd seen him in a gay public setting since we'd broken up. Although it had been eight months since he said he wanted to take a timeout, I was still fixated on him, still hoping for my second chance.

To me, there wasn't anyone else. We had one of those painfully awkward, post-breakup exchanges.

"How's your sister?" I asked.

"She's good. Good."

Silence. We sipped our beers and looked around the club.

"How's the rest of your family?" I asked.

"They're good. Real good."

More silence. We sipped our beers and looked around the club.

It was awful, knowing how close we had once been.

Three weeks later, on Labor Day weekend, I went five nights without sleeping more than an hour or so each night. In ten days, I lost about twelve pounds and had a strange rash on my thigh. I thought, somehow, I was HIV-positive. I called my friend Walter Batt in Miami.

"Walter, I've lost all this weight in a week, I can't sleep. I think I'm HIV-positive."

"Have you done anything unsafe the last year or so?"

"No, nothing even close to unsafe in a decade. And my sex life is pretty much non-existent at this point."

"Then you're probably not HIV-positive. There's something else going on. If you want to fly here, you can see a doctor I know."

Instead I went to see Ken Fisher, a local gay doctor well known for treating HIV-positive patients. I met him at 6:00 A.M. at his office before he opened for the day. He drew the blood, and we talked a bit about what was going on, but not in-depth, not specifics. I knew I was sick, but I did not want to say I was depressed and lost over a former boyfriend.

Walter was right. The HIV test was negative. I called my CIGNA health plan and said I wanted an appointment with a counselor.

"Are you feeling like you might hurt yourself?" the nurse asked.

"No, I'm hurting enough without hurting myself. I just want to talk to someone."

I went to see a counselor who asked me a few vague questions and I shared the nutshell of the story. He agreed I was suffering mild depression. It seemed more than mild to me, but he noted that my outward performance and behavior had not been negatively impacted, so he would only call it mild. He would give me some anti-depressant medication if I wanted it. I got the impression he didn't take me seriously at all, even after I spent nearly an hour sharing the situation and how awful I felt. He ended our hour together by saying simply, "Well, if you want to see me again, you know where to find me. You can call."

I didn't take the drugs and I didn't call for a follow-up. I had to deal with this myself.

I sought out my good friend Lawrence, a successful businessman, who is several years older than I. I hoped he would have some words of wisdom to impart, he usually did. I had unexpectedly run into Lawrence at Trumpets, a gay bar in Washington, D.C., back in 1995 before coming out publicly. It was one of those awkward moments when, even though I had already been discovered, I struggled with whether I should talk to him. I did and our friendship grew from there. Lawrence already knew about the break up and how hard it had been for me, so when we met for dinner, he was ready to cut to the chase.

"Why do you still want someone who no longer has any interest in you?"

He was giving the best and most direct advice I could receive. He was right, and I was finally ready to hear it. It truly was time to let go, and I would.

That Christmas, I gave Jason a basket of sailing-related gifts: some framed photos from Provincetown, a great coffee table book, a small sailboat—all things I had been collecting throughout the year because I knew he loved sailing stuff. I included a card that said that I knew it was time for me to let him sail away for good and that I wished him well and that I wanted him to find happiness. If Adele's "Someone Like You" had been out then and playing in the background, it would have been the prefect scene.

Jason gave me a $50 gift certificate to OfficeMax. That sums it up.

He had already sailed away, rightfully so, and finally, so would I.

In March 2000, I won re-election for my fourth term as mayor by a huge margin. My "Bridging to the Future" agenda had advanced with tremendous support. More and more people were becoming involved with the community. Two of my big supporters, Barb Carter and Pam Goronkin, got themselves elected to the city council, making me feel good about one important tenet of leadership: to bring others along. We had brought many others along and the community was stronger. Voters also approved a mayoral term length change from two years to four years, effective with that election, so I would serve for twice as long. I had not taken a position on the ballot issue, and was willing to accept whatever the voters decided.

2000 Primary Election Results
Neil G. Giuliano   11,612 (70.3%)
Tom Head   4,315 (26.1%)

Jason's sister and her husband were contributors to my campaign and came to the election night victory party at Beeloe's in downtown Tempe. As I saw them walk in, I couldn't help but think of 1998, two years prior, when I stood as the victor with Jason by my side.

Then to my surprise, I saw him coming down the stairs behind his sister and brother-in-law. I hadn't seen him in a long time. He was now, finally, on the periphery of my emotions and of my life.

I thought about all I had learned from my time with Jason, the importance of communication and just letting go. And for a fleeting moment, as I briefly caught his eyes and we smiled across the roaring crowd, I wondered what would have happened if I had left my comfort zone sooner and let his love in. What if we had met at a different time in our lives and had not been first boyfriends for each other? I know it just wasn't meant to be. But still.

Just as quickly, the thoughts left me as I turned my attention back to my supporters and felt grateful that I had survived politically, again. And it was more than that, I truly had a large mandate to continue to lead and serve the community as mayor. I had a lot of political capital and would have four years to bring "Bridging to the Future" to its final chapter. We had accomplished so much already, but much remained to do, too.

In March 2000, I stood before my community as a complete

man, knowing now what it meant to truly love and be loved—
and having learned powerful lessons about living, learning,
loving, and letting go.

CHAPTER TEN

Bring It On

> *You know what the problem with the greater Phoenix area is? If you can't think of it on your own let me help. That problem would be the gay problem. Homosexual. Fag. Flamers. But rompers ["butt" pelled incorrectly]. Fudge packers. Queers. Funny boys. OKAY, the problem has been addressed. Our town, Tempe especially, has been infested with faggots like you and your people. I say burn the fags. Burn them all and we have no problem. Then the Boy Scouts will live long and prosper. Death to fags.*
>
> —email received October 5, 2000

The controversy arose from an innocent and honest conversation with a local reporter, whose story ignited a fire in the community that was then stoked by my adversaries, and yet I still couldn't believe what I was hearing. "They want a recall election over *this*?" I shook my head. "This is going to get very ugly," I said. I wasn't wrong.

One morning in mid-September 2000, a reporter from a

local alternative weekly newspaper, *Phoenix New Times*, phoned me at my ASU office where at that time I was director of federal and community relations, given the mayor's position was technically a part-time one, although in reality it was more than full-time.

The initial question was, "What are your thoughts about the United States Supreme Court's 5-4 decision to allow the Boy Scouts to discriminate in selecting their membership."

I answered, not really weighing my words carefully, but giving my opinion in a thoughtful way. The questions moved to the city United Way campaign, and the mixture of the two would take me, and the city, on a path no one was truly prepared for, especially me. The story that ran on September 21, 2000, read:

> The U.S. Supreme Court may think it's okay for the Boy Scouts to bar gay men and boys from participating in the venerable youth service club, but some Tempe city leaders say the organization should be prepared to lose the city's financial support.
>
> On Thursday, city administrators plan to tell the Tempe City Council that the city will sever its relationship with Valley of the Sun United Way if it continues to funnel hundreds of thousands of dollars a year to the local Boy Scouts organization.
>
> Tempe Mayor Neil Giuliano, who is openly gay, says the city has a clear and specific policy of non-discrimination and that it's wrong for the city to ignore that policy when it comes to charitable contributions.
>
> "If the United Way isn't living up to that [same policy], then we can't do business with them," Giuliano says.
>
> In a 5-4 June decision, the U.S. Supreme Court upheld a Boy Scouts executive board rule that prohibits openly gay men and boys from membership. The board believes gay men in particular are not appropriate role

models for boys, a position that many see as the kind of blatant discrimination that governments, political factions, and other organizations have been moving away from in recent years.

Giuliano says Tempe is one of those entities that has taken a strong position against discrimination—and needs to continue to hold the line.

"The Supreme Court has said the Boy Scouts can discriminate, and they have a right to do that," he says. "But then we have a right to say we think that's wrong."

The comments that I made to the reporter short-circuited what should have been a relatively straightforward matter. After reading my remarks in the newspaper, my ever-present and always alert detractors—and some new ones, too—seized their opportunity. They re-framed the issue not as a simple matter of making the Boy Scouts membership decisions comply with federal, state, and local policies about the use of public funds, but as the mayor advancing his "gay agenda" against the beloved Boy Scouts. Of course, I'd done nothing of the kind, but in politics, perception often overrides reality, and the whole issue spun out of control from there.

At the next city council meeting, Interim City Manager John Greco presented his recommendation to disallow the Boy Scouts from receiving United Way campaign contributions. No action was scheduled yet; it was on the agenda for information only.

The next day, I left for a Tempe Sister Cities trip to Zhenjiang, China for a week. The trip was bad timing, but I really believed that when I got back, the council would have ratified John's proposal and moved on to the next piece of business. Another case where I couldn't have been more wrong.

There's a saying that a politician must disappoint their constituents at a rate they can tolerate. I had not calculated that accurate advice.

While I was on the other side of the world, the issue blew up and out of control. Two of my council members, Hugh Hallman and Ben Arredondo, wrote a guest editorial that was published in the *Arizona Republic*, blasting the proposed policy and me. Some of the same forces that had marshaled themselves against me in earlier campaigns found new momentum and added their energy to the issue. The issue of whether the Boy Scouts should be disqualified from the United Way campaign—even though it was really the only alternative if we were to be true to our own policies—provided them with a new rallying cry. As always, I was the focal point for their homophobia. By the time I returned from Zhenjiang, the political heat had become beyond a flaming furnace—and some in the community wanted me to burn *literally* as well as politically. The emails and calls were flooding City Hall.

Every day the entire week I was away, stories ran in the both the local Tempe newspaper and the larger Phoenix metropolitan daily on the issue of the Boy Scouts and Tempe's United Way campaign. The perception was that I was attacking two beloved institutions: the Boy Scouts and the United Way. As it turned out, the chairperson of the metropolitan Phoenix United Way campaign that year was also the publisher of the *Arizona Republic* newspaper. A friend of mine worked for the newspaper and told me later that when the story broke, word went through the organization to crush the mayor in Tempe. If true, that would explain the unusually high amount of coverage of a Tempe issue in the statewide newspaper. You know what they say: never fight with those who buy their ink by the barrel. I had not heeded Betty Asher's advice very well: this was a battle poorly chosen, but I really had not thought I was choosing a battle when I stated my views. I was simply sharing my take on a public policy issue.

What's ironic is that I had led ASU's United Way campaign for several years in the mid-1990s. I was an insider and huge supporter of the organization and major donor, too. But I did believe what I had told the reporter: if the United Way wanted to support organizations—including the Boy Scouts—that discriminated, they were just wrong. In sharing those truthful, philosophical and innocent comments on a slow news day, I had unknowingly created a political tempest beyond my wildest expectations. More fuel was added to the blaze when John Greco was interviewed by the newspaper and said some inappropriate things that incited people further. To make it the perfect storm, we faced one of the biggest media controversies ever without a public information officer. Tempe's talented public information officer, Nachie Marquez, had just moved on to another job and hadn't yet been replaced. So we had no one to field questions from the press or to advise us on a media response while the issue unfolded.

When I returned from China in early October, this issue consumed my city. At first, I hoped that I could figure out a way to contain it, but it couldn't be done. There was no putting the toothpaste back into the tube this time. I issued a statement trying to clarify myself and explain how limited my role actually was in determining who was allowed to receive funds and who wasn't. I even encouraged city management to forget about any policy changes for the time being and leave things as they were. I apologized publicly for the way the entire issue was handled. Still, that was not enough for my adversaries on the council or in the community. They wanted a public flogging of the gay mayor who had dared to suggest money might be snatched away from the Boy Scouts in Tempe. Although the boys were often mentioned in the rhetoric and debate, in fact, the issue was never about the kids in the program. The real issue was, and remains, about the adults who teach kids that excluding people because they are different—specifically, because they are gay— is acceptable.

By speaking to that reporter, I had unintentionally created an issue that was perceived by some as an effort to promote a single-minded gay rights agenda. But the real issue was homophobia, not the Boy Scouts or the policy; when a straight colleague publicly shared the same view as the issue unfolded— in much harsher and more strident rhetoric than I—no one raised an eyebrow. There was no effort to throw him out of office, as had happened with me.

The reality was my comments had more to do with basic fairness than a gay rights agenda. I would have felt the same if the group had chosen to discriminate against blacks or Muslims or anyone else, but the perception was that it was a gay issue, and since I was gay, I was the leader. Religious right and other far right folks grabbed the reins early and ran with their long-awaited operation to oust me.

They filed the all the proper paperwork with the city clerk, and it was official. The recall process was under way. It involved collecting enough signatures to force another election and the timing in this case made it relatively easy for my adversaries to collect enough names: the 2000 U.S. presidential election was just a few weeks away. All my opposition had to do was position someone with a clipboard at each polling station and state their case to voters as they went in to do their civic duty. That was a highly contentious and very close presidential election; if you recall (no pun intended) it took a court decision to declare George W. Bush the victor over Al Gore months later— and in Tempe the turnout was high. My adversaries collected the nearly 4,000 signatures required to force a recall election for the office of mayor and attempt to have me removed from the office I had just been re-elected to with 70% of the vote just four months prior.

I was in my last term. I thought my days of campaigning were behind me. I had donated $10,000 of my remaining campaign funds toward an effort to build a new performing and visual arts center in Tempe. Aside from it being a cause I believed in quite passionately, I was sure I wouldn't need the funds. As they say, "If you want to make God laugh, tell Him your plans." I'm sure God was laughing as I assembled a team and marshaled the troops. I had to raise money all over again. I was running for mayor yet again, thanks to the recall effort. I was amazingly fortunate that nearly all of my previous campaign team and volunteers immediately regrouped. We organized fast.

This would be a different campaign. I had to choose my tone and words carefully. I was angry and annoyed by all of it. But the democratic process had advanced and as the sitting mayor I was determined to respect it even if, in my view, this tool of democracy was being misused. I was determined to retain and demonstrate my integrity and maintain the dignity of the office I held. I felt that was extremely important, not just politically, but as the right thing to do for the community.

According to Arizona recall election law, to remove an incumbent from office someone must *run* against the incumbent. If the recall is successful, that person assumes the incumbent's seat. Strategically, for me that meant that the first order of business was to keep any strong, credible candidates from entering the race. A strong challenger might just give the recall movement the weight and depth it needed to transform from a nuisance to something much more serious. This wasn't a public effort at all. Instead, it involved asking for the support of friends—and even former adversaries. As it turned out, I needn't have worried. Smart, political savvy, and educated people in the community knew the recall effort was not about my overall performance as mayor. They knew the recall wasn't about the Boy Scouts—or any of the other seven issues listed in the recall petition. They were much smarter than that.

Several former top city employees were approached by the recall leaders and asked to run, including a few who had been recently replaced by the interim city manager. The recall leaders hoped that those former employees had an axe to grind against my administration; they were wrong. They then turned to a former mayor, a very respected leader in the Mormon Church, and just about every former elected official in the community. All of them turned down the opportunity. While many of them disagreed with my views on the Boy Scouts and United Way, they did not see that disagreement as a reason to throw me out of office. Ultimately, only a part-time actor agreed to represent the recall and run for mayor. He wasn't fanatical over the Boy Scouts issue, but he was the only person they could convince to take on the part, and he could act. After all, the entire effort was political theater.

After my return from the Tempe Sister Cities China trip, I saw I had been deluged with hundreds of vitriolic emails. Clearly, my comments had touched a nerve with people in Tempe, and had been spun in such a way that brought out a bigotry and hatred that had been lurking below the surface. Late on the night I got home, I was going through the emails trying to get a sense of how I would respond to what were clearly religious-based views about my being gay and the issue itself.

Among the hateful messages was something very different: an email from one of the students enrolled in my Personal Leadership Development class at ASU. He was a young man who was attending ASU on the Leadership Scholarship I had created for out-of-state students. It read:

Your office said you were in China, but would be back soon. Please give me a call as soon as you can, I need some help with something. I'm not sure you know that my younger brother came to ASU as a freshman this semester. Last Friday night he tried to kill himself and almost jumped off the stairway on top of the Life Sciences Center on campus. He's gay and having a hard time with it all. My parents back east are deeply religious, and I heard once of some parents support group and am wondering if you know how to contact them. My brother has to move out of the dorm tomorrow and is seeing a counselor. I'm not sure if he can stay in school. I think my parents are flying out here. I'm just not sure what else to do or say and thought you might be able to help.

Good God.

The email was a few days old by that time. What had happened since he wrote it? Even though it was late, I called the student and spoke with him for quite a while, listening to his fear, frustration, and uncertainty. I told him about how his parents could track down their local chapter of Parents and Friends of Lesbians and Gays (PFLAG) and tried to be supportive of both him and his brother.

I had received calls like this one from people in search of answers, information, and support numerous times. One evening, I received a phone call from an agitated man. "My wife and I voted for you in every election," he began, but I could tell it wasn't going to be your average constituent call. "We know you're gay and heard you have talked to gay groups around town. We didn't know who else to call...our seventeen-year-old son just told us he is gay. We reacted terribly. Actually, we were more hurt he didn't trust us and tell us sooner. He got angry and ran out of the house. We don't want to call the police, we're not homophobic, but we don't know anyone who's gay, and we don't know what to do."

"Does he have his cell phone with him?" I asked.

"Yes, he always has it with him."

"Call him and calmly tell him you're sorry you over-reacted. Tell him you love him and you want him to come home, that he can always come home."

I gave them the number of the Phoenix-area PFLAG and encouraged them to call and asked them to let me know how things worked out.

I never again heard from that Tempe father, but years later while I was GLAAD president, a twenty-something guy came up to me in the grocery store when I was back in Tempe.

"Hey, are you the mayor?"

"Former, yes," I said.

"I think my mom and dad called you when they freaked out the night I came out to them about seven years ago."

Despite all the time that had passed, I remembered.

"Did you go home?"

"Yeah," he said, smiling. "They called me and asked me to come back. I didn't go that night, but I did go back. It was tough at first but now they are very supportive and we're pretty close."

"You're lucky they're your parents," I told him. Not all parents try as hard to come to understand as his had done.

"I know, and they're lucky I'm their son," he said confidently, and I'm certain that is true, too.

There were other encounters like this one. As I reflect on my years as a mayor and my years as a full-time activist, I see that those roles complimented each other and helped me grow and become the person and leader I am today. I have always been glad to help young people in the transition into their full identity, but there was something special about the email I received upon my return from China, coming when it did during the heat of so much homophobia in my political career, that gave me perseverance and strength of purpose.

Until I read that student's email and talked with him about his brother's life and death issues, I had been fearful of the recall. I was initially put on the defensive by the actions and intentions of this small group of misguided people, some of whom are still politically active in the community today, although they would probably not like the community reminded of their leadership in the recall against me. The current chair of the Republican Party in Tempe was the leader and spokesperson for the recall in 2001. Republican leadership in Tempe has become far Tea Party-right and very out of touch with most Tempeans. The wife of a former Republican state representative from Tempe was a recall effort leader as well. It's not an influential list, but not insignificant either. Some have professed the error of their involvement in the recall to others in the community. I am glad they might have evolved to a better place than where they were when they tried to run me out of office; I would hope we all evolve. None have ever said a word to me, however, and that's fine, too.

I had been thinking mainly about how to derail the recall with a strong show of support or with legal challenges. I was worried, too, because some of my supporters felt I said too much and pushed the envelope too far. I wasn't sure they would all rally to my defense as I would need them to. I honestly could not predict what would come of the situation. A few supporters did fall away in silence.

But when I read that young man's email and talked to him on the phone, my fear left me. Fear was replaced by resolve and strength of purpose. Maybe I had pushed the envelope and made people uncomfortable being so vocal about the discrimination we all knew was taking place. It had not been my intention, but I did not regret that I had said what I had said. I had spoken the truth.

That young man's email reminded me that, whatever the political storms of the moment, living in the open meant something important—not just for me, but for others like this young man and his family. I had a valuable role to play in the larger community and I would not run scared. I would not let these people throw me out of office because I spoke up about an issue important to gay people—to all people—whether they understood that yet or not.

My conversation with that worried undergraduate student in the quiet darkness of my home office late one night was a moving moment for me and convinced me that I had done the right thing. When I hung up the phone, I knew I would do whatever was necessary, within the law, not only to beat back the effort of a few closed-minded individuals, but defeat it so strongly and resoundingly that they understood once and for all their hate and fear would never succeed. If they wanted a fight, they would get one. My attitude was "bring it on."

My recall campaign team met a couple times and tossed around the required components of the campaign: budget, core responsibilities, timing, and other factors. Message was the most important, as it most always is, and we came up with a brilliant and perfect strategy. The issue, we decided, was not Neil Giuliano as the mayor, not his sexuality, not anything related to me personally, not the way I had performed my duties as mayor of Tempe. The issue for voters to determine was whether the recall effort itself was valid in the first place. Our message to Tempe voters would be simple and finite: "The recall is wrong. Just wrong."

That message appeared on road signs, in mailings, in speeches, everywhere. It wasn't about how good a mayor I had been, what we had accomplished as a community; none of that mattered because none of that was the real issue. The message was that the entire recall election was bogus, organized by anti-gay bigots, and hate and bigotry were not legitimate reasons to oust someone from office. That was it, plain and simple. Although our opposition tried to cloak their campaign in other issues, people knew the truth. Editorial after editorial in the local newspapers and on radio echoed that truth. The recall was wrong, just wrong.

In late spring 2001, with the actual recall election over three months in the future, several of the area mayors and I met with Senator McCain to discuss those issues where our local concerns and federal money intersected, among other things. As the meeting ended, he asked me to stay behind. We chatted a bit and he was very direct.

"Do you need any help?" he asked.

"No, I think we're going to be okay."

"I want you tell me if you need help," he said. "We'll do anything we can to help you. Both Cindy and me."

"Thank you, I will," I said. "I really appreciate it."

It wasn't the first time Senator McCain had helped me. During my first "openly gay" campaign in 1998, he endorsed me and allowed us to use his remarks and his photograph on a postcard mailing. The Religious right leadership in the Phoenix area was furious that he had endorsed the campaign of an openly gay mayor, but as I've said, John McCain and I have a long history. Despite his current public positions on LGBT issues, which I find indefensible, he has always been helpful and loyal to me personally.

As the recall battle began in earnest, another problem cropped up. My one-time-opponent-than-supporter Barbara Sherman had become an opponent again, perhaps because I refused to accept and take her positions on many of the issues of the day. She and eight of her followers challenged the legal validity of the voter-approved mayoral term increase from two years to four years. They claimed the vote was illegal because of an alleged missed deadline for a required election publicity pamphlet mailing. In May of 2000, Proposition 100 had passed by a vote of 9,155 votes in favor and 5,650 against. It had not been a contentious issue, no one really campaigned for or against it; it was just put on the ballot by the city council, without my participation or vote, and left for the citizens to determine. And they had.

But this group wanted the mayor's seat open in two years and not four, so it aligned for Councilman Hallman to seek the office at the end of his four-tear council term. In fact, he filed paperwork, started a campaign, and prepared to run for the office just in case his friends' court case was successful.

I sought out Andy Hurwitz, a well-known and respected attorney in Arizona, to represent me. I had been told he understood these issues well and might be willing to help.

"Sure, we'll defend it," he said. "They don't have a case. This is just a distraction."

Ultimately, all this small group of dissatisfied people accomplished was to waste time and taxpayer money in service to their own political motives. Pretty transparent, but fine, we dealt with it.

Within days of learning of the plans for a recall election, we held a rally, and even with only a few days' notice, hundreds of people attended to support me, including former Republican Arizona Attorney General Grant Woods and five of the six city council members. We received letters of support from Senator McCain, Governor Jane Dee Hull, and others who were going to stand with me against the threat of removing me from office, and read them to the assembled crowd. We had hoped that such a strong showing of support from a wide array of community leaders might convince the "recallers" to drop their misguided campaign, but they were determined. And so it continued.

After the recall petition signatures were counted and verified, the recall election was scheduled for a day that would change us all: September 11, 2001. That tragic day would put into sharp focus just how trivial the entire year-long recall effort truly was.

In many ways, the period from October 2000, when the recall process started, through to January 2002, when the Arizona Supreme Court ruled on the voter-approved term extension issue, was more stressful for me than the events leading up to my public statement coming out as a gay man. It was a prolonged and continuous battling, week in and week out. As I reflect back now on what was accomplished during that time period, however, I have to acknowledge those difficulties made me a stronger leader and taught me a great deal about other people. Although the protracted fight took its toll on my emotions and personal life, I never once considered resigning and my ability to govern through the tough times was actually empowering. Even after a four-and-a-half hour city council meeting with hundreds of very angry people calling for me to step down, I refused to give in to the bigotry and hatred encouraged and created by a small group of zealots. I might have been exhausted quite often, but I was determined they would never get the best of me. They would not win.

Any campaign, recall or otherwise, takes coordination and funding. We raised about $70,000 locally and nationally, including from many supporters from the gay community. The Victory Fund in Washington, D.C., which raises money for openly gay candidates, contributed to my effort. I found the recall campaign to be even more engaging, more fast paced and intense, than my four previous mayoral campaigns because there was so much at stake; no one wants to end their service by getting *thrown* out of office. The core of my campaign operations team once again included stalwarts Manjula, Rob, Charles, Luke Lucas, and about 100 volunteers. They were determined and focused beyond previous campaigns as well. In some ways, this was about their reputations as well as mine, since they had spent many years getting me elected and re-elected. A successful recall election was not going to be the way it would end for this team. My public campaign team once again included Virginia Tinsley and Rudy Campbell as my co-chairs. Their longevity and respect in the community was an immeasurable asset to the campaign and to me personally.

We targeted our core voters: the more long-time Tempeans who lived in the two geographically middle zip codes in Tempe and who had voted in the legislative elections but had not voted in city elections. We sent 15,000 pieces of mail to those people twice. As recall Election Day approached, the campaign intensified. From July until September 11, 2001, I was focused and engaged daily on winning the recall election, even while continuing to govern and lead the city.

I had decided that the truth had to be told, so we created and sent mailings exposing the champions of the recall effort for the right-wing bigots they were. They actually assisted us in the effort because we simply reprinted their hateful messages on the back of an oversized postcard. Rob designed it and on the front of the card was a photograph of an angry skinhead, mouth wide open in a scream, with the headline: "Don't let hate and bigotry change the future of Tempe."

It was a radical approach that could have easily backfired, but we accepted that possibility as a calculated risk. The image and the reactions to the mailing got us newspaper and TV coverage, giving our message far more exposure than we could have afforded. And it reminded everyone what the root of the recall effort was all about.

I also did something just ten days before the recall election that could have become an issue, but I was fully prepared to accept the fallout if it had. Two great friends, a gay couple in Phoenix, asked me to preside over their "marriage" ceremony that was going to be held in Bisbee. I had randomly met Jim before my first city council campaign while biking through the city—we both stopped for a drink at the same location and struck up a conversation. He and Sam had become great friends of mine over the years and as such I would not deny them my involvement in their most special day because of the recall campaign. I drove down to Bisbee to spend the night and "officiate" at their ceremony on September 1, 2001. It was all flawless and fabulous, with a hundred or so of their family and friends gathered for their special day.

Finally, September 11, 2001, arrived.

Very early that morning I was standing in a church parking lot waiting to be interviewed live on our local Fox affiliate station. I was used to being at polling places early on election days, it was my ritual.

Suddenly, the reporter said, "Wait a second, we are going live to New York—a plane has crashed into the World Trade Center."

My first thought, beyond the obvious tragedy underway, was very local and specific, involving air travel and the issue of where a new publicly funded football stadium was to be built.

As I huddled with the TV crew around the tiny monitor and watched the story unfold, I quickly realized how unimportant the local stadium issue really was. We saw the second plane slam into the second tower, and the horror of that moment is forever stamped into my memory. I remember thinking, *This is an act of war*. Shuddering at the images flickering on the reporter's monitor in that church parking lot, I understood instantly that the United States had just been attacked. This was not random.

The interview was canceled and the group disbanded. As I drove to City Hall, I heard the news of the Pentagon attack.

Our city emergency operations center was convened, putting all police, fire, and emergency personnel on the highest alert status. It was similar to Y2K preparation when I also reviewed ready-to-go, unsigned documents to initiate certain duties and responsibilities as mayor in times of war and terrorist attacks, in case the city needed to take sudden action to provide for and protect our people. The uncertainty over what was happening, as well as when the next strike might come, weighed heavier on me than any other time during my tenure. The recall election became the farthest thing from my mind. The safety and security of my community was my only priority.

I asked questions and listened intently as various briefings took place during the day. Was our water supply protected? Power stations, bridges? How would we communicate with citizens? Were all emergency operation plans in a ready state? What were we hearing from state and federal authorities?

Unlike those in New York City, the voting polls in Arizona remained open. By 9:00 A.M. I had suspended all of my recall election campaign efforts and was on-call at home or present at City Hall. Not surprisingly, the voter turnout was almost non-existent in the morning and early afternoon. But then something unexpected happened. When people began arriving home in late afternoon, earlier than usual because of the horrific events, they went to vote in droves. It was surprising. Perhaps voters turned out in an effort to restore some semblance of normalcy or claim some small measure of control during a day that had turned everything upside down. Perhaps they voted to express their patriotism and appreciation for a country where democracy is real and individuals play a crucial role in the operation of government. Perhaps it was simply to tell the terrorists responsible for the catastrophic events of that day, "You will not defeat us."

Whatever those voters' reasons were, they turned out in record numbers. The recall election brought out the largest voter turnout in modern Tempe history to that point, topped only by the year when eighteen-year-old citizens first had the right to vote. Too bad today's eighteen year old citizens don't vote in similar numbers.

We switched TV channels from CNN to our local Tempe 11 when we thought the election results would be available. We did not wait long. Within a couple minutes, city clerk Kathy Matz, who had been my very able and dedicated chief of staff for almost three years prior to taking that post, appeared and read the recall election results.

2001 Mayoral Recall Election
Neil G. Giuliano   16,125 (67.7%)
Gene Ganssle   7,689 (32.3%)

A landslide victory with sixty-eight percent of the votes in a bitter recall election would normally have been cause for huge celebration—especially when the election symbolized a triumph over hate and bigotry. But, of course, on that sad day the congratulatory cheers were muted and brief. There was no real celebration that night.

I took a phone call from a council colleague who informed me that friend and Tempe resident Gary Bird, a member of our Industrial Development Authority Board, had been in one of the towers and there had been no word of him. The worst proved true, and the community lost Gary that day, the only Arizonan to be murdered in the terrorist attacks of 9/11. His widow, Donna, and I share mutual friends and philanthropic interests, as well as love for the Tempe community and we get together occasionally. Once she called for advice about how to help the child of a neighbor she was sure was gay. Donna's concern for others—even in the face of her own tragedies—is one of the many things I admire about her.

Though my emotions were very raw, I had to say something to the small group of friends and family who gathered after the election results were announced. I had to acknowledge the end of an eleven-month political war, the hard work of everyone involved with the victory, the consequences to me personally and to the Tempe community, but also its insignificance compared to the war that had just begun that morning. I knew I would have to talk about how we would all have to summon the courage and strength to move forward together.

It was difficult. I remained composed, as I knew I had to be, but it was emotional. I shared a few words of thanks and said we should all take stock of what's truly important, and come together beyond where we had been, to form a stronger community. We had been tested that day, locally with a senseless political fight and nationally with an attack on our soil that took many lives. We would rise again and be stronger.

With the recall election behind me, the only remaining challenge to my authority and tenure was the court case challenging the length of my term.

The case wound through the Superior Court of Maricopa County, where we won, then on to the state Appellate Court, which vacated the lower court opinion ruling the issue was vague, and ultimately arrived at the Arizona Supreme Court.

On January 11, 2002, I had just stepped out of the elevator on the third floor of City Hall when my phone rang and I stopped to answer.

"Hello," I said nervously.

It was Andy with the news: "You're going to be the mayor until 2004. It was unanimous. We won."

I took a deep breath, sighed, and thanked Andy, telling him he had been fantastic and how grateful I was for his work. I thought to plan a dinner with Andy and supporters to celebrate and toast the victory, but it never happened. I neglected to show my deep appreciation for his stellar defense. I know better, and my father in particular would be disappointed in me, as I am in myself.

As word spread around the third floor of City Hall, there was a bit of cheering, unusual since city employees are civil servants and not political appointees. Whether I was their mayor for two years or four had no impact on their job security, but to hear their enthusiasm for us continuing to work together was appreciated and affirming. The staff members always know what is really going on, and they knew the motivation behind the court case from the get-go. I should have been jumping up and down with cheerful excitement, but in reality I was just glad it was over. I held no animosity toward the political moves of my adversaries. It was not a time to gloat, it was a time to move on. Their effort had been exposed for what it was, and that is their legacy.

Yet another major political battle was now behind me.

I had two years remaining in office and plenty of work left to do, but in the back of my mind, I had already begun to think about what might lay ahead for me, as soon as this final term as Tempe's mayor was history.

CHAPTER ELEVEN

Good Transitions

Some of my close friends and supporters put it to me very directly.

"You *have* to run again," they insisted. "There isn't anyone else."

I appreciated the sentiment, but I knew that it wasn't true. There just wasn't anyone else they thought could do the job as well and they wanted to support me.

After winning re-election in 2000 with 70% of the vote, beating a recall election with 68% in 2001, and then in 2002 having the state Supreme Court determine that the legal challenge to reduce my term from four years to two had no merit whatsoever, my constituents seemed to really want me to run again. "You have to run." I heard it everywhere I went.

It was flattering to hear and I admit I listened to their arguments for why I should seek a fifth term. My political profile was higher than ever and my leadership of the council and the community had never been stronger after having weathered non-stop political storms for two solid years. My adversaries had thrown everything possible at me, and I survived. By 2003, things in my political world were a far cry from where they had been in 2001— a lifetime from where they had been when I first ran for city council in 1989. I had grown so much, as one would hope and expect. As all of us experience, things that are new and perhaps even make us uncomfortable at first become second nature as we learn, stretch and become more than we once were. It was a great feeling and one of the best reasons for taking on new assignments, tasks, and obligations. That internal feeling of accomplishment and growth is the fuel for reaching beyond our grasp.

There was a little part of me that was willing to be persuaded to run again, but in my heart, I already knew that I wouldn't do it. From the very beginning I had said I would run for mayor four times. Back then, it was a two-year term and I expected to serve for eight years. It turned out to be ten. Fine.

Of course, politicians change their minds on self-imposed term limit commitments all the time, and I believe I could have done so and been successful—but I just didn't want to be that guy. People have said a lot of things about me—and I'm sure they'll say plenty of things about me in the future—but going back on a promise to voters isn't going to be one of them.

By the end of my term in 2004, I would have been mayor of Tempe for a decade. I knew of the good work in that decade, but as I mulled over all the pleas that I run again, I pulled out my initial campaign booklet, "Bridging to the Future," and looked over the initiatives that I'd identified when I decided to run in the first place, back in 1993.

Like most brochures, it was really just bullet points— highlights of what I saw as critical needs and issues for the city of Tempe—but it was very special to me. I had crafted the content with thought and careful intent. Rob Kubasko designed it, making it look very cool and futuristic, and it had captured the attention of the community at time when few really knew me well and I was little more than the "also ran" candidate. One newspaper had cited that booklet as one reason for endorsing me. It had been my initial guide and agenda for becoming and serving as mayor.

I was still in the closet then, but one of the things I identified in 1993 was the need for Human Relations Commission for the city. I could see that the city was more multi-racial, more multi-ethnic -and of course, multi-orientation—than it had ever been. Cities and towns across the country were engaging their citizens in this type of participation, and it made sense for Tempe. I remember suggesting the idea to Mayor Harry Mitchell while I was still a city councilman, and his response was that a diverse group of people was already involved in the city. True, but I saw challenges and tensions that required sensitivity, and I thought that education and information could help us address them as a community. We created the commission and today it is a very vital part of the fabric of inclusiveness in Tempe.

Check.

Transportation issues had been of great importance. In 1993 I had promised the citizens of Tempe that, if elected mayor, I would work on building a more comprehensive, more multi-modal transportation program in Tempe. This had taken a great deal of work, including getting voters to approve a .05 percent sales tax in an election just a few weeks after I had publicly come out, in order to provide a local match to the federal funding we had applied for, working with the politics of metropolitan Phoenix and obtaining multiple feasibility and ridership studies. The result: we have a twenty-one mile light rail line that runs through Tempe, expanded bus service and bike lanes, and an overall system that is exceeding all expectations in terms of community ridership and usage. During my last two years as mayor, I served as Chair of the Transportation Planning Committee of the Maricopa Association of Governments, helping to shape the $14.3 billion twenty-year plan for the entire region that was approved by voters in November of 2004. Over 50% of the funds would go toward increased freeway capacity, but we ensured 33% of the funding for mass transit projects, vital to a land-locked city located in the geographic center of an urban area like Tempe.

Double Check.

In the materials for my first campaign, I outlined my plans for the Rio Salado urban redevelopment project. Rio Salado was the name of a dry riverbed and the project for revitalizing it into useable public space. It was one of those projects that everyone thought would be a great thing—until it was time to pay for it. It had been talked about since 1966 when an architecture class at ASU had been given the assignment of designing how to return water to the dry river bottom. In 1987 a regional property tax increase to fund a valley-wide Rio Salado project failed, but within the city of Tempe, voters supported it. People in Tempe never stopped talking about trying to make something happen in the dusty riverbed that cut like a scar through the area just north of downtown. Most Tempeans thought reclaiming Rio Salado would make a wonderful addition to city life.

While running for mayor I used the image of the dry river bottom in campaign materials and talked about Rio Salado as a visionary project that was important for our economic development and our sense of community. It would give us a gathering place, reclaim our city center, help define the city as a destination, and one day be an economic engine. After I was elected, we did another study on the feasibility of the project and created a finance plan. Pat Flynn, Dave Fackler, and Steve Nielsen comprised the city staff trio that drove the day-to-day work of a talented team of professionals while I gave voice to the vision and solidified council and community support. There remained a small but vocal group of residents who felt the river bottom should stay as it was, but they were far outnumbered, so we marched on to make the Rio Salado dream a reality.

Someone should write an entire book on the creation of the Tempe Town Lake and Rio Salado Project; I won't attempt to share the entire story here. I will say this much: it is an amazing story of how a community held on to a vision and made it a reality, overcoming challenge after challenge, creating partnerships that others would have thought impossible.

On August 8, 1997 we held a groundbreaking ceremony to begin construction of Tempe Town Lake and by June 1999 we began to fill it with water from Central Arizona Project. You would think that filling the lake once it was constructed would be a "no-brainer" but instead it became a political issue. One member of the council, who would be a future mayor, spoke out against filling the lake for economic reasons, setting off a duel of guest editorials in the local newspaper. My view was practical: if we did not fill the lake while the project had momentum, the dream of Rio Salado might not ever happen. We had to grasp our destiny rather than wait for the "perfect moment." The truth about perfect moments is they never appear. You have to create them.

Fortunately, my philosophy won the day, 6-1.

By July 14 our community's lake was full, and it was a beautiful and overwhelming sight. Water was once again in the Salt River and it was, as we used to say "a river once more." Today the area is the second most visited destination in Arizona, behind the Grand Canyon, and many consider it the "Central Park" of the entire region. It hasn't been without problems and challenges; one of the rubber inflatable dams burst in summer of 2010, giving the naysayers some air-time, but it has since been repaired. The project is far from complete, and will continue to evolve and add value to the community for decades to come.

Triple check.

The Tempe Performing Arts Center and the adjacent seventeen-acre park was approved by voters in May 2000 and was built right on the banks of that man-made lake at Rio Salado. None of that complex project was easy to advance either and, of course, we had political resistance from some of the usual folks, including about where the facility should be located once it had been approved. But it was always my vision to have it become our little Sydney Opera House on the water, and it has become just that for our region, now with an awesome pedestrian bridge connecting the center to the north side of the lake. Much of the initial work on the center happened during the time of the recall and the lawsuits challenging my election. But we pressed on and persevered. Supporting the arts in Tempe had been included prominently in my "Bridging to the Future" vision, and with the help of a lot of people, we had exceeded all expectations.

Triple check again.

Neighborhood activist and friend Dan Durrenberger helped me formulate a comprehensive neighborhood engagement and enhancement program we called Tempe Neighborhoods Tomorrow (TNT). With great staff support from MaryAnne Corder, it became a wonderful way to keep in touch, hear ideas, and respond to concerns of the many community leaders throughout the city. In 2000 it morphed into an official city commission with a respected and influential voice. It was yet another example of what I had learned from all my research of leadership: you actually have more power when you empower others. And for an elected official desiring to build a strong connection with constituents, that is critical.

Quadruple check and extremely significant because this was about what people experience outside their front door, not what they read on the front page.

Crime prevention efforts, economic development, city council operations, regional issues, youth violence, city/university relations, recycling, zoning issues, and even the Mayor's Youth Advisory Committee were all topics I created an agenda for, either before or once elected. I made sure others on the council and people in the community took the lead on an area or two, never forgetting what I had learned in high school leadership activities with Key Club: people support what they help create. Most of the time it didn't need to be done "my way," it just had to happen. And, for the overwhelming most part, it did.

I felt particularly proud of what we'd been able to do for Tempe when the city won the 2003 All-American City Award, a recognition of the National Civic League for outstanding success in community problem solving that is considered the "Oscar" for a local government. My chief of staff at the time, Steve Zastrow, took the lead lining up those who would be involved and, along with Josh Lader and others on my team, was a lead architect of the presentation that brought it home for Tempe. It certainly wasn't my award alone, but it was especially rewarding. I had been so embattled during my tenure as mayor, receiving that recognition toward the close of my fourth term really made me realize how much one can accomplish if you respect, but don't empower, the naysayers. Governing is an art, and staying focused on the big picture and not getting pulled in on the little issues that pop up every day can be a challenge.

When I am asked to identify critical characteristics for successful leadership, I always respond: discernment. If one can't successfully discern when to engage, and more importantly when not to, it is possible to spend too much precious time putting out fires that others should be handling.

But when you keep your head down and do your work, and empower others to the best of your ability with the welfare of the citizens in mind, you end up with a thriving, well-governed city—something that requires more than just functioning streetlights, reliable trash pickup, and city services. You end up with a place where people gather together, where they feel included, where they offer the best of themselves and participate in making things better. You end up with a better community.

One thing I wasn't able to accomplish was bringing a new stadium for the Arizona Cardinals and the Fiesta Bowl to Tempe, thanks to the city of Phoenix leaders and their relationship with the Federal Aviation Authority (FAA).

First, you have to know that the Arizona Cardinals have a great relationship and history with the city of Tempe. In fact, their corporate headquarters and training facility remain in

Tempe. We wanted their new stadium in our city limits, too—the voters of the county approved a rental car sales tax to pay for it, and I was one of the only mayors in the region to spend political capital campaigning for the proposition.

We submitted a proposal to the entity that would decide on a location for the new facility; so did the cities of Phoenix, Mesa, and one of the Native American communities. Tempe won.

But it was a short-lived victory. Before long the city of Phoenix, who had lost out in the site competition, opined: "It's too close to Sky Harbor Airport, it's going to cause an air traffic hazard issue. We don't want a tragic accident."

In my view, Phoenix had decided the site was too close to their downtown core, near a site where they wanted to build a new convention center, and used the proximity to the airport to shoot down our stadium site. It would be an "air navigation hazard" they claimed and proceeded to line up the FAA and other officials to back up their position. It was bogus; there were clearly mitigation efforts that could have been applied and have been applied in other jurisdictions to make the stadium location work. But with Tempe's history of complaining about the airport's noise, Phoenix was not inclined to be an ally.

Of course, several studies had been conducted before we won the stadium—and no one had seemed to find the location's proximity to the airport to be an insurmountable problem, the challenges could be overcome and it was the best location, right on the proposed light rail line, from a taxpayer investment standpoint. The airport is as close to downtown Phoenix as the proposed stadium site and no one had ever found the lights and tall buildings of the city to be a navigation hazard.

We came up with a plan to move the stadium to the west to appease the FAA. We worked a quick deal to buy an existing apartment complex to make room for it. I had met with the mayor of Phoenix at the Doubletree Hotel during the height of the controversy, seeking a solution that could keep the stadium in Tempe. He stated quite clearly: "You can have your stadium, but we have to agree to talk about other issues with regard to the airport." That seemed reasonable, and I took that commitment as good news. But that commitment did not hold, perhaps it was never intended to. There's not a nice way to say it: we were screwed. And we had no capacity to make it otherwise.

It was time to pitch yet another idea, not a new one, but it was my Hail Mary.

I approached Arizona State University. I had a very respectful and open working relationship with President Lattie Coor, who remains one of the leaders I admire the most in Arizona. Too bad he never wanted to enter the elected office arena, not that one can blame him for that fact. There was suitable space available on the perimeter of the university campus: the golf driving range not far from the current ASU football stadium. Perhaps the university and the professional team could partner to build a stadium that could be shared between professional and university activities. The university could then reclaim and repurpose the land where the current stadium was located. I knew there was no love lost between the university and the professional team, but this could be a win-win for everyone.

The university leadership was not warm to the idea, and I understood the pressures Lattie was facing from his constituency; suggesting the ultimate tearing down of Sun Devil Stadium was heresy to many. As a loyal alum who had been student body president and in charge of the Alumni Association, I understood. But I still thought it was a sound public policy option to the benefit of taxpayers.

We had a meeting to discuss it. I was both an employee of the university and the mayor, and I believed I had a good and respectful relationship with my colleagues at ASU. I didn't know that inside the university administration, some were fuming that I would dare suggest ASU share a new stadium with the Cardinals. They had been sharing with the professional team since the Cardinals had arrived from St. Louis; it was supposed to have been a short-term arrangement, but the powers that be in Phoenix never lived up to their promise to build a new stadium for the Cardinals. They remained in the collegiate facility, which had not been designed to professional football standards for fans. And, of course, it was all about money, too. Stadiums bring in revenue, and sharing revenue is a tough concept for many.

It became clear that the university would not work with us to carve out a site that would work for a new joint-use stadium, which I still think was a missed opportunity on behalf of county taxpayers, although I was not blind to the level of unhappiness that would bring to my fellow Sun Devils. If I had been blind, the call from a member of the Arizona Board of Regents made it crystal clear:

"Mayor, we're not doing business with the Cardinals ever again."

We tried. The Hail Mary would not be caught. Ultimately, the stadium was awarded to Glendale, Arizona, on a site in the far west valley that had previously been home to nothing but cotton fields.

An epic failure on my part.

It's ironic because as I write ASU is trying to figure out how to create the tools needed to help fund the vast improvements necessary for the aging Sun Devil Stadium. I hope they are successful. But we could have had a brand new state-of-the art stadium, built and operated to the benefit of taxpayers for both teams. It would have been a facility and complex that any collegiate recruit would have been thrilled to share with a professional team. Collegiate athletes want to be close to professional sports. The upsides outweighed the challenges and downsides, in my view. One memorable quote I offered came during this saga, at a news conference when we were addressing all the obstacles in our way to remain the home of the Fiesta Bowl and the Arizona Cardinals: "Our challenges will equal the greatness we desire." It was true, we desired to make something really great happen, and that is never easy. In this case, it just was not to be.

Even more ironic are the current reports that the ASU baseball program is now considering the concept of a new stadium partnership with the Chicago Cubs for their spring training games in Arizona. The deal would allow ASU to reclaim the land where their baseball stadium now sits, which is prime real estate. It's the same kind of resource-driven deal that I was trying to broker for the university with the Cardinals.

In the end, we lost the stadium fight, but I'm not one to dwell on losses. We immediately started talking about luring the Insight Bowl from downtown Phoenix's major league baseball park to Sun Devil Stadium—and that did happen, although I had left the mayor's office by the time the deal came together.

Win some, lose some.

Looking back at my "Bridging to the Future" campaign materials from 1993, I realized I had accomplished just about everything I set out to accomplish as mayor. I had grown into the role very well, had risen to be a leader of my peers in the region and even nationally in some respects, and advanced some very significant policies and projects that would far outlast my tenure in office. I felt that I was ready to move on and discover what else life had in store for me. I admit, there was also an element of "leave while they want you to stay" too.

Though it was wonderful to have so many people supporting, believing, wanting to help, I knew I was the one who would have to do the job and four more years would be a long time. I issued a public statement in November of 2003, thanking everyone for their support but making it clear that I wasn't going to seek a fifth term under any circumstances.

That statement was the beginning of a long farewell tour—à la Cher—culminating with two big events in April and May 2004, not counting the one with sixty-three friends from across the country who joined me on a cruise around Hawaii in March. We called it the "Mayor's Farewell Cruise" and it was an amazing week of parties, a group excursion to Little Makena Beach, great meals with friends, and a ton of laughs. The first

Tempe farewell event was the fancy tribute dinner at Tempe Mission Palms Hotel with lots of speakers and testimonials from members of the business community and private citizens. Senator John McCain and Governor Janet Napolitano sent video greetings. The attendees donated $75,000 for a piece of public art to be installed in the park at Tempe Town Lake in my honor. Virginia had talked with the Municipal Arts Commission, and some key leaders had said they would match the funds we had raised, which would mean $150,000 for a public art piece. It hasn't happened yet, local politics being what they are, but it's quite an honor and I think it's appropriate given my very public support for the arts in the community. Someday it will happen and it will be grand.

Just having a piece of art dedicated in my honor one day would have been tribute enough, but there was more. The council had passed a resolution naming the entire south bank of the town lake, between Rural Road and the Mill Avenue bridges, the Neil Giuliano Lakeside Park. When they made that announcement at the tribute dinner, I was completely overcome, as I know I will be again someday when the park dedication event is held and the signage goes up. That will be something I wish my parents could have seen. It was tough not to burst into tears as I told the assembled audience how, when I moved to Tempe, Arizona as a seventeen-year-old college freshman, I hadn't even known where Tempe City Hall was and never dreamed I would learn, grow, and rise to one day be elected mayor and serve for ten years. I tried to thank all the many people who had helped me. It was a marvelous and tremendously emotional evening.

The second event was held down at Tempe Town Lake and was an open picnic for the community. I talked with everyone, we took group photos that I later signed for the hundreds of residents who came by, and it was a very fun time. My mom attended and she made a point of thanking the many people who had helped me over the years. The photo we took that day is a special one to me.

The various city departments created and made some very nice presentations to me as I prepared to depart after a decade. It took a few weeks just to box things up, and a good number of boxes of papers and materials were provided to the Tempe Historical Museum. I carried home just three boxes of items and things I had accumulated over my tenure, including the pen set Mom had given me the night of my first swearing in, in 1994, that had sat on my desk for all ten years.

One presentation by the Public Works Department was not to me, but had been something I had pushed for a long time. As a university community, Tempe has a lot of young people, and we couldn't afford to be blind to the fact that they drink alcohol. In a phrase, they party. There is a stretch of curved road around Gammage Auditorium that one can't avoid when driving around campus. There was a place on a traffic light pole to add a large "Don't Drink and Drive" message, back-lit at night, to remind everyone to be careful and not risk driving after drinking. The Public Works Department created the sign and invited me out to the site to see it up close before it was installed. It is still there today and if just one person heeds the message and thinks twice about driving drunk, it will have been worth the effort.

My many friends and supporters in the gay community wanted to help me celebrate my mayoral years, too. I had been "out" as mayor for eight of my ten years. We planned a weekend of "Red, White, and You" events—and friends from all over the country flew in for my final weekend as mayor, which would include the annual July Fourth events for the community. About 300 people came to a backyard pool party at my friend and former state legislator Steve May's Paradise Valley home. A group of about twenty of us stayed at the Buttes Resort for the weekend and attended the Fourth of July celebration at Tempe Beach Park. The male couples were quite comfortable holding hands or standing with arms around each others' shoulders as the fireworks blasted into the hot, dry Arizona summer sky. Most were from large urban cities where standing arm in arm with your boyfriend watching fireworks would have never been seen as out of place or a big deal. But we were in Arizona, in 2004, and men showing affection for other men in public simply did not happen outside of a gathering specifically for the gay community. Yet here we were. I stood back and behind the crowd and observed them, interspersed with local dignitaries and others in the VIP section, and thought of the journey I had been on, and that I had led my community on, to get to this night. I thought back to that night in 1996, just eight years prior, when I feared my truth being revealed, and the recall campaign press conference that had been held on the very spot where we now stood to watch the fireworks. My community had been transformed, and had adjusted to a new norm of acceptance. We were welcome. What a journey it had been to get to that night. I am certain no one else thought much of it at all, but it was absolutely one of my proudest moments.

After fourteen years on the city council, ten of them as mayor, I left office officially in July 2004. I exited on my own terms and timetable. And I felt very good about my tenure, what I had accomplished and what it meant in a much broader sense. The broad accolades that had poured in helped erase the doubts I still had about the things that did not go as planned, the projects that tanked, the battles I had not won. On balance, those who had watched elected officials govern for much longer than I had been around were offering a pretty darn good critique of my years of leadership. I had accomplished nothing by myself; working with others is the true essence of leadership in my view. I had sought and accepted the opportunity to have influence within my community, on the views and beliefs of others, to leave a mark and make the city a better place than when I had arrived. That average skinny high school kid who yearned to fit in and make a contribution had done okay after all. If one had told me as I arrived in Tempe in 1974 that in thirty years I would be concluding a decade as mayor of the city, I would have thought it an outrageous and preposterous projection. And yet it came to be.

Former Mesa, Arizona, mayor and friend Peggy Rubach had given me a framed copy of the ancient Athenian Pledge when I was first elected mayor:

We will never bring disgrace to this, our city, by any act of dishonesty or cowardice, nor ever desert our suffering comrades in the ranks. We will fight for the ideals and sacred things of the city, both alone and with many; we will revere and obey the city's laws and do our best to incite a like respect and reverence in those above us who are prone to annul and set them at naught. We will strive unceasingly to quicken the public's sense of civic duty, that thus, in all these ways, we will transmit this city not only not less, but greater, better and more beautiful than it was transmitted to us.

Those Greeks were pretty spot on back in 335 B.C. The framed pledge hung in my office for a decade. I read it often as mayor, and it's in my home office today.

* * *

The mayoral election to select my successor, sadly, was as ugly as they come. I supported the man who had stood with me for many years, even though I had won and he had lost in the city council election of 1990. Dennis Cahill was the council member who had rushed out of City Hall that July night in 1996 to give ol' Fritz a piece of his mind after he intimated he knew I was gay. He wasn't slick or especially articulate; he was a bricklayer by profession, led with his heart, knew the issues, was qualified for the position and had earned the right to seek the office as a credible candidate. I knew it would be a long shot for him to win, but he had stood with me in tough times, so I would stand with him. He would have to beat the former council member who *was* slick and articulate. Dennis lost, partly because of the very negative campaign employed against him by his one-time ally, and partly because of his own stumbles. I had backed the losing candidate, and offered the full support and capacity of the mayor's office to Mayor-elect Hallman for the nearly two-month transition period.

My last day as mayor was a full one. I walked around City Hall and thanked staff, as I had been doing for a few weeks throughout the city offices. I sat in my now-empty office and made some phone calls to long-time supporters and friends and reviewed my comments for the evening's ceremonies. I chatted with my chief of staff, Steve Zastrow, who had been with me since April of 2001. We both took a risk with his hire; he had worked over in Culver City, California, though never at such a high level, but I liked that he was from outside and would bring a fresh perspective. That was my risk. His risk was obvious: he was becoming chief of staff to a mayor facing a recall election in five months, which meant he could be hired and gone in less than six. We both survived just fine, accomplished some great things together, and had a lot of fun along the way. During his first week on the job, the recall leaders said in a newspaper story that he was an "illegal waste of money." His response was to say he had not yet had a chance to learn how to waste any money, let alone do so illegally.

My comments that evening would be brief; I had already said my farewell at a previous council meeting. That evening should be, and was, about the new mayor and the journey he was about to begin leading the city.

On the night I was first sworn in as mayor, my predecessor, Harry Mitchell, gave me a small "T" lapel pin, made of gold. Not a lot of gold, but gold. I only wore it on special occasions because I was always afraid of losing it. I decided I would pass it on to the new mayor as part of this swearing-in ceremony.

After the new mayor was sworn in, I walked back to my car with my Soleri bell and my City of Tempe flag—the traditional parting gifts for those leaving office in Tempe. I tossed them in the back seat, just as I had placed my jacket in the rear seat that long ago summer night in 1996, when my political future was so uncertain because I was soon to be exposed as a gay man.

But that night, after passing the torch of Tempe's leadership on to my successor, I stood proud of my own truth, my public service and leadership. I took a moment by the car just to look up at City Hall and take one last look at the office window behind which I had spent ten years of my life.

The next day, when I woke up, the phone wasn't ringing and I wasn't expected to be anywhere other than at my job at ASU, working on the details of the final U.S. presidential debate to be held on campus in October. The whole day was strangely quiet. The full impact of my decision not to run hit me in that silence. Someone else was now in charge, and it was okay. It felt good to have gone the distance, accomplished a great deal, won many important battles, personal and on critical issues facing the city, and then leave on my own terms, my head held very high.

I was used to the phone ringing. I was used to having a full schedule. I was used to being busy from the moment I woke in the morning until late at night. Weird, how as difficult and stressful as all that kind of schedule is, you can get addicted to it. You can become addicted to the feeling of being needed and wanted and sought after. Then, when it's gone and many of the people who had surrounded you disappear, you understand that many people wanted to be with you, not because of *you*, but because you were mayor.

Of course I knew this, but once out of office, I was a bit surprised at just how many people fell into that category. For the first few weeks there was a sense of loss. Fortunately, I had a lot of other things to keep me busy.

That's one of the important lessons I've learned about holding a special position and visibility. It's important to stay grounded, and one of the best ways to do that is to develop and maintain solid relationships—both in the job and outside of it. As I transitioned from public figure to private citizen, I was grateful for the good friends I had made along the way; some had been interns—young people who started with me who I got to watch grow up, finish their education, start their families, and begin their own successful careers. Others were staff and some business and community leaders whom I had gotten to know along the way. Their years of service to me, and the community, made all the difference. I believe it was Jimmy Carter who once said: "A president, or any leader, can encourage and inspire a vision, but it takes the people to bring it about." True indeed.

My political and public service life wasn't the only thing in transition during this period: my long relationship with Arizona State University was also changing.

When I first ran for city council 1990, I was Director of Constituent Relations at the ASU Alumni Association. Shortly after I was elected, I was asked to become Director of Federal Relations, the job I held when I ran for mayor. To run for mayor, I needed the support of Brent Brown, who was Vice-President for University Relations. Brent was a Democrat and a Mormon, a very conservative man in many of his views. His brother had been a state senator for many years and he had worked in state government himself. When I told Brent of my aspirations for higher public office, he said, "Neil, I've been trying to get close to politicians my whole career. I feel like I'm in politics myself. Go for it, you'd be a great mayor!"

That kind of genuine personal support was invaluable to me. By this point, I had been at the university for sixteen years, as either a student or staff member. The combination of my work as mayor and my job as Federal Relations Director really worked well together. The two gave me a public face, both in Tempe and in the political community at large.

But in 2002 that comfortable and mutually beneficial relationship began to alter.

The university had a new president and he brought with him a new Vice President. "University Relations" became "Public Affairs." The new President, Michael Crow, was someone I knew and had worked with for many years. He had been a consultant to ASU on federal government initiatives, and I had been in countless meetings and conference calls with him. He has a brilliant mind, he's a long-term thinker and strategist. He had been a contributor to my final political campaigns and attended my post-swearing-in party at Harrison's Marine Center. I knew from the beginning things were going to significantly change under his administration.

A few weeks before the new vice-president was to officially start, I happened to be working quietly in my office while the Director of State Government Relations was giving him a tour of the department. They couldn't see me, but I could hear them talking in the hallway.

"Down there is Neil Giuliano's office, our Director of Federal Relations. Neil's also the mayor of Tempe."

"You have the mayor of the city working at the university?" The new vice-president sounded incredulous and taken aback; "Why on earth would you permit that?"

Uh-oh. I guess the new president had not provided his new vice-president the details of the university-community relationship at the time, or the fact he was very aware I worked there and was a contributor to my campaigns.

There was a part of me that strongly considered stepping out right then and introducing myself. But another part of me understood that it might be better to take this information to heart and consider it carefully by myself. One thing was obvious, however: I was living—or rather working—on borrowed time.

We worked on a lot of projects together, they were all successful, and it was never an uncomfortable situation. I never had a less than stellar evaluation in my entire career at the university, but one day that new vice-president, Virgil Renzulli, popped in my office, sat down and said, "There's a job opening up, doing fundraising at Channel 8. I think you should apply for it."

Then he got up and left. The entire episode was less than

sixty seconds. I don't think I even had a chance to respond; it was not a conversation.

Curious, indeed. But I got the message. And university leaders had been great to me for a long time, so I would not make waves.

I would plan my exit. If having the mayor on the public affairs team was not considered a plus any longer, I would just have to respect that view. Mutual respect is vital for a healthy working relationship. I would create my own exit strategy.

What did make that conversation even stranger was that I was the one who had written the proposal to bring the 2004 presidential debate between John Kerry and George W. Bush to the ASU campus and was co-chairing the planning committee. I was the one that had championed the opportunity to put ASU on the front page of every newspaper on the planet, and not for an athletic scandal, a party-school reputation, or girls gone wild video.

In April of 2003, ASU had been named a finalist to host one of the debates. In November we were selected, and it would be the capstone of my career at the university.

I had been working and trying to bring a presidential debate to our campus for many years. Initially, for me, it was just about the thrill of meeting such powerful figures, something that I had enjoyed since I had the opportunity to meet Barry Goldwater and Ted Kennedy on the campus in 1974. I did some research in the late eighties and in my youthful enthusiasm even called the Commission on Presidential Debates. I was completely clueless on the millions of dollars, the years of planning, and the application process that preceded what I saw, on television. Janet Brown, Executive Director of the Commission on Presidential Debates, took the time to talk with me in 1991. She was very gracious to a then-naïve, lower-level university employee in the alumni association. She explained the whole process: how the university had to present a proposal, far in advance, the funding process, the level of detail and support required to prepare for the onslaught of media and security. I pitched it to university leadership every election cycle: 1992, 1996, and 2000—and I could never convince the university to apply. There were always other priorities in the way. The idea of having a presidential debate at Arizona State stayed alive in my mind, but unfortunately, it never caught on anywhere else and even after I was a city councilman and mayor working on campus, no one shared the vision for what it would mean for the campus and community.

But all that changed when Michael Crow became president and the new vice-president for public affairs took over in 2002. I first made sure I had the support of Colleen Jennings-Roggensack, ASU Assistant Vice-President for Cultural Affairs, a wonderful colleague and friend. She oversaw the major facilities on campus that would be needed to make this happen and had the full respect of the university hierarchy. It would not happen without her unflinching support. My star had lost some of its shine from when I had suggested the university share a football stadium with the Arizona Cardinals, and I'm sure for other reasons too, but that was fine by me. Fortunately, she had been involved with a similar event when she worked at Dartmouth years earlier. She understood the benefits of being selected to host a debate and helped sell it to the powers that be. We made the pitch to the top brass of the university to apply to host a presidential debate in 2004 and they agreed. I wrote the proposal for the Commission on Presidential Debates and we sent it in.

By then, I'd been in touch with Janet Brown for nearly thirteen years. We'd built a nice relationship, casually keeping in touch, especially after I became Director of Federal Relations and then mayor. I also met with her in person during trips to Washington, D.C. I'd been joking with her for years, "I'm going to get ASU to apply one of these days." She was always kind and gracious and never discouraging, even though I'd never yet been able to talk my school into making good on that promise.

For 2004, though, the timing was right. John McCain had run for president in 2000. Janet Napolitano—who was the governor at the time—wanted the debate at ASU as she had ambitions of her own that it served well. Everyone in our congressional delegation was on board with the idea. We were able to show unanimous political support; this was a win for everyone.

Co-organizing that debate ended up being my final job at ASU. Although my professional handwriting was on the wall, my expertise and my political relationships were critical parts of pulling off the event. They couldn't fire me—not yet—but I knew it was time to start thinking about my next moves.

Once I had decided that I wasn't going to run for mayor, I started putting out feelers and soon I was getting calls about job opportunities. In the summer of 2003, I got a call from a search firm. The Human Rights Campaign (HRC), the nation's largest LGBT advocacy group, was looking for a new president to replace Elizabeth Birch, who had brilliantly branded the entire movement for gay equality with their new, yellow equal sign on a field of blue.

"They'll never hire me," I said, laughing. "I'm a Republican. Their constituency is Democrats; all their money comes from Democrats. They rarely even lobby Republicans. They are *not* going to hire me."

But the recruiter convinced me to throw my hat into the ring, and I finally agreed. I made the first cuts and was interviewed by an entire hiring committee. It went really well except for two questions.

"We're looking to fill this position by the end of the year and bring in our new president in January 2004. Are you willing to resign the mayor's position in Tempe six months early and move to Washington now?"

"No," I told them bluntly. I knew there was no way I would resign before the end of my final term. HRC had an interim president, and to my mind, that person could serve a few more months so that I could complete my responsibilities to the city of Tempe.

I'm sure that answer did not go over well with the interviewing panel.

The other question went like this: "What's the difference between a mayor and state legislator in terms of the skills they bring to a job like this?"

I wasn't sure where the question was coming from at the time, but I answered it honestly.

"A mayor's job is leadership. With respect to my friends serving in legislatures, they really just need to have an opinion and show up and vote. Successful leadership is not a requirement to be a successful legislator."

I didn't get the job, which turned out to be a blessing. Still, it was nice to be considered, although I doubt I was ever a serious candidate in their minds. I just helped broaden the pool of candidates, which is fine too.

But when I saw whom they did hire, I understood the questions better. HRC's new president was Cheryl Jacques, a Massachusetts state legislator. She lasted eleven months and was unceremoniously let go following the 2004 elections. When the recruiter called again and asked about my interest in the job, I politely told him I had already heard they were going to offer the position to the man who ultimately accepted it, Joe Solmonese, so why were they pretending to have a selection process?

Although meeting with HRC turned out to be futile, even being considered got me in the loop and on the radar of executive search firms that specialized in not-for-profit organizations in the gay movement. The Center on Halsted is acommunity and resource center in Chicago and I had a wonderful conversation with leaders there about their executive director position. I'm not sure where that might have gone, but when I got word that ASU would host the 2004 presidential debate, I called them and withdrew from consideration.

I was working on creating my own exit strategy, but I also respected protocol and sought approval from my supervisors. I also let Michael Crow know my plan, and if he wanted me to stay at the university and take on new responsibilities outside of Public Affairs, I would be open to it, but I shared that I would not stay in Public Affairs since it had been made clear by the vice-president that I did not have a future there. Michael sealed my departure, for which I would later be thankful, when he indicated he didn't necessarily think I should leave the university, but that my role should somehow remain within the Public Affairs arena. Translation: move on. My immediate supervisors and I came to an agreement that I would begin telecommuting to complete a few projects shortly after the debate, and six months following, in April 2005, I would retire. I was pleased with that decision.

The debate came together perfectly. Over fifty-one million people watched it live from Tempe, and the ASU campus. The building, the set, the staging was in place and prepared. To dress up the building, I had suggested we hang US flags in between the high columns of the Frank Lloyd Wright-designed auditorium. It was a technical challenge, but the ASU staff did it perfectly and that view became the backdrop for nearly 3,000 members of the media who would be sending images of the facility around the globe. I could not have been more proud—or exhausted—but it was beyond worth it all. Colleen, and her organization and talent, were a requirement for pulling off an event of that magnitude. It wouldn't have happened at all without her and her team, and the fantastic cooperation we had with the city of Tempe, too. Colleen understood teamwork, we each handled our aspects of the event, and working with her made it a great experience.

The week leading up to the debate was like the last week of a mayoral campaign. Twenty-hour days, a draining number of details and activities coupled with a sense of destiny that is empowering and strengthening. It was a tremendous honor to work on the inside of it all, and as the co-chair of the event I was able to sit-in on the negotiations between the two campaign teams during the week. Every last detail was negotiated; exactly where tents were to be placed, the minute dignitaries would arrive, their every movement once on site, everything. Not a single detail was left to chance. I flipped the coin to determine the podium assignments: Bush staff called heads as the quarter fell to the table, and it was tails. Within a nanosecond, the Kerry lead staff person said, "Stage right."

Two friends flew in to help out with the actual debate. There was Kim Fuller, who served as Activities Vice-President when I was student body President in 1982-83 and had worked on presidential and cabinet member advance teams for years and knew the drill of such events very well. My friend Guy Padgett, the young mayor of Casper, Wyoming who I had met at a Victory Fund event, flew in too. They were both tremendous assets to me those final preparation days and it was fun to have them involved.

On debate day both candidates arrived for their pre-scheduled walk-through of the facility. They each had up to an hour in the hall, on stage, with absolutely no one in the room beyond who they brought with them. The President arrived first with Karl Rove, Condoleezza Rice, Karen Hughes, and Andy Card and was not in the hall for more than thirty minutes. John Kerry arrived at his appointed time with Bob Shrum, Mary Beth Cahill, and some other advisors and used every last second of his time. We did the obligatory welcome and had photos taken as each candidate arrived and included the student body president, too. Having been one, I knew what it meant to her to be included at an event of this magnitude.

About a half hour before the debate was about to start, I gave my ticket, my actual seat in the auditorium, to a student who had been volunteering outside of the event in the media hall.

"Use this, go in, sit down, and take it all in. You'll have a great seat." She thanked me profusely and ran off to get into the auditorium. I had my all access pass, so I just walked in through the side entrance, past the Secret Service and other security, who all knew me by that point. I stood near the back of the hall, next to the broadcast booths for the various networks. I could see Tom Brokaw in his booth to my right, scribbling notes and listening intently. Janet Brown walked out on stage to kick off the event, before it would be broadcast live around the world. She acknowledged the team effort it took to get to that evening and closed with the following:

"While many, many people worked very hard on tonight's event, we would not be here if it had not been for the former mayor and university staff member, who I first met in 1991 when he first sought to bring this event to this facility, so thank you, Neil."

Exactly thirty years prior, in October 1974, a longhaired, skinny freshman political science major had heard Barry Goldwater and Ted Kennedy speak on the ASU campus. Standing there, watching Kerry and Bush debate, was surreal to that kid: me. My decades with ASU had truly been life altering and defining. It would soon end, but it was time, and I could not have scripted a better closing.

* * *

In April 2005, after thirty-one years on the campus as an undergraduate student, student employee, graduate student, student body president, faculty associate teaching a personal leadership development course, and in various professional administrative roles, I left ASU. Walking off the campus that final time as an employee, I made a point to walk through the Best Hall residential complex, the first building I had walked into in August of 1974.

Had I stayed too long? Perhaps, but fortunately I was always growing, being challenged, and taking on new positions. For fourteen of those years, I was concurrently serving in public office. I could not have had that opportunity without the tremendous support of many university officials over a long period of time. Even as I tell the full story about my exit from the university, it's all good and I remain forever grateful and honored to have been a part of the institution. I'm actually very thankful it all played out as it did, or I would not have had the incredible leadership opportunities and life experiences that have come my way since. There truly was a world awaiting me beyond the borders of the ASU campus.

My retirement party was held on campus, with Virgil Renzulli as MC and a good number of folks in attendance, which made it very special. The local politicos, the Governor, and others sent representatives and it was a warm, emotional, and fun time. Some campus people I had known since my early days as a student attended, along with former colleagues, supervisors, and many of my former students too. At the annual Founders Day dinner, the ASU Alumni Association recognized me with its highest honor: the James W. Creasman Award of Excellence. That was a huge surprise to me and very heartwarming. The Alumni Association had been the place where many of my initial community relationships had formed, and I had served as the Interim Executive Director of the organization for exactly one year, July 1994-July 1995, my first year as mayor, while they searched for a permanent Executive Director.

On the whole, my personal, professional and political transitions worked out very well for all involved.

I was ready for change. It was scary to walk toward the unknown, but I knew I would have significant opportunities to choose from. In fact, I already had one consulting position with a real estate development firm in Las Vegas. I knew I wanted to stretch and grow, do something different. My entire identity had been wrapped up in being the mayor and working on the ASU campus. Change would be good.

Now I had to ask myself the very question I had posed to the students in my leadership course annually for over twenty years:

What could I become?

At the time I had no idea my next major leadership role would reconnect me to my past and give me the chance to make good on the silent promises and passions of my heart.

CHAPTER TWELVE

On the Front Lines of a Movement

When the search firm recruiter looking for a new president for the national Gay and Lesbian Alliance Against Defamation (GLAAD) first called, asking if I, or anyone I knew, might be interested in the position, I told them I would certainly identify some people for them, but it would not be a leadership role I would pursue.

By then, spring of 2005, I'd already been interviewed and rejected by the Human Rights Campaign a couple years prior, had traveled the country raising money and supporting openly gay candidates for office on behalf of the Victory Fund, and was visibly supportive of the efforts in Arizona via our statewide organization the Arizona Human Rights Fund, now Equality Arizona. I knew the local and national gay advocacy landscape pretty well. I was happy being a donor and occasional spokesperson in the movement for gay equality on a volunteer level, but I had doubts about whether I was the right person for a full-time leadership position in gay advocacy. Both because of my political affiliation and because of my own personal journey,

I was, in many ways, "late to the party" in terms of representing the issues of LGBT Americans. I now knew so many people who had been involved from the very early days of the 1970s, and my many years of being closeted made me wonder if I was truly worthy of such a role. I didn't feel confident that I was, so when GLAAD called the first time, I passed.

Besides, other opportunities seemed to be swirling around me. By then, I was up in Las Vegas each week, working with a truly great group of people, led by businessman and philanthropist Michael Saltman. Michael had a vision to undertake a redevelopment project that was, in many ways, similar to what we'd done in downtown Tempe. As mayor, I'd been the public face of our urban redevelopment projects and had been intimately involved with every aspect of what was considered by many to have been a very successful effort. Michael wanted my expertise and had asked me to work on the project, which was planned for land he owned on Maryland Avenue, directly across from the campus of University of Nevada, Las Vegas.

It was, challenging, complex, and visionary. I was working on a project that might do for another city what we had done for Tempe. When I retired in April 2005, I started working with Michael full-time and I probably would have stayed with him and that project had life not aligned so strongly in a different direction. In the end, when the economy turned for the worse and recession set in, the project was put on hold. It has not significantly advanced beyond a strong vision and amazing potential. It has been personally rewarding and enjoyable to keep in touch with a man of Michael's accomplishment and passion for quality and full equality and we will remain allies on other projects into the future.

The developers of a controversial high-rise condominium tower in Tempe had approached me about joining their team, and there were other private sector opportunities and inquiries as well.

I was therefore a little surprised when my good friend Steve

Culbertson in Washington D.C. forwarded me the position announcement about the GLAAD job, and then another friend, Curtis Steinhoff in Phoenix, did the same, both of them suggesting that I would be perfect for this organization. I'd already told the search firm to call back, and I would give them the names of other people to consider. Founded in 1985 in response to inflammatory anti-gay coverage of the AIDS epidemic (which ironically ties to my current professional work as CEO of the San Francisco AIDS Foundation), GLAAD's work spread to Los Angeles and had focused on being a watchdog for the portrayal of gay people in media, an advocate for gay issues, and a place where gay people could share their stories honestly, without judgment or shame.

GLAAD wasn't politics or federal relations—the areas where I felt most comfortable. The organization involved media and national advocacy, sponsoring the huge GLAAD Media Awards with all the big gay celebrities and straight supporters; fun events I was sure, but things with which I had far less experience.

I was also concerned about becoming a "professional gay."

Your life narrows when your job and an aspect of your identity merge. I knew that taking the GLAAD job would bring my sexual orientation into a much larger sphere of my life that it ever occupied before. I had mixed feelings about that. While I was proudly gay and knew I could do the job, being gay wasn't all there was to me. What I had always liked about government service was the variety of issues. Being "professionally gay" meant the opposite: Every issue in my work life would be, at least in that respect, on the same topic.

On the other hand, it was a compelling and unique opportunity. Friends, mentors, and others I respected encouraged me to seriously consider the opportunity. It was suggested I fly over to San Francisco toward the end of June and attend the Media Awards event there, meet some people, and just observe it all. I did. I stayed with my good friends "the Jeffs," one of whom was on the GLAAD National Board of Directors, and had a great weekend. The event was well-produced and delivered strong messages about the significant influence the media has on the hearts and minds of people with regard to their views about gay people and our equality in society. I was impressed by what I learned about the content of GLAAD's work—and the strong platform the current leader had built—and I found myself excited about working for the organization.

Even more than that, however, was the part of me that *did* want to make a difference for the cause and my tribe. I still had a deep desire to serve. I owed much to the gay community. They had fought for me, and helped create the cultural environment that enabled me to be a successful and out elected official in the first place. I wanted to give back. I could see myself in this national leadership role. I realized there was a reason why the opportunity kept coming back to my doorstep. In the next conversation with the search firm, I said clearly that they could advance my name.

Then something happened. I had been asked to moderate a town hall-style panel of Phoenix-area clergy on the topic of homosexuality, religion and the Bible at the Phoenix Art Museum on August 5, 2005. When I arrived I met a charismatic guy by the name of Daniel Karslake who was finishing a documentary film about how religion had been misused against gay people called *For The Bible Tells Me So*. We hit it off well and I shared privately with Daniel that I had been in conversations with the folks at GLAAD about their leadership vacancy; he was very encouraging about the opportunity that existed for GLAAD to have influence in the media beyond the entertainment world. Talking with Daniel helped me see the potential for GLAAD to expand its influence.

I had told the hiring committee that media and entertainment weren't my background, but they saw other qualities and skills in me that they felt would serve the organization well. In the interview, I spoke about the vast potential and role of media in changing hearts and minds and preparing our society for the legal and political equality that would follow. In my view, media—both mainstream and gay— would be critical in leading the way toward achieving full equality.

In mid-August, I was offered and accepted the job. I was a bit surprised since I had heard I was up against a woman who was a well-respected and successful activist with a long history of deep engagement on behalf of the gay community. But I was excited for this new opportunity to serve and all the possibilities and life changes it would bring for me.

That meant the end of my Vegas work. My developer friend Michael Saltman was very sorry to see me go, and I was sorry to leave. I do love projects like his, where you are literally creating something out of nothing, but I felt that the opportunity to work with GLAAD was an important and significant one. I would start in September, first visiting the New York office to meet the employees there, and then go on to the Los Angeles office. I wasn't sure where I would be based just yet, and my learning curve was very steep.

I was surprised, too, when one of the members of the GLAAD board—Phil Kleweno, the co-chair who hadn't been on the actual hiring committee—said to me, "I voted for you."

Of course, I was thinking that he'd lived in Tempe and voted for me for mayor or even city council. I said so and thanked him.

"No," he said, laughing. "I voted for you for student body president in 1982. I was at ASU at the same time."

It's true what they say: the world is small. He and many other board members, major donors, and other activists in the gay community have become dear friends who have truly enriched my life's journey. Taking the GLAAD position was clearly the right opportunity and leadership role for me to accept.

* * *

Most people know about GLAAD because of their Media Awards events, which were televised nationally for a few years while I served as GLAAD President and Executive Producer of the Media Awards, including seasons on the Bravo, VH1, and Logo networks. Throughout its history, GLAAD had effectively focused its work primarily on defamation in the media — newspapers, television, and film — but when I got there, I realized that they'd done so much good work there that the entertainment and news industries were no longer where the most blatant and visible defamation occurred. For that, one would have to look at the world of religion and communities of faith, and in sports. Those were the places where it was — and still is—perfectly fine to defame and discriminate against an entire class of people based on sexual orientation. One can also look at advertising—arguably the most influential media platform on our planet. In my analysis, by focusing on TV, film, and print media, the organization had limited its strategic plan. I decided that to reach the full potential of the GLAAD mission, I would need to broaden GLAAD's work into those industries and begin to tackle the defamation against gays, lesbians, and transgendered people in religion, sports, advertising, digital media, and beyond. Broadening the organization's reach would take some time—and be a bit controversial within GLAAD too—especially since its established mission had enjoyed such strong support from existing constituencies. There were also other entities doing some work in similar areas, particularly with regard to advertising and moving into that territory would be a delicate and sensitive activity that would have to evolve through building relationships and trust with those groups. But the potential of a GLAAD Media Awards in Advertising was a powerful idea for the industry, for the gay community, and as a revenue producing activity. I was committed to seeing it through.

I'm happy to say all of the above programs were started during my tenure at GLAAD. They all came about by expanding the capacity of the organization and strengthening the entertainment and news media aspects of its work as well. Working with a great board and talented staff, we grew the organization to over $10 million in revenue from a budget of just over $7 million when I arrived.

I was about a year into my tenure at GLAAD when the controversy surrounding the popular television show *Grey's Anatomy* broke.

We'd heard that something had been brewing on the set. Hollywood is a very small community in many ways and GLAAD had developed deep and far reaching contacts throughout the industry. There was a great deal of rumor and speculation surrounding an alleged on-set argument between two of the biggest stars of the show, actors Patrick Dempsey (who plays Dr. Derek Shepherd, aka "McDreamy") and Isaiah Washington (Dr. Preston Burke). A few months before, in October 2006, Washington had supposedly referred to their fellow cast member T.R. Knight as a "faggot." That slur was the source of the on-set tension, with Washington having allegedly made a comment about Knight in the course of an argument with Dempsey.

For several months, however, there were very few details of what had been said and no one was willing to go on the record. T.R. Knight shed some light on the affair when he made a statement to *People* magazine on October 19. He didn't refer to the incident at all but said, "I guess there have been a few questions about my sexuality. I'd like to quiet any unnecessary rumors that may be out there. While I prefer to keep my personal life private, I hope the fact that I'm gay isn't the most interesting part of me."

Darn well stated, if you ask me—and I know a bit about having to make public statements about one's sexuality!

It did seem that everyone involved hoped the incident would

be viewed as a one-off and that it would blow over, but Knight's statement indicated that the problem was more serious. He'd had to go on record to acknowledge he was gay as a direct result of the publicity surrounding the on-set incident. It reminded me of my own experiences as mayor of Tempe in many ways, but until someone was willing to go on record and tell us what had happened, there wasn't much we could do with just rumor and Knight's statement to *People*.

It wasn't until much later, in a January 2007 appearance on Ellen DeGeneres' talk show, that Knight confirmed that Washington had called him a "faggot."

It was a "teachable moment" and at GLAAD we were determined to use this unfortunate situation to educate people about the harmful use of such language, and help move the culture toward a place where the "F" word is no longer tolerated. Eliminating the "F" word is just one more small but important step toward full equality in our society. Cultural change leads; policy and political change follow. In drawing the line on unacceptable language, GLAAD was forging that cultural change.

One of the mistakes made by the producers of *Grey's Anatomy* was attempting to keep the initial incident under wraps. The harder you try to keep a secret, the more it seeps out. Someone always talks.

In the end, we didn't need to search for signs of unrest among the cast or get someone to speak off the record. Instead, the powder keg of pent-up anger and emotion spilled over backstage at a major awards show with cameras rolling and was forever preserved as a textbook example of the wrong way to respond to a public inquiry about a private dispute.

After receiving a Golden Globe Award for "Best Television Series-Drama" on the evening of Monday, January 15, 2007, the entire *Grey's Anatomy* cast made itself available to answer questions and talk about the show. Shonda Rhimes, the program's creator and executive producer, stood alone at a microphone, with the cast standing in a straight line behind her. Questions were shouted from the crowd. A voice in the room asked her something about the cast getting along and inquired about rumors of disharmony among them.

"What happened?" a reporter yelled from the crowd.

Rhimes laughed nervously. "Seriously? Seriously?" But behind her stars Eric Dane and Patrick Dempsey looked uneasy. Their faces didn't reflect the joy that should have followed winning such a prestigious award for their work.

Then Isaiah Washington unexpectedly left the line of cast members, grabbed the microphone, and proclaimed, "No, I did not call T.R. a faggot. Never happened, never happened."

With those words, he climbed aboard a full-on train wreck of a PR disaster.

The next day, the story was everywhere. As soon as I saw the video of his outburst, I asked the GLAAD staff involved with entertainment media and communications to prepare a statement to fully frame and define Washington's use of the "F" word as a significant act of defamation. For months we had been aware something bad had taken place on the set of the show. Now that it had become an even larger story, we went to work. We contacted the appropriate people at ABC and with the show, asking for a meeting, demanding an apology, but stopping short of demanding that Washington resign or be fired. The latter would render us on the outside of the issue moving forward when what we needed was a greater opportunity to drive the public conversation about such defamation.

The meeting with Isaiah went as well as could be expected. To a great extent it had been scripted ahead of time, like a well-choreographed dance. The high-level ABC official involved with handing this PR crisis was an openly gay man himself, and he had suggested in one of our first conversations following the incident that we include Kevin Jennings, the Executive Director of the national Gay, Lesbian, and Straight Education Network (GLSEN) in the meeting. Most executives at organizations in the movement for gay equality would probably have resisted including the leader from another national organization in a very high profile media moment. Indeed, GLSEN works primarily in the education sector, not with celebrities who engage in blatant acts of defamation. Two factors made me quite comfortable with the suggestion, however. One, I liked Kevin and thought him to be one of the brightest leaders in the movement, and we got along well. Secondly, the ABC executive running interference on the entire saga was a member of the GLSEN National Board of Directors.

I was born at night, but not *last* night.

To his credit, Isaiah Washington had issued a solid, and apparently sincere, apology in response to my statement calling for him to do so. He had nothing but positive things to say about T.R. Knight, calling him "courageous, talented" and stating that he held T.R. in high esteem.

He was definitely right about that: T.R. Knight handled himself perfectly. He was brave and strong. He was willing to be outspoken, to use just the right tone in expressing a level of frustration and guarded anger. His actions and demeanor spoke volumes about the kind of person he was. He was a person going through a very public discussion about what he had long kept private and it had to be a difficult and very emotional time for him and those close to him. I knew what that felt like; I'd been there. We had a friendly private email exchange about the situation, and I tried to let him know that GLAAD was there for him if he needed support, and that I personally hoped to meet him soon under better circumstances; later, I did, at the 2007 GLAAD Media Awards. The crowd gave him a standing ovation when he walked on stage to share some comments about the importance of our visibility in changing hearts and minds, and introduce me to the 3,200 people seated in the Kodak Theater. I have had some amazing venues and speaking opportunities in my life, from those deeply personal nights at Camp Laforet in the Black Forest of Colorado to the million or so people gathered at the Millennium March on Washington in 2000. But walking out onto the stage at the Kodak Theater in Hollywood is an experience unto itself, and the four opportunities I had to do so were fantastic and a blast.

On the day of the meeting, "Dr. Burke" entered the conference room. I say "Dr. Burke" because he came straight from the set and was still in his character's surgical scrubs. We exchanged pleasantries and greetings, and then Kevin and I sat on one side of the table and Isaiah and the ABC executive sat on the other side. Some bottled waters were passed around. The turkey wraps on plates in the center of the table would go untouched.

Washington apologized for his behavior and comments and the harm they caused. He said he did not know where such actions and language had come from. He seemed very sincere, but then again, he is a pretty good actor. Kevin talked a bit about the impact that anti-gay language has on kids, how it is used on playgrounds as kids are pushed to the ground, kicked and beaten. I emphasized the opportunity we had to educate people that such language is wrong, that we expect them to apologize and to make clear the severity of their bad judgment in that word choice. I reminded them that it's only by calling it out again and again that we will be able to change what is considered acceptable in our society.

You can have all the meetings in the world and talk all night long, but if nothing concrete comes out of it all, at the end of the day, it's all just talk. I wanted to make sure that by coming together, we made something better out of a bad situation. GLAAD had an awareness program called "Be an Ally and a Friend" that Rashad Robinson and Damon Romine of the GLAAD staff had discussed with ABC in advance of our meeting with Washington. We talked about featuring Washington in one of our public service announcements to continue the national dialogue about the harmful consequences of anti-gay language and other hurtful behavior. He knew our request was coming, so it was not a surprise when he agreed to do it.

In the end, I felt the meeting was productive. Once it became public, ABC handled the situation well; but if the on-set difficulties among the cast had been adequately handled in October 2006, the media explosion in January 2007 probably wouldn't have happened. The cast members involved, and specifically Washington, would have had the opportunity to deal with whatever personal issues led to the outbursts and you and I would not have known anything about it.

As it was, however, the producers discomfort and uncertainty about the best way to deal with the situation had only made it worse. You can't just ignore these things. You can't just sweep them under the rug and expect them to go away. GLAAD became involved because it was necessary for us to speak out. We did our job and tried to make sure we did it well. We were excited to have Isaiah Washington as a new partner in helping to eliminate hate and discrimination toward gay people.

Not that everyone was pleased, of course. Some in the African-American community charged that I, and GLAAD, was being racist, alleging we were going after Washington because he was an African American. Some in the gay community were very upset that I had not called for Washington to be fired on the spot. I can understand the anger and frustration behind that sentiment, but sometimes taking the hardest line is in opposition to the main goal: to create an ongoing dialogue about the topic. Demanding that the guy be fired would have pretty much ended our ability to have any serious conversations about the incident. We would be left yelling from the sidelines instead of sitting down at the table with the parties.

The incident reaffirmed what I knew from having been mayor: whether it's gay community politics or city politics, there will always be people with different views about how I handle and approach issues. I understand that and am fine with it. Feedback and input can be a valuable part of decision making, but in the end a leader has to lead with authenticity and do what he or she feels is the correct course of action, given the best information available and considered.

In this situation, I had done the right thing; GLAAD had taken the right and balanced approach for our mission. And in reality it is a mission with enormous value to our entire society, not one that only benefits gay people. By working to reduce hateful language and defamatory behavior toward one group of people, we are all advanced to a better place. Imagine if it were still common and allowable for women to degraded and verbally abused. We observe the places and cultures in the world where that is still the norm and acceptable, and we have collective relief that we have advanced beyond those beliefs and attitudes. Imagine if the use of the "N" word to defame and dehumanize African Americans had been allowed to persist. All of us have experienced life and been touched in positive ways, as a society and as individuals, because certain words, behaviors, attitudes, and actions have been curtailed through cultural change.

Washington's PSA aired May 2006. Leading up to its premiere, there were hundreds of mainstream and LGBT print and digital stories, broadcast news segments, feature segments, and blog entries about the entire affair. In our view, that was a good thing. Conversations move people to think and rethink topics, and over time they change their hearts and minds, too. One of my former colleagues in Las Vegas, Mike Crisp, called to say there was a serious discussion about the issue in the office lunchroom. People talked about their own personal situations with similar outbursts. He said that overall, most people were changing their views about the "F" word.

"I've never heard people having a conversation like that before," he told me.

We were making a difference. It was a great feeling of accomplishment, not unlike a major community initiative being successfully advanced while I served as mayor.

During the Isaiah Washington incident, I was asked to appear live on the *Paula Zahn Show* on CNN to discuss the harmful effects of anti-gay slurs. I arrived in the studio, chatted with the producer about the live segment, sat for some make-up, and was ushered on to the set where Paula Zahn was already seated. We had a couple minutes before the interview would start, so we talked generally about the incident and all the media coverage surrounding it. Then she leaned toward me and said, "Now, when I refer to this incident, I shouldn't use the actual word, right? I mean, I shouldn't repeat the very slur that is so offensive, right?"

Wow, I thought, *she gets it. This is significant; a national news show host is modeling the very behavior that will educate others in the battle for cultural change we need to win in order to achieve equality.*

"Correct," I said. "Please refer to it as an anti-gay slur or the 'F' word, but don't say the word itself."

Then the on-set producer counted down the seconds; five, four, three, two, and then a finger pointing right at us. We were live on CNN and the world was watching.

CHAPTER THIRTEEN

Another Farewell

The challenges in our lives—and how we deal with them—define us more than the good times. It has been true for me at every critical point in my life. Sometimes you make good decisions, sometimes you make bad ones, and sometimes you just have to play the cards you are dealt and do the best you can to survive.

The end of 2005 and most of 2006 proved to be that kind of time for me.

I had just started my new job as president of GLAAD and most of my family had gathered for Thanksgiving at my sister's home in San Ramon, California. Mom was complaining about some pain in her side and had scheduled an appointment to see a doctor right after the holiday weekend. She was seventy-four and seemed to be reasonably healthy—especially considering she had been a smoker for a good part of her adult life.

On December 5, 2005, I was in my Manhattan office when I saw "Mom" flash on my cell phone caller-ID. I took the call and stood by the window, looking out toward the intersection of 29th Street and 6th Avenue. Nothing prepared me for what she was about to say.

"They did all kinds of tests and the doctor told me it's liver cancer, and I've had it for a while," she said calmly. "It doesn't look good, Neil," she added.

"What do you mean, 'It doesn't look good?' What did he specifically say?"

I needed a moment to think about how to react and what to say. I could hear the fear in her voice, she was afraid, as was I, but I had to somehow be the solid one for her.

She added that the doctor was going to review the tests and she was to go back to see him the following day. I said something reassuring like, "We'll see what he says then, it will all be okay" to which she said, "There's nothing they can do, Neil."

Once off the call, I phoned my sister Kim, who had been with her at the doctor's office and was now in another room away from Mom, and she laid it out clearly: "He said it was stage four liver cancer. And he said she has about six months."

By then I was sitting down and the weight of what I was hearing was starting to sink in. "Six months? With what treatment?" I asked.

"Pain medication, he said the cancer was already wide-spread, so surgery isn't an option. He doesn't think chemo would increase that timeframe, and Mom said she doesn't want that anyway."

"Jesus, how is she doing?"

"She is pretty calm, scared. He gave her some pills to sleep and said they will help her rest."

"Okay, well, I will get there right away," I offered and we ended the call.

A few times in my life I have experienced this weird warm sweat break out everywhere at once—my body's physical reaction to a very extreme situation. I was a bit overcome and just sat there in my office with my mind racing, backward and forward in time. Feeling so sad and worried, and pretty darn helpless, too. I wouldn't cry until later that night, back in my small studio apartment a couple blocks from the GLAAD office.

My mother had a wry sense of humor. Her response to the news was classic Jackie: "Liver cancer? Not lung cancer? I should have kept smoking and drank more."

She took the horrible news much better than the rest of us.

We asked if she wanted to do anything special in the next few months, but she insisted she didn't want anything; no final family trip or anything like that.

"I just want us to all be together for my last Christmas," she said. "That's all."

We all amended our holiday plans: Mom, Kim, and Jia had planned to go to Hawaii with friends. That trip was cancelled. I was planning a trip to Cape Town, South Africa with friends; I too cancelled. Everyone was doing what they needed to do, wanted to do, in such terrible a situation; all we could do really, which was just be there for her and each other.

Being in a new high-profile job and having to deal with the pending death of my mom should have been enough drama during that first year at GLAAD, but there was more, involving an escalating crisis in the life of my best friend that reached the danger zone during that same time period.

Some back-story is necessary to understand the relationships and my chosen family of friends.

Memorial Day weekend of 2002, I met a young man who had just moved to Phoenix from Yuma, Arizona. He was a sharp, young gay guy, who had been student body president at his high school. Mutual friends thought we should know each other so they brought him to a pool party at my place in Tempe.

Ultimately, after working at a local bank for a couple years, Martin was offered a job working for Steve May, who had served two-terms in the state legislature as an openly gay Republican and was now running his family business. Martin became his executive assistant and before long was considered a part of the family, with Steve and I as his adopted "dads." Martin is as much the "son" as I will ever have, and that is very meaningful to me.

I had met a great guy named Tim while chatting online, and we dated for a short while. He had been a fraternity president at ASU, was a smart, good-looking guy, and we hit it off really well. The crazier experiences with online dating would come after I left the mayor's office and was up in Las Vegas. In Tempe, I once met a guy named Brian and had dinner with him at the Outback Steakhouse near my house. We had a great conversation talking about politics and issues of the day. The chemistry was not there for a romantic scenario, but I knew immediately he needed to meet my friend Luke. A few months later, in September of 2002, Luke was coming to town and I arranged for us all to meet at a fundraiser event for a candidate for Arizona Attorney General. They met that night, started dating, fell in love, and have now been together for nine years. They got married in California during the window when it was legal.

With Tim and Steve, Martin and me, our little family was strong. On Sunday nights we would have a family dinner that usually grew to ten or more people. It reminded me of the days when Peggy Rubach from Mesa would have "Price Club" dinners for large crowds of folks. I still make Rubach Chicken every once in a while.

By 2006, Steve and Tim had been together a few years. But some major challenges with the family business were taking a toll on Steve. Over time he turned to drinking to try and disappear from it all. More and more at parties with friends and even at public events, he drank past intoxication. He was out of control.

In February while I was traveling for GLAAD, Martin called me in a panic.

"Steve's passed out real bad. Tim's out of town." He sounded truly frightened. "What should I do?"

"Get him in the car and take him to the emergency room right away," I told Martin. "And if you can't do that, call 911 immediately."

This is really Steve's full story to tell, and I share only part of it with his permission.

I headed to Phoenix on the next flight, and Martin, Tim, and I drove Steve to The Meadows out in Wickenburg and admitted him to a six-week residential rehab program. It helped for quite a while. But by March of 2008, the situation grew worse. A few of us, including some former legislative colleagues, were convinced Steve was using more than alcohol to deal with his challenges. It was time for more drastic measures.

We arranged for a mutual friend, a doctor, to invite Steve to dinner and to meet him at his house. Unbeknownst to Steve, Martin, their friends Bill Lewis and Kyrsten Sinema, and I would also be there waiting with Dr. Doug. Also present was a local friend and real estate broker who had successfully overcome meth addiction. He was proof treatment could be successful. It was a full-on intervention. We told Steve we knew of his substance use, that he needed help, we loved him, and he needed to get into treatment.

It was just like a television show—we each took turns telling Steve what his using had created for our relationships with him, and then he had a chance to speak. He broke down and thanked us, admitted he needed help, and agreed to seek it immediately. I'll always remember one comment he made, and it guides me to this day. He said, "I wish you all had done this months ago." Maybe we should have, but Steve is cunning and super smart, and he hid his addiction quite well.

That advice would be thrown back at him when he fell off the wagon in a huge way in the fall of 2010. Some local Republican leaders, who did not know Steve's full story and how fragile he was in his recovery, convinced him he should run for the legislature again as a write-in candidate. Steve sees much of this part of the story in a different light and recalls it differently, but I am convinced all they really wanted was his money, since he could bankroll his campaign and that would help others on their ticket as well.

It was spiraling out of control. Kyrsten and I, learning that his previous personal history was going to become an even bigger and more public issue, helped him see that staying in the race was not the right choice for his health and well-being. In fact, he should get away from Arizona, seek treatment, and get away from all the drama surrounding him and his candidacy, of which there was plenty. He finally agreed, although the paranoia of addiction had him questioning our motives and changing his mind often over the period of a few days. I drafted a statement of withdrawal for the press and Steve made plans to go visit his sister in Kenya, where he stayed for about seven months.

He is on a much stronger road to recovery now and no longer in Arizona full-time, which is a good change for him. I am confident he will return to his more than successful and happy self. But it has been a long road for six years, and, as others in recovery have told me, his sobriety must be something he wants and handles himself every day.

Aside from all those challenges, we have had some amazing experiences together. In September of 2002 we were both invited to observe the national elections taking place in Macedonia. I was invited to be part of a team from the International Republican Institute (IRI) and spend time in Skopje, which happened to be one of Tempe's Sister Cities. I made sure not to speak to the press about any pressing LGBT issues before I left town; one firestorm created while I was traveling internationally had been enough for my mayoral tenure.

Watching the electoral process in an emerging democracy was incredible, and like something lifted right out of a movie plot. Over 700 United Nations troops were in the country along with nearly the same amount of election observers from organizations like IRI. The political rallies in the streets of Skopje leading up to the election were phenomenal to witness in person. Nearly everyone was participating for the party of their choice.

I was assigned to a polling place in an Albanian village

outside of the city where someone had been killed in the previous election. People walked for two hours to get to the voting location, only to wait three hours to actually cast a ballot.

When the voting period ceased, the room filled with representatives from each party and the doors were locked. Several of the representatives had been drinking a lot, and one got sick over in the corner of the room, which only had one window. The person in charge took the two plastic tubs with ballots, cut open the seal, and then dumped all the ballots on the table in the middle of the room. They made tall neat piles, and I was positioned behind one "counter" and another observer was positioned behind another "counter." Our job was to ensure each ballot was placed on the new pile created for the candidate for whom it had been cast.

The ruling party was removed in that election—a common scenario in an emerging democracy, since it is nearly impossible for the politicians to "deliver" in such situations. There is little or no economic infrastructure and so the people choose the opposition at almost every turn, hoping they will be the ones to make things better.

Interestingly, the new Prime Minister of Macedonia was a man who had lived in Tempe for six months in the late 1980s, when Tempe's Sister City relationship with Skopje was just beginning. Elections observer rules did not permit me to meet with him while I was there, but I did meet with the mayor of Skopje, who had been to my home in Tempe when I hosted a welcome reception for him.

I will never forget the police-escorted ride back to Skopje with the counted ballots in a vehicle with no one but the driver. People stood along the curved mountain road shooting their rifles in the air as the motorcade rode past them.

Meanwhile, back in the United States that year, more people watched *American Idol* than voted in our November elections.

We sure take our democracy for granted sometimes.

We take family for granted, too, sometimes. I thought about that as we prepared for Mom's passing at the close of 2005.

On December 22, we had a very casual dinner together, seated around Kim's kitchen table. Mom told us her last wishes for her memorial service and the handling of her affairs, and then we just talked, sharing stories of our family life together.

I updated everyone on the progress, or lack thereof at that point, of this book. They all knew I had been working on it off and on for years.

"Can I read it before I go?" Mom asked.

Of course I told her she could, but it would never happen. After that dinner, Mom's health declined quickly. By Christmas Eve, hospice services had brought in a hospital bed and provided instructions for how Kim, my brother John, and I would care for her in her final days with us. So much for the "six months left" the doctor had estimated. We learned how to administer morphine to help ease her pain and provide comfort.

My last conversation with her came in between her whispered "Hail Marys" late one evening after I had helped her get to and from the bathroom and settled back in her bed, caring for her as she had for me when I was a child. She was on painkillers, but otherwise fairly alert, not overly emotional, resigned to her fate.

"Can I ask you some things?" she said to me.

I wanted to appear strong, stay in control, so as to not open the floodgate of her emotions in a way she would not be able to manage in addition to the physical dying process, which was well underway.

"Anything," I said with a smile, holding her hand.

I hoped she would not raise anything from long ago, which for me were long over and just didn't matter any longer, but I had read once if someone dying wants to talk about anything, you should let them, so I would go wherever she wanted to go with the conversation.

"Are you happy you took the gay job?" That's what she called my work with GLAAD: the gay job. Mom was not the most sophisticated activist, but she had become quite a defender of her gay son, the mayor, over the years since I came out in 1996. I remembered during the recall how she jumped into the debate and educated some of the senior citizens in her community in Peoria, Arizona, when they started popping off about me. She told me later, "These crazy old people here think you're just out to recruit more gay people, and I told them your father and I raised four kids and recruited all of you to be straight. It just doesn't work that way. You are who you are."

For all her defense of me, Mom hadn't really understood what I was embarking on when I decided to become the president of GLAAD. At the time, she just said, "If it makes you happy — and if it's important—you should do it."

So in response to her hesitant inquiry, I told her, "Yes, I am happy I took the gay job. It's important and fun, too."

"Do you really think people will change and you'll be treated like everyone else some day?"

"I'm sure of it," I told her. I elaborated, telling her how I thought it would just take more time for people to realize no one chooses to be gay. The more people like her spoke out, as she had for me, the sooner that day would come.

Then she asked the question that only a mother on her deathbed could get away with—and the one that turned me into her little boy once again: "Do you think you'll find someone to love, who loves you, so if you get sick, you won't be alone?

God, I thought, *I don't know*. Lasting success in the intimate personal relationships department had been elusive, as much as I wanted it to occur.

Through some tears I told her I would try, maybe it would happen someday, and that I would be fine no matter what, and not to worry about me.

"Okay," she said. "I hope so, Neil. I hope so."

She fell asleep and was out of it for quite a while after that. We thought the woman we had known and loved all our lives was entirely gone after that night, but we were wrong. The evening before she died, we were all just sitting around in her room, waiting. We knew it was near the very end; she was heavily medicated to keep the pain under control, yet propped up in the hospital bed. My siblings and I were alternately talking to each other and to her. Longtime family friend from Arizona, Ann Marie Forster, was with us, too, and was a tremendous help. Then, all of a sudden, Mom perked up, opened her eyes very wide, took a deep breath, and as we expressed our love and goodbyes, she just looked at us, tried to nod her head and said "bye-bye" before closing her eyes and going back to sleep.

I'm not sure where that strength and focus came from, given all the medication and final stages of death she was enduring, but to witness that and say goodbye was the most powerful human experience I have had. It was a witnessing of the powerful and mysterious strength of life and death at the same time. She peacefully slipped away early the next morning.

The funeral and services over the next few days were executed exactly as she had wished. She had told us in a funny yet serious way, "I want to be cremated. If you bury me, I will come back and haunt you!" I carried her ashes back to Arizona the day after the service in San Ramon, and we had a short ceremony at the cemetery in Phoenix to place them in the same plot, which had been dug up a bit, where my father had been buried some twenty-eight years earlier.

Mom's death was a bit harder for me to navigate than when Dad had died. It's a weird feeling to have both parents gone. In a sense, your parents are the only other humans who are, in a way, obligated to love and care for you no matter what. There's a sense of complete loss that one has to work through when both parents pass on.

I hope she doesn't think placing her ashes in with Dad is burying her. I haven't been haunted yet, so I think she's in a good place, and I'm okay.

CHAPTER FOURTEEN

Something Significant Yet to Do

"And you'll live as you've never lived before."
—"The Music of the Night" from *Phantom of the Opera*

Former Supreme Court Associate Justice Sandra Day O'Connor said it best in 2003: "Real change, when it comes, stems principally from the attitudinal shifts in the population at large. Rare indeed is the legal victory—in court or legislature—that is not a careful by-product of an emerging social consensus."

Culture leads, politics and laws follow. I knew that prior to becoming a leader in the national movement for equality, but my full-time, on-the-front-lines social justice work taught me the truth of that statement. GLAAD has played a tremendous role in that cultural change for twenty-five years, helping to create the emerging social consensus by working to evolve the way the media portrays gay people, ensuring it is fair, accurate and inclusive. And hearts and minds changed. That cultural change has enabled marriage equality in seven states, the repeal of "Don't Ask, Don't Tell," and advancement in many other areas.

Leading GLAAD provided many wonderful experiences with truly talented individuals, experiences I would have never enjoyed had I not left the confines of the ASU campus.

In June 2007, I was invited to make a presentation aboard the *Queen Mary 2* on her journey from New York to Southampton, United Kingdom on a special trip just for the LGBT community. My GLAAD board chair, Phil Kleweno— who had voted for me for ASU student body president—was now consulting with the company that had chartered the ship for the voyage. It was packed with luminaries who were providing seminars, speeches, and presentations on all sorts of topics, from politics to entertainment. Mine was on gay and lesbian portrayals in television and film. I talked about the progression from *Three's Company* to *Will and Grace*, and from *Boys in the Band* to *Brokeback Mountain*. It was received well and the clips are powerful. When you watch them chronologically you can see and hear the culture changing: moving away from hostility and toward openness, acceptance, and soon, I hope, full equality.

One of the performing guests on board during that magical trip was Franc D'Ambrosia, who performed as the "Phantom" the longest in the history of the musical up till that time. It is hard to describe what it is like to sit close to someone with such awe-inspiring talent, and to observe it firsthand. His voice was so powerful it moved many of us to tears. We became friends on that trip and a couple of years later, as a favor to me, Franc came to Tempe to perform at the Tempe Center for the Arts at our annual fundraiser. He closed that show with my favorite: "This is the Moment" from the musical *Jekyll and Hyde*.

Among the many cherished friends I made while leading GLAAD was the wonderful and incredibly generous Marc Cherry, who has frequently allowed me to call his beautiful house my home while in Los Angeles. Marc is the creator of the hit TV series *Desperate Housewives*, and shortly into my tenure he hosted a successful fundraiser for GLAAD. Nearly his entire cast attended, which was a lot of fun. It's always exciting to meet celebrities, but whether I was there to work or just to hang out and relax, Marc has always gone out of his way to make sure I feel comfortable and welcome.

Once while staying with Marc he included me at a small dinner party he was having. During the usual get-to-know you banter that night, I learned his guests were from the theater world. To be honest, I recognized the names of the roles they had played on stage rather than their actual names. Aaron Lazar had been in *Les Miserables* and *The Light in the Piazza* on Broadway, while Davis Gaines had performed as the "Phantom" over two thousand times.

Yes, you know where this is going.

Marc has a huge grand piano in his home and after dinner Michael Feinstein—yes, *that* Michael Feinstein—sat down at it and started to play. Aaron stood next to him and sang a couple songs that were beautiful, and then Davis got up and walked around those of us sitting casually on the floor on huge pillows to the front of the room where he sang "The Music of the Night." "And you'll live as you've never lived before," is how the lyric goes—and for me, in moments like those and many others during my tenure leading GLAAD, that was certainly true.

One of the great honors of my public life came in early 2009 when I was invited to be a Distinguished Lecturer at the Clinton School of Public Service at the University of Arkansas-Little Rock, on the grounds of the William Jefferson Clinton Presidential Center and Library. In addition to a public address on cultural change and state of the movement for LGBT equality I would speak to a class of graduate students and tour all the facilities. I would also meet some students who I have come to know and have stayed in contact with, too.

The entire complex is beautiful and the library, museum-like for the public part, tells quite the full story of our former president. I was impressed that I was able to review his public calendar for October 31, 1996, the day he visited the ASU campus in Tempe while I was mayor. As protocol dictates, I was there to greet him, along with university president Lattie Coor, as he emerged from the presidential limo. It was an energizing campaign rally just days before his re-election that drew well over 10,000 people to the Gammage Auditorium parking lot.

The library is fully inclusive and the story of his personal failings is presented. It acknowledges the facts, stating clearly that his own activities gave his adversaries the opportunities they desired to try and bring him down. That seems pretty accurate. I had made mistakes that gave my adversaries the opportunities they desired, too. Nothing on the same scale, but mistakes nonetheless.

GLAAD provided the opportunity to travel our great country, from small towns to large cities, and hear the stories of everyday people who had experienced defamation or discrimination because of who they are. I learned in powerful ways the huge impact the media has, on a local level, in telling our stories and changing hearts and minds. I also came to better understand the enormous influence and power of online media in shaping our culture. The Internet has become a staple of our lives as much as coffee in the morning, certainly for the better. And it's impacted my personal life as much as my professional life.

Like tens of millions of Americans and people around the globe, I have met some good friends in the online dating world. I've had my share of blunders and misjudgments, too. They ran from the ridiculous to the unbelievable. The online dating world for the gay community is not so different from that for the straight, except that it is much smaller.

Early one night while traveling I was chatting with this guy who was not far away from where I was staying, and we agreed we would meet for a drink. Easy enough, let's exchange photos so we'd recognize each other. Sure. It's important to know that at this point we had not shared information about our work, or even our real names, we were both just a person sitting at a computer. Beyond that fact, there was no verification of any information until his photo arrived, before I had sent mine. And that provided quite a shock. It was a hazy photo of a shirtless *me* from my Facebook page. This random guy was sending me a picture of myself. "That you?" I typed into the chat box? "Yup," came the response. Um, I don't think so. It's always better not to incite crazy people, so I just said I was going to pass on the drink.

Another time while home from GLAAD travels, a guy who said he was a lawyer in Phoenix, who seemed pretty smart from the conversation, said we should maybe meet that weekend for a bite to eat. Sounded fine to me, and he sent me a picture of himself that had been taken in my pool at my house! I laughed and typed in "Nice place, was that a big party?" To which he replied, "Yes, from last summer." I had missed the party that Martin had hosted, one of many I am sure.

We all have read the headlines about the straight married men, some in politics or other high-profile roles looking for secret affairs online, sometimes they are closeted and looking for other men, sometimes not. The media loves those stories. Simple advice: If you are married and want to have a secret affair, go back in time and do it the old-fashioned way. The online dating world, for both straight and gay people, may be the modern equivalent to the corner bar but it's much more public. Still, even knowing that, I have made mistakes and have met people who I suspect would betray private moments, photos, and conversations shared in confidence or in the heat of the moment. One ex-fling has even told a mutual friend that he secretly taped us without me knowing it, because he knew I was somewhat high profile, while vacationing in San Diego years back. If that is true and the tape is someday public, I hope I look as good as Rob Lowe.

The annual GLAAD Media Awards are without question the most star-studded events benefiting the gay rights movement, once called the "Gay Oscars" by a Hollywood publication. The executive producer role I held was one of oversight and direction, not day-to-day details and implementation. For the latter, I would enjoy a tremendously professional and top-notch team throughout my four seasons of the shows. Having run and staged large-scale public events while at ASU, and participated in many as mayor, I understood their work very well. And my exposure to people of great visibility, importance, and influence from all professions had prepared me for meeting the likes of Janet Jackson, Ellen Degeneres, Jake Gyllenhaal, and other stars at the pinnacle of success in the entertainment world.

A special moment happened at the 2008 GLAAD awards when I was backstage with a brilliantly successful film director and fashion designer who was a big supporter of the organization. Tom Ford is even more attractive in person than in the gazillion photos of him all around the planet. Remaining professional was vital, but given the opportunity to be otherwise, I would have fallen from grace. No doubt.

"Can I tell you something, and you promise you won't feel bad?" he said to me as he put his hand on my shoulder and looked right at me.

"Of course," I mumbled, already nervous and worried that something that should have been done for him or his husband fell apart. I was already preparing to apologize when he said, "I understand that you're wearing the same suit that you wore last year."

That caught me off guard. I was so relieved that was all he was worried about that I laughed a bit and smiled at him.

"I run a non-profit," I replied. "Of course I'm wearing the same suit."

"We're going to take care of that," he said, and then we were interrupted. It was time for him to step out on stage again for the closing part of his presentation.

I was flattered and blushing. After all, this was the man who had almost single-handedly brought the House of Gucci back from financial irrelevance.

A few weeks later someone called from his store on Madison Avenue to arrange a time to take measurements. To make a story of multiple fittings and measurements short, I have an amazing custom Tom Ford suit thanks to his generosity and kindness. That generosity extended to every detail — I was told that Tom had selected the fabric and style.

When at the final fitting the tailor asked me if I preferred a flat hem or cuffs, the store manager leaned in to inform him, "Mr. Ford prefers cuffs."

Okay then. If Tom Ford prefers cuffs, then cuffs it would be.

It's a gorgeous suit—so gorgeous that I could not wear it with my $145 Cole Hahn dress shoes. I had to upgrade to a pair of Ferragamos and a Prada shirt and tie. I wanted very much to buy my accessories from his store, but the staff person there suggested I diversify the look, and the only thing I could really afford in the store was a small leather billfold. I bought it and carry it every day. It's so well made that I'll probably be carrying it the rest of my life.

Toward the end of 2008 things were beginning to shift for me at GLAAD. Just as I had done with the mayor's office, I had set a time commitment in my mind: three to six years would be a good tenure working full-time in the movement. I'd served three, and had just begun a second three-year contract when there was a change in the leadership of the board of directors. I had worked with every style of personality, leadership and social status that exists, and had great success throughout my life. But there comes a point when you know in your gut something isn't right and not aligned with your personal integrity. When you have that feeling, you have to act.

I enjoyed a supportive and wonderful board overall, but the contention with a couple members of the executive committee, however noble their intention, made it clear they were not going to allow me to fully use my judgment to make the day to day decisions for of the organization. Nothing I couldn't handle, nothing even close to my mayoral experiences from an intensity standpoint. Unbeknownst to them, the larger issue was stirring at the back of my brain, too. I'd been "professionally gay" for three years.

There was so much more I wanted to do. My messaging work at GLAAD actually helped me think about this in a clearer way: What did I want my personal brand to be moving forward? Should I limit myself to being an activist for one cause I deeply believed in, or might there be other opportunities and other capacities to serve and make a difference? What part of my larger journey was I experiencing, and what risk would be involved in uncovering what would be, should be, next? I wanted some time to consider my future.

I spent part of Thanksgiving weekend with my great friend David Mixner, an accomplished activist, author, and voice of tremendous influence in progressive social justice causes for fifty years, at his place in Turkey Hollow, New York. I had always felt a kinship with David, perhaps stemming from the fact that he spent a couple years as a student at ASU in Tempe. I had read his best-selling autobiography, *Stranger Among Friends*, long before we met. His story is an incredible one of advising presidents and wielding significant influence, and I had been looking forward to getting back East and separating myself a bit from the daily grinds at GLAAD. Over the course of the weekend with David and Steven Guy, who shared David's charming bright yellow home in the wilderness, I expressed my feelings about the state of my full-time activism, and David's assessment and response really resonated with me.

"There are a lot of people who can do the GLAAD job, Neil," he said. "There aren't a lot of people with your background and skills. Don't limit yourself. There's something significant yet for you to do, and in time you'll figure that out, it will present itself."

Something significant yet to do. It was exactly what I needed to hear. I started thinking about how I'd been working in one capacity or the other since I graduated college—and how much of that time I'd had multiple jobs with responsibilities that kept me running from morning until midnight. I'd never taken any real time for myself. I'd never traveled just for the experience. I'd never focused on myself for any length of time, even as I professed its importance to all my students over the decades. Even after retiring from the university, I had not taken a break.

After the holiday weekend, I went back to GLAAD with a different attitude and put that mental transformation into motion. I had a great conversation with board co-chair Yvette Burton, who I trusted and respected immensely, and she said we would work through all the difficult issues with the executive committee together and it would be okay. I appreciated her support, so my response was, "Yes, it will all be fine. We'll work through it all." What I didn't share with Yvette was that my version of "working through it all" necessitated "moving on." I wouldn't put her or the organization through any higher level of drama by taking the challenging issues to the full board, where I knew I would find great support. I should have confided in her or one of the past co-chairs with whom I worked so well and successfully, but I decided on my exit path and was very comfortable with it. I had great respect for many of the people I worked with at GLAAD and they might have influenced me to stay had I given them the opportunity.

And I again remembered the words of my friend and mentor, Betty Asher, from years before when I was student body president at ASU: "You've got to choose your battles wisely." I had chosen that this would not be a battle at all, even though I was confident I could win it. I felt it better for all parties for me to just rise above the drama of the situation and move on. I came to understand Betty's advice in a completely different way. Yes, we choose our internal battles, too.

At the end of January 2009, I wrote a letter of resignation to the board, and then headed off to the Super Bowl in Tampa, Florida to watch the Arizona Cardinals and the Pittsburg

Steelers. When I got back to my Los Angeles office, I sat at my desk and reread my resignation letter. I quickly scheduled a meeting with my senior leadership team, all very talented people doing great work. I knew the impact my decision would have on them: most would probably transition from the organization within twelve to eighteen months. That is usually what happens when leadership transitions and it did happen. I'm pleased that each of them landed solidly on their feet in new and more senior positions within that time frame, their own professional growth advancing as well.

Sitting at my computer, I was calm when I hit "send," but I knew it would not be a calm day once my email was received by one and all. I felt strongly that I wanted to inform the entire board of my resignation at the same time, although I knew that was not a "best practice." I should have informed my co-chairs first, and then shared the news with the rest of the executive committee and board. I let challenges with a couple folks interfere with my better judgment of how to handle the situation and that was a mistake.

I know my decision left friends on the board disappointed that I chose not to take on the individuals and issues that in my view were going awry — and I felt bad I would be letting them down. It took a bit of time, but the larger board handled it all themselves after my departure, as I knew they would. They understood what had been going on and it didn't need to be spoken or protracted in a discussion with me.

In my heart, I knew my work at GLAAD had taken me to a new place, a better place. Many people I respected in the movement acknowledged the work I had accomplished and the advancement we had made with GLAAD's strong media advocacy and anti-defamation work; it too had been taken to a new and better place. I had initiated new media advocacy programs, strengthened the anti-defamation aspect of the work, created a solid strategic plan for my successor to initiate, updated the GLAAD brand to "Words and Images Matter," and created a new logo, all while growing the organizations revenues to over $10 million for the first time in its history. Not a bad run for just forty-six months on the job. I feel very good about my tenure as a full-time activist and feel honored to have had the opportunity to serve. And in the end, the people and relationships have added tremendous value to my already very full life.

The farewell parties in New York and Los Angeles were great fun, and my last day as GLAAD president arrived on June 12, 2009. I felt extremely proud of the GLAAD staff and volunteers who did great work while we were together. As I told them often, they didn't make a bit of difference, they made *all* the difference.

I know some dedicated, courageous, and heroic people who have spent twenty years or more in the fight for full equality. I have tremendous respect for them. But if there's one thing my own experience has taught me, it's that our gay organizations are just the formal and institutional piece of the movement for full equality. The true influence and success of the movement is really the tens of thousands of LGBT people living openly, more and more each and every day, making contributions in all aspects of our society, bringing about the tremendous cultural change we have witnessed in just the last decade. That cultural change has paved the way for the political and legal changes now underway, state by state and nationally. And now that we have straight allies more and more visibly supporting full equality, the change will come about even sooner. In January of 2012 over seventy mayors from across the country took a visible stand for full marriage equality. When I read that news release, it took me back to 1996 when I came out while mayor and Tempe became the largest city in American with an openly gay mayor. The cultural evolution our society has experienced in such a short time period can only be attributed to the fact that full equality is the moral and just position for our society, and before too long will be the law of the land.

Someday, when full legal equality has been achieved and our government recognizes gay people, as it does all other citizens, there will be a conversation with some young LGBT people. They won't comprehend that there was a time when gay men were huddled off to jail for gathering together in a club, and that a bunch of men in drag fought back in the late 1960s and took an underground movement out into the open, beginning the contemporary gay rights movement. They'll be amazed and disappointed that a gay soldier had to hide who he was even while being willing to give his life protecting our societal freedoms or that a woman could be fired from her job if a supervisor did not like the fact she had a photo of her same-sex partner and family on her desk.

They will ask older people like me what it was like in the early part of the twenty-first century, as the movement for full equality reached its peak with public sentiment swinging significantly in favor of full equality for gay people, even if it took a while for national policies and laws to catch up to public opinion.

Someone will ask, "What was it like then and what did you do?"

And I will reply, "I did far less than many, but I like to think somewhere along the way I made a difference, be it as a mayor living openly or a full-time social justice activist. It was a time of great national dialogue, highs and lows, wins and losses. It was exhilarating and a tremendous honor."

CHAPTER FIFTEEN

Never a Finish Line

In January 2011, ten people gathered on a top floor of a skyscraper in downtown San Francisco. The view was expansive, from the downtown business district to the famous Bay Bridge reaching out to the East Bay. The people assembled comprised the board of directors of San Francisco AIDS Foundation, a thirty-year-old organization dedicated to ending HIV/AIDS in the city where it first reached epidemic proportions.

I had dinner in New York the prior summer with a friend from San Francisco, who I had first met on an Atlantis cruise in October of 2009. Lorenzo Thione, a successful entrepreneur and a Tony Award-nominated producer, chatted with me about his various projects while I shared about the adventures and projects I had undertaken in the eighteen months since I had stepped down from running GLAAD. At one point Lorenzo said, "The San Francisco AIDS Foundation is still looking for a CEO. You should think about it."

I was a little surprised by that information.

Many months earlier I had been approached about the

opportunity and passed on it, since I was still on my self-imposed sabbatical. What was surprising was that they had still not filled the position.

Lorenzo wasn't sure whether they had or not but said he would find out. Then our conversation moved on to other topics.

Not long after that, though, I received a phone call from the executive recruiter for the organization. By then I had heard via other contacts that they had interviewed candidates, made a selection, and been prepared to announce that person as the new CEO, but then their candidate accepted another position.

"Would you be open to discussing the opportunity?" the recruiter asked.

I had not shifted my thoughts or actions from "time off" mode to "searching for a new leadership opportunity" mode, but I knew it was almost time to do just that. My sabbatical was winding down, but I wasn't in a particular hurry to re-enter the work force.

The San Francisco AIDS Foundation centered its work on HIV prevention efforts, public policy and advocacy and a variety of care programs. I was aware that they operated the large gay men's health clinic in the Castro neighborhood, Magnet, and their public policy and advocacy voice was among the most influential in the country. Clearly they played a significant role in HIV prevention, education, and advocacy. Their successful model of care was well known in HIV/AIDS activism circles.

I was deeply concerned about the cause, but my basic knowledge of and interest in HIV/AIDS issues stemmed from the reality that I had lost friends to the disease and have other friends who are HIV-positive, though most keep their status private due to the stigma that still comes with contracting the virus. I wasn't sure I was the right person for the job. I didn't have a background in the fight against HIV/AIDS, and I am not HIV-positive. I worried that those two factors would limit my effectiveness.

On the other hand, I did have plenty of experience leading large, complex organizations and communicating a vision for advancement toward greater purpose and accomplishment. I had plenty of experience with fundraising within corporate, foundation, and individual portfolios. And I knew a thing or two about staging major events, which was something the organization did annually with its AIDS Walk and, AIDS/Lifecycle bike ride fundraiser. I had a national reputation in the gay community, and while president of GLAAD had opened a San Francisco office, so I knew some of the community there, too. I had to acknowledge that this was a compelling opportunity to be of service to others and make a difference.

After weighing it all, I told the recruiter I would be open to talking about the opportunity. I wasn't sure that I'd take the job if they offered it to me, but I didn't think it could hurt to find out more. I made some calls to former San Francisco Supervisor Bevan Dufty and State Senator Mark Leno. They both underscored the strength and significance of the organization and its influence on and benefit to the community.

By mid-November 2010, I had met several board members of San Francisco AIDS Foundation, and they had made a compelling case for their organization and for what they believed I could offer as their new CEO. The more I talked with them, the more confident I became that I could provide the leadership and vision for the next chapter of this important organization, and learn what I needed to in order to be effective in the role. With my sister Kim and niece Jia over in nearby San Ramon, it was an opportunity with a geographic upside from a family perspective, something I had not experienced in quite some time. We agreed to terms and I accepted the position in December. An exciting new adventure was underway.

January 8, 2011 was my first working meeting with the full board. It should have been a great opportunity to begin the work of learning about my new position, but before the meeting had proceeded past the continental breakfast and coffee, I noticed that the red light on my Blackberry, which I had set on silent mode, was flashing. At the same time Dr. Carol Brosgart looked at her messages and announced suddenly, "There's been a shooting in Arizona—a Congresswoman was shot. Giffords."

I must have looked white as a ghost.

"You must know her," said Tom Perrault, the board chair.

I grabbed my BlackBerry and started to read what the flashing was about. Several messages had come in about Gabrielle Giffords, or Gabby as most know her, and the shooting rampage at one of her "Meet the Congressmember" events.

My stomach sort of lurched tight and my mind raced to Arizona, even if my body was still at the meeting.

"Yes," I told them. "I do."

We're not close friends—Gabby was rising to prominence in Arizona as I was exiting elected office and hails from southern Arizona, but we are political allies and have met on several occasions. I co-hosted an LGBT community fundraiser for her and we had been together not even a year prior for the Equality Arizona annual awards dinner. She was a bright and rising star in Arizona, having beaten back a tough challenger in the 2010 election. She proved that she, too, was a survivor. And as we all know now, she remains so in exemplary ways.

There is a tight kinship among elected officials; we understand each other, even if we are of different parties and hold different views. We share having to handle difficult constituents, strained issues, and the challenges of leading a very public life, by choice. I was very fortunate to serve prior to the near constant coverage of one's daily life via Internet coverage, blogs, and the necessity of informing constituents of your every appearance via Facebook and Twitter. Only a few times was my public official threat-level, as monitored by the Tempe Police Department, high enough to require extra precautions. Right after I came out publicly, of course, and once I received a dozen roses at City Hall, with a note written in pencil on lined paper. The writer could not wait to take me out to dinner sometime at Rusty's Pelican, the correct name being The Rusty Pelican. Tempe Police took the letter and the next day brought back a picture of the man who sent the flowers. They told me if I saw him to call 911 and leave immediately. He had just been released from prison and would not be a friendly constituent. Another time at a public forum on youth education, a skinhead from a local hate group got within five feet of me before two officers swooped in and removed him from the room with fast precision. He had been commenting online that the gay mayor needed to learn a lesson. And I'll never forget the guy at a local gay club who talked non-stop and followed me onto the dance floor and handed me his resume in a rather aggressive way, to the point that one of my Tempe police officers had to intervene and tell him it was time for him to leave. I am grateful that our law enforcement members monitor such things, when they can of course.

That they could not in Gabby's case will forever remain a tragedy. For days many feared the worst, as we mourned the loss of innocent lives. Now over a year later, every advance in her recovery has brought a smile to my face and warmed my heart so much.

I was supposed to be focused on what I needed to learn about leading San Francisco AIDS Foundation, but it was very tough to get through that first meeting with the board. I broke away for a few minutes and took a couple calls from people I knew in Arizona, trying to get the latest details. I felt terrible that I was not home. I knew there was nothing that I could do, but being far away in a time of tragedy for my state hit me hard. It left me thinking about my long years of public service in Arizona. It made me realize I still cared deeply about the state and community that gave me the honor of serving in elected office.

In all honesty, my feelings and thoughts about my public role had been evolving since I left the mayor's office in 2004. On the day of the rampage, something crystallized for me: maybe

I am not stretching enough or challenging myself enough or open to accepting that there might be something significant yet to do that remains beyond my current grasp.

To explain, however, I have to rewind a bit.

* * *

In November 2008, the day after the country elected its first African-American president and signaled an era of change, I made my own change; I left the Republican Party and became a Democrat.

I had intended to switch parties for quite some time—the Republicans were increasingly being run by its religious base—and I would have done it prior to the 2008 election cycle if it hadn't been for my long friendship with John McCain. I remember briefly discussing it with him once before he formally announced that he would be a candidate, either in late 2006 or early 2007.

"I'm getting out of the Republican Party," I told him frankly at a social event. "It's beyond time for me."

"Don't give up yet," he told me. "I'd always said I'd just run once, but maybe I'll do it again. Wait a bit, wait a bit, at least talk to me before you do it."

Because he'd always been so supportive of me, I honored his request, partly. I knew what he stood for as a man, even if his political rhetoric and public policy positions did not always match his personal attitudes I witnessed. I knew I would not be involved in the 2008 campaign cycle, so I waited. But when I finally followed through on my decision, I did not re-engage to let him know it was done or that I was leaving the Party. He was about to be defeated in his campaign to become President of the United States. He had more important things to care about than my party affiliation.

Even though I waited until November 2008, the decision became more and more clear, specifically in the months leading up to the election. On two different days of the same week in June 2008, I found myself inside the campaign headquarters of both of the two presidential contenders. The energy difference within the two headquarters was as wide as the Grand Canyon.

First, I joined Patrick Sammon of Log Cabin Republicans, former Congressman Jim Kolbe, and Log Cabin leader Pete Kingma from Chicago in a meeting with Senator McCain to discuss LGBT issues. Trevor Potter, McCain's general counsel and a good friend of mine who had once served on the HRC board of directors, was also present. I trusted that I could attend as a longtime personal friend of each, and of the Senator's, and not have my presence be related to my capacity as GLAAD's president. GLAAD's work was strictly in community education and anti-defamation, not presidential politics. I was committed to keeping GLAAD out of the LGBT political advocacy waters, and as such, had no plans to be officially or unofficially involved with either campaign.

As our small group arrived in the lobby of McCain's headquarters in Crystal City, Virginia, Cindy McCain, a couple of her staff, and her security detail were arriving as well. Cindy introduced me to her staff, and we all rode up in the elevator together. Once in the headquarters, I stopped by to say hello to Rob Kubasko, the former Key Club Governor from Pennsylvania who I recruited to attend ASU on a leadership scholarship, and who had worked so hard and so effectively on all my campaigns in Tempe. Through his efforts with me and with others, Rob had met people in Washington, D.C., and gotten involved with national political consulting. One thing led to another, and there he was on the inside of the McCain campaign at a fairly high level, coordinating their online media and campaign event brand visuals.

We met with the Senator and soon-to-be Republican Presidential nominee and it went about as I had expected.

In our meeting, McCain acknowledged that he needed to move to the center on our issues. We acknowledged that he would be pressed by some advisors to throw gays under the bus to appease voters in more conservative states.

I said to him, "Please don't use gay people, who we are, the way we have been used by Republicans in past elections. The American people have moved beyond believing those outdated views." My comment was supported by the data, shared by Log Cabin leaders, to illustrate just how significantly the views of the American people had changed on LGBT issues. In 2008, most American supported the repeal of "Don't Ask, Don't Tell" in the military. Most also favored legislation that prohibited employment discrimination against gay people. There was still a split of opinion on the subject of marriage equality, but more and more Americans were coming around.

Unfortunately, at the end of the day, there would be no shift in policy or new leadership in the Republican Party supporting equality for gay Americans. McCain's campaign was nothing like President Bush's overtly anti-gay campaign, and I suppose you could say that was a step in the right direction, but overall, it won't be a surprise that I found my friend's 2008 campaign disappointing. I won't even start on the Sarah Palin topic.

A few days later, at the Obama presidential campaign headquarters in Chicago, the energy and excitement was literally in the air. I was there to touch base with a friend from Arizona who was working on the campaign and see some others who were also involved. Obama was not in the building, and I would not have met with him even if he had been, I was only there to see friends.

I had spent twenty years trying to make inroads in the Republican Party and seen very little progress toward the moral and middle ground on social issues. The reality is there is no "big tent" in the Republican Party. Many of my gay Republican friends still see it differently and I respect them, though I disagree. The longer I stayed in the Party as a gay person, the more I came to believe that I was enabling people who find me immoral and disordered. I was tolerated, not really accepted.

Under the best of circumstances, I dislike the word "tolerance": we tolerate bad clothes; one tolerates a bad meal or unpleasant weather. We don't *tolerate* people's basic rights and who they are.

The Republican Party tolerated me and, as time passed, I resented that tolerance more and more. I asked myself, *What room do I want to stand in? Who's fighting for me?* My views hadn't changed—I was and still am a moderate progressive on social issues and fairly conservative on fiscal issues. I always believed in social equality and I want to stand shoulder to shoulder with others who share those beliefs and whose actions speak as clearly as their words.

Do we need and should we seek moderate Republican support for full equality? Absolutely, we should do all we can to find and support those moderate Republicans who will stand with us when LGBT equality is our determining issue and one can put aside party views on immigration, health policy, education, reproductive rights, and so on. As we learned in the fight for marriage equality in New York, a few Republican votes can put us over the top and bring about full equality and we should be grateful. I know I am. But at the end of the day, we should always remember which party got us to the point of only needing those last few votes of Republicans and has stood with us for far longer to change the culture, cultivate allies, and provide resources for our long struggle—the Democrats.

So, the day after John McCain lost, I mailed my "change of party affiliation" card to the Maricopa County Clerk's Office.

For a while, I gave some thought to becoming an Independent or non-affiliated voter. Right now, in Arizona, more voters are starting to identify themselves as Independents than any other affiliation, but "Independent" means different things to each of them. Some are further right than the furthest right wing on the Republican Party; others are further left than the most left-leaning Democrats. They are all "Independent," but there's no common ground or link between them, other that disliking both parties. It will be difficult for Independents to be a true party of like ideas and values, because they don't share like values and ideas.

I believe in working within the party system, though ultimately we have to reach beyond the labels if we're really going to forge the changes necessary to make our nation what we all want it to be.

One could make the case that my longtime friendship and mutual support with John McCain and his family warranted that I should have stood with him in his final quest for the presidency. One could also make the case that Obama's historic candidacy and progressive views on most social issues—especially on LGBT rights—would have won me over since they were in perfect alignment with my own beliefs, and would have made him my choice. I love when people guess, "You voted for McCain because you know him personally and you might have ended up with a job in the White House." And I equally love it when people guess, "Of course you voted for Obama. You'd be voting against your own equality as a person if you did not vote for him."

There's truth in both statements.

But I must acknowledge this truth: the advancement toward full equality that has taken place with Barack Obama as President would not have happened if my friend John McCain had won the election. If McCain had won, we would not have seen the end of "Don't Ask, Don't Tell" or the passage of the Matthew Shepard-James Byrd, Jr., Hate Crimes Prevention Act or the changes on restrictions on people with HIV who travel into the United States. I do think McCain would have had many LGBT appointees in his administration, and if asked, I would have served, too—a fact which surely would have infuriated the base in his party. To his credit, McCain has never had an issue working with or empowering the gay people who work for him. Unfortunately, that personal support just does not translate into public policy support, which I have to admit, has been difficult to understand over all this time. People learn and evolve; our entire culture has evolved. It's perplexing to me why a man who has been so personally accepting has not allowed his public policy to evolve. I wish he was more like his predecessor Barry Goldwater in that regard, but it's not to be. Fortunately, both Megan McCain and her mother, Cindy, speak out for the gay community, which is wonderful and great advancement for the cause. When I saw Megan at a Trevor Project event in 2009 and told her I might run for office again someday, she was excited about the prospect. It seems the women in the Republican Party will lead most of the men on the issue of equality for gay people. Laura Bush has spoken publicly in support of LGBT issues and is another fine example of the voices we need to hear, speaking loudly and clearly.

My transition from Republican to Democrat was in many ways an echo of my transition from the closet to living openly as a gay man. I've gone from being willing to compartmentalize my politics—and my identity—to appropriately placing them as a part of my story, something my Log Cabin friends remain unable to do. I understand. I was there, and I was wrong. Obviously, I didn't feel that way at first. When I first came out in 1996, it felt okay to be a Republican and a gay man. I felt proud of the response my openness received in my community, in my state, and within the Party. I wanted to believe that it didn't matter as much as I feared it would, and at first the reception I got supported that belief. But it was hollow.

As the Republican Party leadership began to evolve further toward religious-based positions on social issues as the litmus tests for the Republican brand (although not for issues like poverty, immigration, education, and health care), it became clearer that my voice would have little influence. As I've said, I am a man of personal faith, but I don't see it my personal responsibility to get others to believe and see faith as I do, especially not via my political involvement. My existence as a "gay Republican" became useful to the extent that it provided some with the opportunity to boast about inclusiveness when the truth is quite the opposite within the Republican Party.

* * *

I stood in the hallway at my first meeting with the board of San Francisco AIDS Foundation, thinking about Gabby Giffords, about my friends at home, my own public service, the trajectory it had taken me on, and about Arizona. A text came in from a friend who had been a long-time supporter: "This is all so terrible. Why aren't you here to help us? Where are you?"

If I were to return to public service, I'd do so because I love Arizona and my country and know I can make a difference. One of the many things I have learned working outside of government the last eight years is that the successful leaders are those who are the best at talent acquisition. And yet, most people who run for office claim to be singular leaders, as if any single leader accomplishes anything alone. My reputation and track record for attracting, retaining, and empowering talented people to collaborate and work toward accomplishing the shared vision I have articulated, along with my knowledge, credibility, and years of working hard for the good of the many, is unassailable. Not perfect, no ones is, but very, very strong.

In 2009 I flirted with the idea of becoming a candidate for Governor of Arizona, mainly at the urging of some Democrats who felt Arizona Attorney General Terry Goddard would be a weak nominee, having lost twice before. But he was a lifelong Democrat, and I was a twelve-month one. While many groused over his candidacy and ability to put together a successful campaign, none wanted to step out against him either, which was quite understandable. His connections and party support were formidable. I may seek to serve as Governor in the future, or another position, but in October of 2009 I decided against it; the timing was not right—and timing is everything in politics. I still maintain it would have been good for Goddard to have an opponent in the primary election; it would have made him a better general election candidate, although it probably would not have changed the outcome. After Governor Jan Brewer, who had been elevated to the office when Janet Napolitano took the Obama cabinet appointment as Secretary of Homeland Security, signed Senate Bill 1070 concerning immigration, she sealed her re-election. I don't think Goddard, or I, could have won against her under those circumstances.

Recently I reread one of my favorite political books of all time, *Changing of the Guard: Power and Leadership in America* by David Broder. He died recently, but Broder was an immensely insightful political writer, columnist, and Sunday morning TV talk show guest who I enjoyed and respected. In my view, he was among the most reasonable and straightforward commentators who explained his views in simple and practical terms and did not have a haughty demeanor, like many of his peers. Broder had a name for people like me, "inners and outers." We are people who spend some time in public service, then move out of government for a while to serve in other ways, and then can better determine if a return to politics and public policy is desired, even warranted, once again. There is a valuable place for the long-time career politicians, who climb from office to office over the decades of their lives. And there is a place, and a greater need, for those who do not choose that permanent path of politics, but whose contributions hold no less value for public service when they choose to serve.

My role as CEO of San Francisco AIDS Foundation is invigorating, compelling, and important. I work with and serve a talented staff and deserving clients. Our influence on public policy issues related to HIV/AIDS is global. I'm certain I provide the strong and focused leadership that the organization needs as it takes on radically reducing new HIV infections in the city where it first reached epidemic levels. Politically, I am not sure San Francisco and I align well, but it is an exciting and beautiful city. I thought I was fairly progressive, yet not so much when compared to most San Franciscans. When I share with people that my permanent residency remains in Arizona, even as I fly back and forth to the Bay Area, I explain that my vote and influence are needed much more in Arizona than California. And they universally agree.

There will be a lot to think about; my commitment to lead the Foundation is at the top of that list and I believe I am making a difference, especially as we embark on a vision for a new health and wellness center in the heart of the Castro neighborhood.

I hear the calls from friends and people I respect from Arizona and all over the country suggesting I should return to public life. They have continued to come since I left office as mayor in 2004, and I am flattered and feel compelled to listen. The fall of 2011 provided an opportunity to consider seriously running for Congress, representing the newly-created district for central Arizona, which as of this writing includes all of the city of Tempe and pieces of Phoenix, Scottsdale, Mesa, and Chandler. It was a compelling opportunity in a swing district with nearly even registration of Democrat, Republican, and Independent voters. The opinions of many seemed that if I could emerge from a large Democratic primary field, I had the strongest path toward winning the seat in the November election. After a great deal of listening and conversation with supporters, consultants, and friends near and far, I decided to pass on re-entering politics in 2012. I will let a trio of thirty-something's battle for the Democratic nomination; there will be other opportunities in the future to consider a return to elective office. The timing was wrong and I simply could not disengage and walk away from existing commitments because the political opportunity was bright and appealing. That's just not how I operate.

Our challenges are great right now. There is a monumental divide between the rhetoric coming from those serving in office and the needs of the people. That rhetoric is not advancing us toward shared solutions to our problems. Many seem content to further that divide rather than make the attempt to bridge it and bring us together. After all, bringing people together will mean greater compromise. Some people don't want to compromise, but they fail to understand that is what has made our nation the great one that it is.

Is there something out there beyond my role as a foundation CEO? Is there something significant yet to do in my future? Will there be an opportunity for me to make a more significant contribution to my state, my country? Is the time approaching for me to step into a different role—for all the people I might try to bring together? As an elected representative or in an appointed role? Where best can I serve and where am I truly needed?

There remains time to consider all of the above. For now, my commitments are clear; I am at peace and confidant that whatever my future holds, it will all unfold as it is destined. I do believe that my path is not entirely directed by me. There would be no full accounting for the success I have enjoyed in life if I believed it to be otherwise. Indeed, we all must consider how we can better serve our community, our country. We must all consider what we need less of from our government and how we can better serve our country. I will dig deep, listen, and look within for the answers as much as I speak out and offer ideas and pathways for a better future.

This much I know: any future political campaign or work assignment will be easier than those I've already experienced for one very important reason: I've already won the greatest victory.

I've won the campaign within.

EPILOGUE

There's nothing like a 545-mile bike ride to clear your head about life on a variety of levels. Often during my first year with San Francisco AIDS Foundation, I was pedaling my new orange and black FELT road bicycle, training for the San Francisco to Los Angeles annual AIDS LifeCycle ride. It's the largest fundraiser for HIV/AIDS in the world, and in 2011 raised over $13 million. Just under $30,000 of that came from my family of friends and supporters, most of them probably shocked that I would take on that huge physical undertaking. With 2,300 riders and over 600 roadie volunteers, it is a life-changing experience and I am a better person—and in better shape—for having accepted the challenge. The riders range in age from the teens to the eighties and people come from nearly every state and a dozen countries. It is an incredible experience and open to all.

Aside from the exhaustive tasks of preparing for and then enduring the ride itself, the experience gave me hours and hours to think about my future. In fact, the solitude I enjoyed during those hours helped me determine how to close *The Campaign Within*.

In spite of my outrage over the right wing's vehement platform against gay people, I am not an angry activist at all. Rather I am a thankful and hopeful one—someone who sees the finish line. I am still impatient, but having witnessed firsthand how fast our culture is changing, I am more understanding of the path we are on as a society. More understanding that the advocacy groups for most issues of the day play to their base to secure support and funding, but that most miss the importance of the bigger picture of changing hearts and minds first. It is the changing of hearts and minds of our opponents and those who don't fully understand what it means to be gay that will result in full equality and freedom for all gay, lesbian, bisexual, and transgender people. That day will come, too. The powerful social transformation and trajectory in play has passed the tipping point in many ways, and cannot be stopped because, again, it is the moral and just path.

History is a great teacher. The Bible and religion were misused to justify slavery in this country, misused to justify denying women equality, misused to deny marriage to couples of different races, and misused for a whole host of other issues, about which we now know better. Are we not better for having left those other false and self-serving religious-based views behind?

Religious-based anti-gay bigotry has been the focus of Faith in America, an organization founded by furniture maker and philanthropist Mitchell Gold of the Mitchell Gold+Bob Williams chain of stores. His book *Crisis*, released in paperback as *Youth in Crisis*, tells the stories of people who grew up facing the hard challenges of being gay, often as a result of harmful religious-based attitudes about sexual orientation. Mitchell's book is a testament to the harm done to LGBT young people and, more importantly, how we can help stop it.

Another enlightened approach to faith is *In The Eye of The Storm: Swept to the Center by God* by Bishop Gene Robinson. I had the pleasure of spending Thanksgiving week of 2009 with

Gene, his husband, Mark, and other dear friends. Gene is a spiritual man of God whose voice is a vital one in our national dialogue about social justice for all people.

One of the chapters of Gene's book is entitled "The Gamble of Forgiveness." It's a powerful chapter because forgiveness, of self and others, is powerful. Forgiveness of self and others has been a fundamental in my life, too.

As a Roman Catholic child, I remember going to confession at Sacred Heart Church. Kneeling in a small box and talking to a priest through a little rectangle of see-through cloth never worked for me. As an adult, my form of seeking the forgiveness of my Creator takes a different, somewhat unorthodox form and does not involve an earthly representative of God, but I believe in seeking divine forgiveness. I believe in humbly seeking the forgiveness of a loving God, and I believe in granting that same forgiveness to others. We all fail, and yet many of us are called to serve.

I find it important to remind myself of my place in God's creation from time to time, and have that forgiveness conversation with Him. For me, it takes place in the middle of a starry, moonlit night, standing knee-deep in the ocean waves, with my swimsuit left on the shore, a humble creation, alone before God's majesty. The sound of the water, the reflection of the light on the endless waves, the great power and splendor of the ocean for as long as you can see.

I'm like Tim Robbins' character in *The Shawshank Redemption*. When he has finally escaped from unjust imprisonment and he stands in the rain for a moment, arms outstretched, looking to the sky. That's me. That's each of us: one tiny part of a vast creation, small but essential. In those moments, I am in harmony with God and myself. It's there that I can lay it all out: my failings, my joys, my fears, my hopes, and my roles in life. If you've never done it, you really should.

Choosing to engage in the public realm, to seek public office, and serve my community has made me stronger and taught me much about myself, and others, too. While far from perfect, then and now, I have come to adopt the line from a song in the musical *Rent*, "No Day But Today," as a personal mantra: "forget regret, or life is yours to miss."

My life has been an extraordinary journey I could never have imagined. I know every experience, relationship, and struggle, however difficult, has made me who I am. My hope is that the simply told and full sharing of my private journey to a very public life will somehow help others along the way. Our journeys are uniquely ours, of course, no two are the same, but we all have a campaign within of some sort. We're human and therefore both divinely perfect yet far from it, too. What matters is that we know it, understand ourselves, and attempt to use that greater understanding to improve our world along the way. Really, that's all we can do. And when we try, we allow ourselves the opportunity to win and grow to become better people.

When I have fallen down, I somehow got up and kept going. When I did stupid things, I usually knew it right away and did my best to act better in the future. When I had great achievements, it was never without the assistance and support of others. Great happiness and joy never visited me alone. However, when I failed, I owned the responsibility for that failure. I see myself as both flawed and near perfect, fragile and unbreakable, shy and gregarious. I'm a contradiction and I wouldn't have it any other way. And the rabbi from that long ago chilly morning in Bloomfield? I'm thinking maybe he was onto something. But he was the truly special one.

In January 1978, while in the middle of my first significant student leadership role as Circle K International president, a fellow Circle K member from Kansas, Kevin Bomhoff, gave me a book entitled *With Open Hands* by Henri J.M. Nouwen. It's a series of essays on trust, and the quote Kevin wrote on the inside of the cover and attributed to "author unknown" has spoken to my heart for all these many years:

Be patient toward all that is unsolved in your heart—and try to love the questions. Do not seek for the answers, which cannot now be given because you would not be able to live them. And the important thing is to love everything. Love your questions now and perhaps— even without knowing it—you will live along some distant day into your answers.

There was much unsolved in my heart back then and I feared the questions for a long time. But no longer.

I may not have followed that advice to the letter, but I have lived into my own answers, which it turns out, were there all along.

ACKNOWLEDGEMENTS

Many people assisted me over many years with telling my story, in making *The Campaign Within* a reality. In the very beginning Bill Davis was a local newspaper reporter covering Tempe and suggested I think about writing a book. We sat down often to talk about it, and the book took early shape with his guidance. Years passed, my story grew far beyond what it was then, but it wouldn't have started without Bill's assistance and encouragement. Landon Napolean helped in much the same manner as my personal and political drama unfolded and there was more to add to my story. Ian Jackman helped me fine-tune several chapters in 2010 and Karyn Folan assisted in a tremendous way as I prepared the final manuscript for delivery to the publisher in fall of 2011. Thank you all very much.

Don Weise of Magnus Books saw the potential of *The Campaign Within* and has been wonderful to work with in bringing it to literary life. His willingness to tell the stories of LGBT people continues to help change hearts and minds. My thanks to Mark McVeigh, my agent, for his support and to Paul

ACKNOWLEDGEMENTS

Aferiat and Peter Stamberg for making that introduction. Love you guys.

Lawn Griffiths, Ted Rybka, Kathy Matz, Seth Anderson, Duffy McMahon, Manjula Vaz, Rob Kubasko, Lynn Vavreck, Ray Delgado, James Loduca, Steve Clawson, John Fees, Chip and Shannon Scutari, and my brother Gregory all read early drafts and parts of drafts and provided insight and suggestions that improved the final work. Countless others provided information and jogged my memory more than a few times to add critical detail that enriched the story. I am grateful to you all.

David Mixner has been a personal inspiration and source of support without which I absolutely know I would not have finished the book.

To Kim, Jia, Greg, and John, and all the other Giulianos, thanks for your love and support. We've all done darn well and are survivors in our unique ways.

Randy Gross, Kathy Matz, and Steve Zastrow accepted the responsibility of serving as my chief of staff while I served as mayor, each for about three and a half years; perhaps that is the limit one can handle me, I'm not sure. Each was invaluable and provided excellent advice, guidance and did more than anyone could ask; not much would have happened without them. Sharon Coffey, Sherri Nunemacher, Josh Lader, Carlos Pastor, Jayson Mathews and a host of interns and assistants all served in the mayor's office and performed great work for the city of Tempe and me. I am very grateful to all of them.

Bonnie Rasmussen and Lori Briese at ASU offered tremendous support as I took on my elected official roles with the city. They knew how to keep me grounded and made me look good.

Many friends and supporters worked on my six campaigns for public office from 1990-2001. Yes, six campaigns in less than twelve years. I am grateful to all who assisted and provided leadership for my campaign teams, many of whom are mentioned in the previous pages. Rob Kubasko and Manjula Vaz were there for the duration of most, and remain trusted allies and friends.

To my many friends and associates from Key Club, Circle K, and Kiwanis International, local and around the country, including the Convention Commandos, from the ASU Newman Center, Sigma Nu Fraternity, Associated Students of ASU, my many roommates at Best Hall, Terrace Road, Ventura Drive, Jen Tilly Lane, Verlea Drive, Palmcroft Drive, Balboa Drive, and former students from my years teaching and working on campus, ASU colleagues and those from GLAAD, San Francisco AIDS Foundation, AIDS/Lifecycle, RSP Architects, and my many colleagues and friends from the City of Tempe and my world of community engagement and social justice activism: You are all a part of my story and I am honored and grateful to know you.

I am thankful for your presence in my life. Individually and collectively over time, you truly enabled me to win the campaign within.